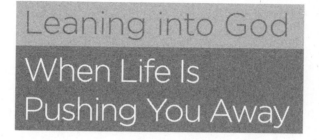

Leaning into God
When Life Is Pushing You Away

Leaning into God
When Life Is
Pushing You Away

ROBERT A. SCHULLER

with William Kruidenier

FaithWords

New York   Boston   Nashville

Unless otherwise noted, Scripture quotations are from the Holy Bible, New International Version®. Copyright © 1973, 1978, 1984 by International Bible Society. Used by permission of Zondervan Publishing House. All rights reserved.

Scripture quotations noted NLT are from the *Holy Bible*, New Living Translation, copyright © 1996, 2004. Used by permission of Tyndale House Publishers, Inc., Wheaton, Illinois 60189. All rights reserved.

Scripture quotations noted NKJV are from the New King James Version. Copyright © 1982 by Thomas Nelson, Inc. Used by permission. All rights reserved.

Scripture quotations noted NASB are from the New American Standard Bible®. Copyright © 1960, 1962, 1963, 1968, 1971, 1972, 1973, 1975, 1977, 1995 by The Lockman Foundation. Used by permission.

Scripture quotations noted *The Message* are from THE MESSAGE. Copyright © 1993, 1994, 1995, 1996, 2000, 2001, 2002. Used by permission of NavPress Publishing Group.

Scripture quotations as noted are also taken from J. B. Phillips: The New Testament in Modern English, Revised Edition. Copyright © J. B. Phillips 1958, 1960, 1972. Used by permission of Macmillan Publishing Co., Inc.; Today's English Version, Copyright © American Bible Society 1966, 1971, 1976, 1992; The Amplified Bible: Old Testament. Copyright © 1962, 1964 by Zondervan Publishing House (used by permission); and from The Amplified New Testament. Copyright © 1958 by the Lockman Foundation (used by permission); and *God's Word*® Translation. Copyright © 1995 God's Word to the Nations. Used by permission.

FaithWords
Hachette Book Group
237 Park Avenue
New York, NY 10017

Visit our website at www.faithwords.com.
Printed in the United States of America
First Edition: November 2009
10 9 8 7 6 5 4 3 2 1

FaithWords is a division of Hachette Book Group, Inc.
The FaithWords name and logo are trademarks of Hachette Book Group, Inc.

Library of Congress Cataloging-in-Publication Data

Schuller, Robert A.
    Leaning into God when life is pushing you away / Robert A. Schuller, with William Kruidenier.—1st ed.
        p. cm.
    Summary: "Robert A. Schuller shows readers how to jump-start an exciting connection with God and stay plugged into His love and presence"—Provided by the publisher
    ISBN 978-0-446-58098-4
    1. Spirituality 2. Consolation. I. Kruidenier, William. II. Title.
    BV4501.3.S385 2009
    248.4—dc22

2009011216

I dedicate this book to Jim Poit, Holly Hagler, Jim Case, Anita Sherbanee, Donna Schuller, Sharon Cleaver, and Paul Park. We met together for the first time on July 9, 2008, as the Consistory of the Crystal Cathedral. We met every week for several hours in the hope of making positive changes for the kingdom of God. They stood by me when I needed them the most. They were there to comfort me when I cried, counsel me when I was dismayed, and assist me when I needed a helping hand. I also want to give a special thanks to Errol Smith and Doug DiSiena for their assistance in special ways.

CONTENTS

ACKNOWLEDGMENTS

Without the contributions of the following people, this book would be nothing more than a thought or an idea. The process from conception to reality is a long, arduous journey. It begins like all works of art or projects with a vision, a dream, or a hope. Those mental images evolve into plans or outlines that when executed, adjusted, and persistently moved forward will produce a desired outcome. This book was no exception.

The idea began with the hope of writing something that would help people establish and maintain a relationship with God and others in spite of the forces that work against them; to create a tool to help build a church without walls; to edify the kingdom of God, not with bricks and mortar, but with the lives of God's children. With this vision an outline was written. In the spring of 2008 Sheila Coleman presented the first outline. This became the frame, the skeleton, and the road map. From there, William Kruidenier put the meat and muscle on those bones as we pushed the dream forward. Course corrections were made. Details were tweaked.

When it looked as if the book was complete in October of 2008, we realized that there was a major component still missing: we needed to help readers integrate the thoughts and the ideas into daily living. We needed a series of questions that could be used individually or collectively. Beth Funk, who has worked with me for nearly fifteen years, was brought onto the team and wrote the questions that you see at the end of every chapter.

I want to also acknowledge the publishing team of FaithWords, the assistance of Sealy Yates, my book agent, and all the other people who have had a hand in making this possible. Finally, I want to thank my wife, Donna, and my children, Chris and Angie Wyatt, Bobby and Hannah Schuller, Christina Schuller, and Anthony Schuller for their faithfulness to the dream of building the kingdom of God—a church without walls.

A NOTE FROM THE AUTHOR

When I first began writing this book, life was relatively predictable. I was senior pastor of the world-famous Crystal Cathedral, a role I was groomed for and expected to fill until it was time for me to retire. In early 2008, I engaged in a new media project at the Cathedral that would have enabled our local and global Crystal Cathedral communities to stay connected to our ministry 24/7 through the Internet and facilitate my dream of an international church without walls. Things were moving in a positive direction and seemed to be unfolding as planned. But life doesn't always go as planned.

One of the great joys of my life has been to serve the Crystal Cathedral Ministries both on the International Board of Directors and as senior pastor of the Crystal Cathedral. But God unexpectedly and radically began changing the direction of my life in July 2008 when the first in a series of decisions—not of my own accord—was made that turned my world upside down. To make a difficult story short, by early September I was no longer part of the weekly *Hour of Power* television broadcast, and in October was replaced as leader of the Sunday morning worship service at the Cathedral. Seeing the handwriting on the wall, in November I resigned from my position as senior pastor of the Crystal Cathedral—I couldn't live with a pastor's title if I had no pulpit from which to preach. I would be less than honest if I said I did not struggle with intense feelings of betrayal and confusion and frequently found myself crying out to God, "Why is this happening? Where are You taking me?" If ever there was a time when I felt like disconnecting from God and others, that was it.

While that transition in life has been a very painful one—one that I'm still processing with my wonderful and supportive wife, Donna, our four loving children, and many faithful and caring friends—I am often reminded in new and exciting ways that the God in whom I place my trust is still good, is still involved, and is still faithful. And in Him I have found hope.

Good things are often birthed from adversity, as I can bear witness in my life. I've held firmly to the belief that God's plans for me are good. That His intent is "to prosper [me] and not to harm [me], to give [me] hope and a future" (Jeremiah 29:11) and that "the LORD will fulfill his purpose for me" (Psalm 138:8). In the early eighties, God gave me a personal purpose statement that I believe is as relevant today as it was then: to *inspire* people to take positive action in their lives. No matter what, no matter how, my heart's desire is to help bring about positive change in the lives of people and society. Preaching has been the primary way in which I've done that in the past. But now, I see that God has given me a fresh opportunity to achieve this purpose in an even greater way using the new media of today.

Early in 2009, in partnership with my talented son-in-law, Chris Wyatt, I launched a new, for-profit, kingdom-based business called ComStar Media®. Recognizing that broadcast pulpit preaching no longer effectively reaches younger generations—and because both Chris and I have a deep love for and desire to reach this generation—we embarked on this journey together. Even as I write this, the details for this new venture are rapidly unfolding. But this much I can tell you—ComStar Media® is dedicated to changing the face of Christian television programming. How will we accomplish this? By integrating an existing television network and companion video Web site using cutting-edge technology. ComStar Media® will offer a new format of kingdom-based entertainment programming including reality television series, daytime talk shows, and weekly magazine series that complement a broadcast schedule of family-friendly, classic television programs from the 1960s, 1970s, and 1980s. By the time you hold this book in your hands, more information about ComStar Media® will have been made public.

Each life is a story to be written. God is still writing my story as He is yours. It's one chapter at a time, and I know that God will provide a happy ending to my story just as He will yours.

—Robert Anthony Schuller

INTRODUCTION

The sixties were supposed to be the decade that ushered in the Age of Aquarius. (Never happened.) According to author Tom Wolfe, the seventies were the "Me Decade." That gave way to what some have called the Decade of Greed in the eighties (remember the 1987 movie *Wall Street*—"Greed is good"?). And the nineties were obviously the dot-com decade. So what about the first decade of the twenty-first century? If I had to give the 2010s a label, I would call it the Decade of Reaching Out. In a way no one anticipated, the Internet Age has created a longing in people—a longing to relate. First, it was cool to relate to computers, iPods, Blackberrys, and smart phones. But having discovered that they don't relate back, we've begun using them to reconnect with people. People are leaning toward one another as never before, hungry for temporal relationships. And hungry for an eternal one as well.

First there were Internet bulletin boards, then chat groups, and now MySpace, Facebook, and Twitter are the eight-hundred-pound gorillas of the social networking phenomenon—all in the name of relating. Time will tell whether all this connectivity turns out to be a hot, cold, or lukewarm thing. Remember: computers in the office haven't yet delivered us *from* paper or *to* shorter workweeks. So who knows what benefits (or not) increased digital-based relationships will bring? Establishing a meaningful relationship is a good thing; wasting time "tweeting"—not so much.

I do believe that social networking is a good development in principle. To the degree it helps us lean toward others and make new connections with new friends who can expand the meaningfulness of our lives, I'm for it. We are people who were created by God to relate—first to Him and then to one another.

I also believe that social networking via technology has become such a powerful force in the world because of the degree of isolation most people feel in their lives. We've lived through several decades of increasing separation in our society. We have become victims of compartmentalized lives. Our homes are compartments, our cars are compartments, our cubicles at work are compartments—and we traffic between those compartments for the majority of our lives. That's an overstatement, of course, but it makes the point: Modern societies have become collectives of intimate strangers. The opportunity to have hundreds of "friends" on Facebook or MySpace—even though we might not know many of them very well—is a bridge over the river of isolation that cuts us off from relating to others.

Social networking—connecting and relating to people—is a backdrop for the subject of this book. I am not going to write about social networking, but something similar: spiritual networking. But not in the horizontal sense—people connecting with people. That's an important subject, but I am writing here about a prerequisite to horizontal spiritual networking, that being vertical spiritual networking—spiritual connectivity of the highest order: connecting with God Himself.

I don't think it's any accident that social connectivity—people leaning toward others—is increasing in our culture at the same time that spiritual connectivity is decreasing. While nearly 70 percent of Americans profess to believe in God, church attendance and denominational growth are either stagnant or falling.[1] And there is little evidence to suggest that, at least for Christians, there is a lot of self-started connectivity with God going on to replace connecting with Him in church.

In a USAToday.com article, the writer said, "Religion in the USA has a new anthem. No longer 'Give Me That Old Time Religion,' now it's 'Don't Fence Me In.'" The article cited a "Pew Forum on Religion & Public Life" survey of thirty-five thousand Americans. The chief point of the article is that Americans are no longer sure of what they believe. People are changing religions easily—as if one is the same as another. "Most" (says the article) evangelical Christians no longer seem sure about who's going to heaven and who isn't. A public policy expert quoted in the article says that "the highest authority is now the lowest common denominator."[2]

Because people no longer see the necessity for connecting with God through church, they are feeling more free to make up their own creeds and criteria for Christian belief—and for other religions as well. And when religion gets redefined, so do the meaning and the method of relating to

God. For any number of reasons, there are many people today who have never experienced or are not presently experiencing that connection.

And using "spirituality" as the fallback position is not a solution. Making up God in one's own image and then relating to that image might work for some. But it is no substitute for relating to the *person* of God—a God who has a time-and-space existence; a God in whose image we exist; a God who longs for the opportunity to relate face-to-face with a person who has somehow lost his or her connection with Him.

That's what this book is about: exploring the ways that a relationship with God is lost and identifying the ways it can be reestablished, *even when life pushes back and keeps you from connecting with Him.*

As the son of a well-known pastor and having been a pastor myself, I've been around "God discussions" all my life. From my own experiences and those of others, I know that people lean away from God for various reasons—there are as many reasons as there are people separated from Him.

The Bible says we are born separated from God. Born in His image, yes—but an image that is tarnished by our own self-will. And that fact puts us all in the same boat. If you are reading this book and have never established a relationship with God, you will discover how to do that in these pages. But I am not writing primarily for those who have never known God. Rather, I am writing for the dispirited, the brokenhearted, the angry, the guilty, the shameful, the wandering, the fearful, the misinformed, the uninformed—all who have allowed something to cause them to lean away from God instead of leaning into Him.

In previous books I have written honestly about the heartbreak and discouragement I felt as a young husband when my marriage ended.[3] It was not something I wanted but rather something I was powerless to prevent. Divorce is a terrible experience under any circumstances, but in my case it was made worse by my being the pastor of a growing church. There I was, a pastor committed to the biblical design for marriage and family who had failed to succeed at it himself. The words "Physician, heal yourself!" (Luke 4:23) echoed in my mind every waking moment. To say I was embarrassed and ashamed in those days is to put it mildly.

It would have been the perfect opportunity for me to lean away from God—to disconnect from my faith. I could have blamed guilt and shame (I certainly felt them both) or anger at God: "God, if You won't help me preserve the most important thing in my life now, how can I trust You for anything going forward?"

Fortunately, I didn't place the blame on Him. I had a social and spiritual network that was strong enough to see me through those dark days. By God's grace, and the loving support of those in my congregation, my family, and others, my relationship with God remained intact—and it has remained intact ever since, even through the recent disruption I described in my Author Note (p. xi). I decided that God's success was bigger than my failures, that His answers were bigger than my questions, that His grace was greater than all my sins. I wasn't holding His hand so much in those days as He was holding mine. And I decided not to pull away; I decided to lean into Him instead of away.

But I realize that is not always how it works in life. All people go through difficulties of their own or others' making, and all people wonder where God is when they are hurting. Without a social and spiritual network strong enough to keep people connected, too often they lean away. They wander off to find solace and support in a godless direction. Sometimes they make it back to Him and sometimes they don't.

I've written this book for those who are trying to make it back—and especially those who don't think they, or God, deserve a "second chance." It doesn't matter to me (and it certainly doesn't matter to God) whether your disconnect from God is based on guilt, shame, rebellion, disobedience, hurts, weariness, fear, or any other human response to the challenges of life. I can only tell you what God has communicated to me in my own hours of questioning: "I am not going to leave you. I am going to stay beside you so that when you are ready to lean into Me, you won't have to look for Me. I am now, and will be in the future, right here."

That's what God is saying to you—to anyone who has lost his or her relationship with Him. You may feel alone, but it is not because He is far away. It is only because you stopped trusting Him at some point. And trust can be restored.

Faith, of course, is the key to restoring a powerful relationship with God. And I want to talk about how to restore and rebuild your faith—to gain confidence and courage, direction and belief. And how to allow God to extend His hand and touch the wounds that need healing—through prayer and praise, joy and forgiveness. Once you have begun again to lean into God no matter how life tries to push you away, there's the matter of moving forward once again with God—building a relationship with Him that keeps you close and moves you through the storms that will surely come again. It's the power of God flowing back through your life that will protect you from ever becoming disconnected from Him again.

Will there be static or noise or crimps in the connection? Of course. We all experience those. But disconnects? No—not if you learn the reasons why leaning into God is always better than leaning away.

Social networking and relationships are helpful, modern phenomena. But spiritual connectivity is powerful and eternal. Without first being connected vertically to God, all the social networking contacts in the world won't be enough. Don't let a temporal way to connect be a poor substitute for an eternal way. Ask God now, as you begin to read, to open the eyes of your heart, and you will see just how close He has been all this time—and how you can lean into Him even when life is pushing you away.

Before turning to chapter 1, pause for a moment and reflect on these questions:

- Do you feel like an "intimate stranger" to God? To others?

- Are you leaning into God for support and comfort or away from Him in frustration? If the latter, are you ready to draw close to Him again?

- If people or events were connected with your distance from God, can you release your hurts to Him for the healing of your wounds?

- How will your life be different if you choose to lean into God? If you don't?

Part 1

Accepting God's Grace

1. Reconnecting When Disconnected by Guilt

BORN INTO THE LATE FIFTEENTH-CENTURY mix of poverty, plagues, and performance-based religion in Europe was a boy named Martin. His parents were taskmasters who treated him harshly but who ultimately saw in Martin a future lawyer. A civil or ecclesiastical lawyer would make enough money to help support the family in the parents' latter years.

Hans Luder, Martin's father (Martin later changed his last name to Luther), was right. Martin earned his bachelor's and master's degrees in law at Germany's University of Erfurt in the shortest time allowed by the university. He was promoted immediately to the law faculty.

Unfortunately for the Luders, young Martin's heart was not set on law. At least, in law he had not found the peace with God he so desired. His father had done such a good job putting the fear of God into Martin that the young man's heart was in turmoil. He knew he was deserving of God's punishment for his sins but didn't know what to do about it. The standard answers of the church—confession and penance—left him unsatisfied.

Nearing his twenty-second birthday, Martin was caught in a thunderstorm one day and a bolt of lightning hit the ground so close to him that he cried out to Saint Anne (the patroness of miners, his father's vocation) for protection: "Help me, Saint Anne, [and] I will become a monk." He interpreted his close call with death as a warning from God that he'd better get on the straight and narrow, and his response was to join a monastery and become a monk.

As far as Martin's soul was concerned, this was a jump from the frying pan into the fire. His legally trained mind soon began to find all sorts of inconsistencies in the teachings of the church, for which his superiors had no answers. Recognizing his intellectual and academic gifting, his spiritual leaders sent him to earn his doctorate in theology so he could become a "teacher of the church." That only encouraged Martin to dig even more deeply into the Bible and the teachings of the church.

During his monastic years, Martin was a model Augustinian monk. Not only did he practice all the disciplines expected of him to attain righteous standing before God—prayer, fasting, and ascetic practices such as sleep deprivation, living in a freezing cell in the monastery, and self-flagellation—he practiced them better than anyone ever had.

But with all his efforts, Martin's guilt—the conscious, continual awareness of his own unrighteousness—persisted. The wrath of God was his tormentor: "When it is touched by this passing inundation of the eternal, the soul feels and drinks nothing but eternal punishment." He applied his logical mind to the study of salvation, seeking the cool water of truth to assuage his burning soul. He tried to understand how it was possible for a guilty sinner like himself to do what Jesus had commanded: "Be perfect, therefore, as your heavenly Father is perfect" (Matthew 5:48). He had executed the formula for perfection that Jesus gave in Matthew 19:21: "Go, sell your possessions and give to the poor.... Then come, follow me"—but he knew he was still imperfect.

The primary biblical stumbling block for Luther was the seventeenth verse of Romans chapter 1, where Paul is quoted as saying that "the righteous will live by faith." Martin focused only on the need for being "righteous" in order to live by faith. He knew he wasn't righteous, so he knew he couldn't live by faith. And he grew increasingly angry with God over this conundrum. The one thing he wanted to do in life—escape God's wrath—was seemingly made impossible by his very guilt. He was guilty and therefore unrighteous. And only the "righteous will live by faith."

Fast-forward: history tells us that Martin gradually began to focus on the word *faith* in Romans 1:17 instead of the word *righteous*. He saw that he could be righteous only by having faith in Christ and accepting God's gift of forgiveness (freedom from sin and its guilt). He saw that he was, just as he thought, totally undeserving of having a relationship with a holy

God. Therefore, if such a relationship were ever to exist, it would have to be on God's terms, not his. And God's terms were simple: "The only way to be righteous—to be resolved of your guilt—is to believe Me when I say you are free" (author's paraphrase of Romans 1:17).

The chain of events set in motion by Martin Luther's discovery included not only his own freedom from the guilt of unrighteousness, but that of millions who have followed in his wake. The Protestant Reformation—ignited by Martin in 1517—recovered the biblical truth that freedom from the guilt of unrighteousness is a gift from God. Receiving it by faith is step one toward experiencing a life of faith.[1]

Marghanita Laski (d. 1988) was a British journalist and author and an avowed atheist and secular humanist. She is famous for making this statement before she died: "What I envy most about you Christians is your forgiveness; I have nobody to forgive me."[2] She apparently knew that she needed forgiveness (like Martin Luther) but lived and died completely unconnected (unlike Luther) from the God who could take away her guilt. Ms. Laski assumed "God" was a figment of the Christian imagination: we invent a forgiving God to release us from our guilt and then say, "I'm free," when He does.

But that's not true of all those who struggle to remove the yoke of guilt from around their necks. There are plenty of people who believe in God's existence and at one time had a fruitful relationship with Him. But then something happened (things always happen) that created a guilt-yoke that was too big to get through the door marked "Guilt Removed Here." They can see the door and they know what's on the other side. But twist and turn as they will, the yokes they're bearing won't allow them to enter. So they live with their guilt and live without God. They know God can remove their guilt, but they think He's made it too hard to get to Him to have the procedure done.

Since everyone has a conscience—that part of us that "hurts even when everything else feels so good"[3]—we are left with only one choice: having our consciences cleared of guilt. This is one of the rare tasks in life that is no harder to do than it is to say. What it took to make it possible to remove guilt was not easy—but that heavy lifting has been done for us by God. All that remains is for us to appropriate the result. But more on that in a moment.

How is your relationship with God? As I see it, you (along with me—and everyone else) are in one of three places:

1. You've never had a relationship with God.

2. You have a relationship with God that has been broken/damaged/ hurt.

3. You have a great relationship with God.

If either number one or two applies to you, this book can help you identify what needs to happen in order for you to connect or reconnect with God. And if you are in place number three, this book can prepare you for obstacles that may appear down the road—bumps and pitfalls that have the potential to short-circuit your relationship with God. And in my experience of talking pastorally with people for many years, guilt is an obstacle that has broken the God-connection in many people's lives.

The famous psychiatrist Karl Menninger (d. 1990) was told the following story by a friend of his who witnessed the event: It was a sunny day in Chicago in 1972 when a stern-faced, plainly dressed man stood on a busy corner in the downtown Chicago Loop. As pedestrians hurried by he would periodically hold out his straight arm, point to someone walking by, and speak a single, loud word: "Guilty!" He would then lower his arm and resume his stance while waiting for his next "victim." The effect of the man's actions was unnerving, to say the least. Those receiving his glaring accusation would pause, lower their eyes, and move quickly away. Menninger's friend was with a person who said, "But how did he know?"[4]

Truth be told, it didn't matter to whom the strange man pointed that day. He could have closed his eyes and pointed or put on a blindfold and thrown a dart, and he would have hit a guilty person. The ones who didn't get pointed out were spared a bit of embarrassment, but not because they weren't guilty.

The bottom line is that everyone is guilty of something. The question is not whether we are guilty, but what we have learned to do with our guilt.

The Bible says that every human being is guilty of two things: Adam's sin and a person's own sins. From our forefather Adam we have inherited, as his descendants, the guilt that he passed as progenitor (and the first sinner) to the human race: "Just as sin entered the world through one man, and death through sin, and in this way death came to all men, because all sinned" (Romans 5:12). (Jesus, having been conceived by the Holy Spirit rather than a human father, did not inherit culpability for Adam's sin.)

While we might have needed the Bible to pinpoint that initial source of guilt, we need no one to tell us about the second—our own sins: "All have sinned and fall short of the glory of God" (Romans 3:23); and "Whoever keeps the whole law and yet stumbles at just one point is guilty of breaking all of it" (James 2:10). You and I know full well that we are sinners—that we are guilty of doing many things that a righteous God would not do. (And He is the standard, after all.)

So, taking the Bible at its word, we conclude that it's not a question of "if" we are going to experience guilt, but what we are going to do about it. Here's the simple remedy for guilt I mentioned earlier: *just as we inherit the guilt of Adam when we are born, so we inherit the innocence of Jesus Christ (the second Adam [1 Corinthians 15:45]) when we are born again.*

This is what Martin Luther came to understand five hundred years ago that freed him from his fear of the wrath of God. We can't erase our own guilt. God provided an innocent (guilt-free) man—His Son, Jesus Christ—to create an exchange: we give Him our guilt, and He gives us His innocence. As I said earlier, the theological mystery that undergirds that exchange is not simple, not to mention the pain and suffering it cost Christ to enact it. But on our side, it is simple: we give Christ our guilt and unrighteousness, and we trust by faith (Romans 1:17) that His righteousness will become ours.

There is one thing we have to do: admit our guilt to Him and allow Him to make the exchange. And deep down, that's something we all want to do. We want to say what we're guilty of—but we want to say it to the person who can do something about it. Ironically, we're afraid that whatever we tell God we're guilty of (as if He didn't already know) will be too gruesome, too wicked, too juvenile—too something—for Him to forgive us and draw close to us. Everybody else's guilt is fixable, but not ours.

In 1993, British police accused two ten-year-old boys of brutally murdering a two-year-old named James. But the two boys insisted they were innocent. There was a two-week trial, during which it became increasingly obvious that the two boys' stories were filled with inconsistencies. They appeared to be guilty. The trial came to an end when one of the boy's parents assured him that, even if he was guilty, they would always love him. At that moment, and in the face of overwhelming evidence, the boy softly confessed, "I killed James."[5]

It was only when he was convinced that his parents' love would not be withdrawn that he felt free to acknowledge his guilt. That's how it is with us. We have to believe that God's love will not be withdrawn, regardless of what we have done, and the Bible assures us of that very thing: "Where sin increased, grace increased all the more" (Romans 5:20). As the hymn says, "Marvelous grace of our loving Lord, grace that exceeds our sin and our guilt."[6]

Children learn to receive God's forgiveness (or not) primarily by how their parents handled the subject. If a child fears unkind or unbalanced retribution will follow his confession of an act of disobedience, he is likely to remain silent. But if he knows that the person to whom he confesses—the authority against whom he has "sinned"—will accept his confession with understanding and forgiveness (and a fair discipline when appropriate), he will gladly confess. Even a child feels the relief that follows the unburdening of a guilty conscience.

That's why removing guilt from our souls should be easy when it involves confessing to God. His response is always loving, forgiving, and just (fair). If you have guilt about something that involves another person, you may need to confess your guilt to him or her. But ultimately, as the psalmist said, all sin is against God (see Psalm 51:4). Even if you receive human forgiveness from another person, you still need to say to God, "Here is what I have done." When you do that, God says, "Not guilty. My Son, Jesus Christ, paid the penalty for what you have done. You are free."

Leonard Jones, a Christian songwriter and singer, writes powerfully biblical songs. Think about the lyrics to this song as you consider becoming reconnected with God:

> Many are they that rise up against me
> Many are they that say of my soul
>
> They say—"There is no help"
> They say—"There is no one"
> They say—*they* say . . . (who are "they," anyway?)

But this is what the Lord says
This is what the Lord says
This is what the Lord says
We're not guilty!

They say—"There is no help"
They say—"There is no one"
They say—*they* say . . . (I don't care!)

But this is what the Lord says
This is what the Lord says
This is what the Lord says
We're not guilty!

If God be for us
Who can stand against us?

Spirit of condemnation
You've got to go![7]

If you will listen to what the Lord says, you will hear Him say, "Not guilty!" God has the authority to remove whatever guilt you are carrying. Asking Him to do so will allow your relationship with Him to be immediately established again.

Questions for Reflection and Discussion

1. There are two kinds of guilt in life. *True guilt* is when we've legitimately done something wrong and need to make amends for it. *False guilt* is when we agonize over something we've done that wasn't our fault or we had no control over and we're just punishing ourselves. Which kind of guilt do you tend to struggle with most often? Think of a time recently when you struggled with either kind of guilt.

2. Guilt over a bad choice can hound you your entire life. Is there anything for which you still feel guilty even though it happened a long time ago? What keeps you hooked to those feelings of guilt? What steps do you need to take to move past those guilt feelings?

3. What are some negative ways people deal with guilt in their lives? What are some positive ways of dealing with guilt?

4. What do you learn from Psalm 32:3–5 about the consequences of not dealing with legitimate guilt? What do you learn from the writer about finding resolution from guilt?

5. What correlation do you see between knowing God's love will not be withdrawn from you in spite of what you have done and your relationship with Him?

2. Discovering Redemption When Short-Circuited by Shame

A YOUNG REVOLUTIONARY WITH A MESSAGE that was resonating among working-class folk had made his way to a nation's capital city to take on the establishment. The powers-that-be were not happy about his arrival, so they put their heads together to find a way to discredit him, hoping he would take the hint and leave town. And they were not above creating trumped-up charges that would land the young firebrand in jail—or worse.

As for the young reformer himself, he had warned his committee of supporters and advisers that their reception in the capital would likely be less than welcoming. When the man who served as his chief of staff brushed off such predictions, the young leader took him aside and shared a personal concern about the man's loyalty: "I've been through this kind of opposition before, Pete. I know what to expect. But you haven't, and I wonder if you'll be strong enough to risk being identified with me if the heat gets turned up."

Pete did not stutter in his reply: "No way, boss. There are a few others on our team that I'm a little worried about, but you needn't be concerned about me. Even if everybody else bails out when the pressure is on, I'll be with you."

Almost as a way of proving his point, Pete actually physically attacked one of a group who came to request the young leader's presence at a meeting with some of the city's leaders. They accompanied the group to city hall, only to discover the young leader was to be arraigned and interrogated about his business in the city.

Pete suddenly saw his life flash before his eyes. Arrest? Conviction? Jail time? Or something worse? He had a wife to support and a business to run back home. Was this really happening? He needed time to think and moved to the edge of the crowd that had formed in the courtroom.

Suddenly a young reporter standing next to Pete recognized him and said, "Hey, aren't you one of his supporters? Can you give me a comment?"

Pete didn't have an answer. He was still thinking about the cost of what he had gotten himself involved in. Before he realized it, he heard himself saying, "I don't know what you're talking about"—and he turned quickly and left the courtroom.

Not wanting to miss the story inside, the reporter didn't follow him, so Pete felt he was safe mingling in the crowd that had gathered in the street. The young reformer's notoriety had preceded him—Pete was surprised at the size of the crowd and the opinions he heard being voiced. People were arguing and taking sides.

When Pete passed by a particularly vocal group, a woman stopped midsentence and pointed directly at Pete: "Hey—that guy is one of them. I saw him a couple of weeks ago at one of their meetings out of town."

This time Pete panicked: "You're out of your mind! I don't know that guy. I never saw him before in my life!"

"Then why do you dress and talk like him?" a man said. "I can tell you're not from around here, and neither is he. How do you explain that?"

Pete was in trouble—his cover was blown. The crowd was angry and he wasn't sure what they might do next. For the third time in a matter of minutes, Pete denied any association with the young leader: "I swear to God I don't know what you're talking about. I'm not here to see him. Now back off—I'm late for an appointment." He broke free from the group and made his way down the street, turning into a dark alley.

As Pete tried to regain his composure, he thought he felt a knife blade go through his heart. But it was only his conscience. His back slid down the wall he'd been leaning against until he crumpled into a heap on the dirty pavement. He wept out loud—deep sobs—as he remembered what his leader, mentor, and friend, Joshua, had warned him about—about succumbing to the pressure. And how brash he had been when he boasted that he would never fold—that Joshua could count on him.

He was not the man he had bragged that he was. He had never before felt so ashamed.

Most people, churched or unchurched, will recognize the framework of that story—when Peter, the disciple of Jesus of Nazareth, denied that he knew his own Lord on the night He was arrested in Jerusalem. In all of world literature, it stands as a dramatic example of a man's failure to live up to his own standard of belief, and his subsequent painful experience of personal shame.

I'm sure there's not a person alive who has not experienced the humiliating pangs of shame. It's awful to be ashamed! We feel shame as children when we're caught with a hand in the cookie jar or telling a lie to our parents. And we have felt shame as adults. Guilt is bad, but somehow, to me, shame feels worse.

What's the difference? From the reading I've done, and from my own experience, it seems that guilt is focused more on something we do—a law or a standard that we violate. I realize there are greater and lesser violations of standards, but think of this simple example as a generalization: Let's say I exceed the speed limit while driving my car. I'm guilty of breaking the law, and a policeman pulls me over and gives me a ticket. I pay the fine, all without feeling particularly ashamed. I'm sorry I did it, and I purpose to myself and the judge (and God) to be more respectful of the law. But I don't normally, willfully violate the speed limit and other laws—I'm not that kind of person. I got careless and broke the law and was guilty. My guilt was associated with my behavior.

But what if I, unbeknownst to my family and church congregation, had run up a string of speeding tickets? What if I employed the latest radar detector in my car *for the express purpose* of violating the law? What if I used my identification as a member of the clergy to weasel out of speeding tickets, protesting that I was on my way to a pastoral emergency? And what if all this came to light in a public courtroom? Would I be guilty or ashamed?

Well, I would obviously be both—certainly I would be guilty of continually violating the law. But I would *feel* far more shame than guilt. I would be embarrassed, mortified, and humiliated for who I had allowed myself to become. Why? Because shame says more about who we are than what we have done. In the case I just cited, over many months, maybe years, I would have built up a persona, a perception, of myself as a man of God, only to have the truth come out: I was actually a deceiver, a manipulator, and a hypocrite. Even thinking about how such a revelation would feel makes me shudder. And it has made many others—from presidents to preachers—shudder as well, publicly and privately.

Mark Twain wrote, "Man is the only animal that blushes. Or needs to." I don't know if that's completely accurate—we've all seen the family dog exhibit that "hang-dog" look when caught lounging on the forbidden sofa or bed. But you get Twain's point. Man knows—*immediately*—when he has been found out.

Take Adam and Eve, for example. The Bible says something amazing about them in their state of innocence: "The man and his wife were both naked, and they felt no shame" (Genesis 2:25). We, of course, cannot imagine what that would be like since we have had the experience of shame. But they hadn't. They lived together in the Garden of Eden in a totally transparent state with each other—no subterfuge, no duplicity, no scheming, no conniving, and no shame.

Until they sinned by disobeying God, that is. And *immediately*, they knew they were naked. When Adam heard God approaching in the Garden, he hid himself (see Genesis 3:10). And then God asked a most revealing question: "Who told you that you were naked?" (verse 11). Think about it—there *was* nobody else! Adam and Eve were the only two people in the world. And I don't think Adam and Eve looked at each other after eating the fruit from the tree "in the middle of the garden" (verse 3) and said, "Hey, we're naked!"

God's point was subtle. Satan had already told Adam and Eve that "your eyes will be opened" (verse 5) if they disobeyed God. And they were. And that's how Adam knew he was naked. I don't know that his shame was as much because he was naked in God's presence as it was that he knew his eyes were opened—which meant he had disobeyed God. Adam knew that his whole person, his whole being, had changed from being an "obeyer" of God to being a "disobeyer" of God. And he was ashamed at what he had become. So he hid; he tried to unplug from God.

We inherited more than our genetic code from father Adam. We also inherited his wide-open eyes (our ability to be ashamed) and our tendency to hide from God because of our shame. Shame is just another way that our closeness to God erodes along the way.

Somehow in the Christian community we have taken verses like 1 John 1:9 and applied them to guilt (what we do) but not to shame (who we are): "If we confess our sins, he is faithful and just and will forgive us our sins and purify us from all unrighteousness." Sins. Those are things we *do*. Somehow we get that Jesus died for our sins and will forgive us our sins if we confess them.

But what we don't get as readily is that Jesus also died for who we are—people who are sometimes so ashamed we can hardly look at ourselves in a mirror, or look at our spouses or friends, much less look at God. Somehow we don't read 1 John 1:9 this way: "If we confess *who we are—a person who is ashamed*—he is faithful and just and will forgive us for the cause of our shame and purify us from all its effects."

I don't mean to take liberty with the Bible by rewriting that verse—but I don't think God is any less willing to forgive our shame (who we are) than He is our guilt (what we do). It's because shame *feels* so much worse than guilt (and often we are guilty and ashamed at the same time) that we run and hide when God draws near and wants to talk. We can't imagine that a person who feels so good (God) would lower Himself to the presence of someone who feels so bad (us).

But He does. God "made garments of skin for Adam and his wife and clothed them" (verse 21). In other words, God took away the cause of their shame by giving them clothes to wear. He couldn't take away their sins of disobedience or their now-open eyes, so He did the next-best thing: He proved to them that their shame would not be a permanent barrier or a permanent connection-breaker between them. He reentered their lives and met their needs. Adam and Eve came out of hiding and stood clothed in new garments before Him—garments procured by the shedding of the blood of innocent animals who knew no sin and no shame. Innocent beings gave up their lives to cover the guilt and shame of those who deserved to lose their lives.

That's the story of the Bible. Remember King David in the Old Testament? Here he was, the man after God's own heart, the king of Israel, the one through whom the Son of David would come as Israel's Messiah—and he found himself covered with shame. He took the wife of one of his loyal soldiers, got her pregnant, had her husband killed so he wouldn't find out—and then concealed the whole mess for nearly a year. David was guilty of adultery and being an accomplice to murder, yes. But more than that, he endured the pain of shame, of being the kind of person who would stoop lower than low to satisfy his own carnal desires.

Here's how his shame made David feel:

> When I kept silent,
>> my bones wasted away
>> through my groaning all day long.
> For day and night
>> your hand was heavy upon me;
> my strength was sapped
>> as in the heat of summer.
>
> (Psalm 32:3–4)

But God graciously sent a prophet to David to tell him that God knew what he had done and it wasn't the end of the world. There would be ramifications and implications, but life would go on. And it did. David's relationship with God wasn't broken in spite of his shame (see 2 Samuel 11–12).

Here's the epitaph by which David was remembered in Israel: "When David had served God's purpose in his own generation, he fell asleep; he was buried with his fathers and his body decayed" (Acts 13:36). And that was many years after David's connection with God was broken for a year due to his sin and shame. David's shame was removed, and he "served God's purpose" in his generation.

And Peter—what happened to the most ashamed man in Jerusalem? A few weeks after Peter's denial of Jesus, after Jesus had been crucified and raised from the dead, He appeared to Peter. And the interesting thing is the example that Peter sets for you and for me when we find ourselves ashamed and disconnected from God: Peter *ran* to get to Jesus when he recognized Him. *Swam*, actually. Peter and the other disciples were back fishing on the Sea of Galilee when John recognized the figure on the shore to be Jesus. And "as soon as Simon Peter heard [John] say, 'It is the Lord,' he wrapped his outer garment around him . . . and jumped into the water" (John 21:7) and made his way to shore. Peter couldn't wait to get to Jesus, the very person he had denied; the very person in whose presence he must have felt unbelievably ashamed.

We don't know everything that happened in that breakfast meeting. But we do know this: before Jesus departed He recommissioned Peter to His service, telling the once-ashamed disciple to "feed my lambs...take care of my sheep...feed my sheep" (verses 15–17). That doesn't sound like a disconnected relationship to me. It seems that shame is not the barrier to connectedness with God that we are convinced it is.

What God did for Adam and Eve in the Garden of Eden was a precursor of what He would do for you and me. In the Garden, innocent animals were sacrificed to cover the shame of Adam and Eve. On a hill outside Jerusalem, "God made [Jesus] who had no sin to be sin for us, so that in him we might become the righteousness of God" (2 Corinthians 5:21).

Let me use a statement by the Russian novelist Ivan Turgenev (d. 1883) to make a closing point. He said, "You should never trust a person who doesn't blush." I see his point—trusting a person who has experienced shame means he or she will probably understand the shame you are feeling. But let me say it a better way: "You should always trust *the* Person who doesn't blush."

Did you know that Jesus never blushed—never felt shame about anything—in His whole life? He was like Adam was in the beginning—innocent to the ways (and resulting feelings) of sin. He is the person you and I should jump out of the boat and run to when our shame has disconnected us from Him. Don't hide as Adam did. Instead, run to Him and let Him restore your righteousness. In that act, there is never any shame.

Questions for Reflection and Discussion

1. The psychologist Norman Wright describes the difference between guilt and shame in this way: "*Guilt* says, 'I made a mistake,' whereas *shame* says, 'I am a mistake.'" Shame can make us believe that everything we are and do is fundamentally flawed. Where have you seen the effects of shame at work in your life?

2. Many people carry shame imposed on them by the negative labels of others. Can you think of any negative labels that have caused you to feel shame in the past or that are still present in your life today? What do you think the solution for overcoming personal shame is?

3. Shame often makes us try to hide our true identity from others and even from God. What things do people "hide" behind to keep their true identity from being revealed? What do you use to hide your shame?

4. To become authentic people we have to quit hiding and let other people see all of who we are—our successes and failures, our strengths and weaknesses. How easy is it for you to do this? Who in your life helps you be an authentic person?

5. God is continually in the process of redeeming (reclaiming or buying back) lives that have been short-circuited by shame and bringing good from that shame. Where in your life have you already seen God do this? Where else in your life do you need to experience God's redemption over shame?

3. Finding Forgiveness
After Fits of Rebellion

H E WAS YOUNG, but his credentials were impeccable. And he certainly looked the part—the CEO part, that is. The founder of the company, now the chairman of the board, had looked across the land for a young leader to bring in and succeed him as CEO. The chairman had been the company's only leader to this point, but it was time to transfer the reins to a younger set of hands.

The new president was the tall, dark, and handsome type, physically speaking. He wasn't hired for that reason, of course, but it didn't hurt. He commanded respect just by entering the room. It was his academic and experiential credentials that made him stand out. He had been at the top of his class in both business and graduate school and had hit the ground running when he entered the business world. Rapid promotions in his first jobs made him seem like a natural. So the chairman hired him to take over his own company.

The young president's first assignment was to close a deal that the chairman had been working on for years. A competing company had made life miserable for the chairman—they had a good product but were a fly in the industry ointment that no one seemed to be able to deal with. The chairman's company was now large enough to make the problem go away by buying them out. And he sent his young president to complete the deal.

The chairman was clear and firm: there were to be no last-minute compromises or changes. The competing CEO would have no role in the company after the buyout, and all his staff would lose their jobs. It seemed harsh—but it had to be done. The young president assured the CEO he understood—and boarded the company jet for the cross-country flight to complete the deal.

The next day, the chairman collapsed in his leather chair when he caught a cable TV business report. There was his young president and the competing CEO standing side by side, announcing plans for a *merger* instead of a *buyout*. The president had completely ignored the chairman's explicit instructions on how the deal was to be done.

The chairman tracked down his CEO at thirty thousand feet on the return flight and demanded to know why his instructions hadn't been carried out. What followed was a lengthy explanation of the benefits of his decision—how he had changed the chairman's instructions with the chairman in mind. "I did this for you, sir," he said. "The amount of revenue this is going to generate will far surpass your original plan. By retaining the other president and his staff, we get the best of what they had, which we can use to our benefit."

"As far as I am concerned, this deal was your first test of loyalty to me and this company—a test you have failed," the chairman said soberly. "You have chosen your own preferences over mine, which means we will have to part ways. Your services as president of this company will no longer be required."

Recognize that scenario? It's the story of the young man God set in place as king over Israel, a strapping young thirty-year-old named Saul. He was "an impressive young man without equal among the Israelites—a head taller than any of the others" (1 Samuel 9:2). But in one of Saul's first assignments as king he completely rebelled against the clear instructions God had given. To use the language of modern business, Saul settled for more of a "merger" than a "buyout."

Saul was creative but not loyal. Instead of doing what God had sent him to do, he did what he thought was better. And when God confronted Saul about his disobedience, He minced no words:

> Does the LORD delight in burnt offerings and sacrifices
> as much as in obeying the voice of the LORD?
> To obey is better than sacrifice,
> and to heed is better than the fat of rams.
> For rebellion is like the sin of divination,
> and arrogance like the evil of idolatry.

> Because you rejected the word of the LORD,
>   he has rejected you as king.
> (1 Samuel 15:22–23)

God talked about Saul's "rebellion" and "arrogance," words that sound rather harsh to us. After all, Saul's intentions weren't evil. He had God in mind when he changed God's assignment, thinking the Lord would be pleased with his creative gesture.

So what's going on here? What's at the heart of this thing called *rebellion*? I have met people who believe they have lost their closeness to God because they disobeyed Him at some point. They may have committed an impulsive, yet serious, sin. Or they may have lived lives of indifference toward God and aren't sure how to find their way back—or if God even wants them back.

Or they may have acted in a way that we normally associate with rebellion: like a child who throws a tantrum in the middle of a grocery store aisle because he can't get what he wants off the shelf. Adults don't normally throw themselves down on the ground and kick and scream, but our rebellion is just as serious. We say to God what a rebellious child says to his parent: "I've had it with You. You never answer my prayers. You let my marriage fall apart. You let me contract a terminal illness. You allowed me to lose my job. You didn't keep my kids from getting into trouble after I've prayed for them for years. I'm done with this. If this is the spiritual life, I want no part of it."

And we leave. We unplug. We disconnect from God.

But then, when we've had time (and sometimes it's a long time) to consider what we've done, we think differently. We find ourselves as frustrated as the apostle Paul sounds in Romans 7:19–20: "What I do is not the good I want to do; no, the evil I do not want to do—this I keep on doing. Now if I do what I do not want to do, it is no longer I who do it, but it is sin living in me that does it."

Is our "frustration" with God and the way the spiritual life works actually rebellion and arrogance? Does God view ours as seriously as He viewed Saul's? And if we know it's wrong (as the apostle Paul did), why do we do it? And if we've rebelled against God and pulled the plug, how do we get reconnected again?

First, let's define *rebellion. The American Heritage Dictionary* says to rebel is to *"refuse allegiance to* and oppose by force an established government or *ruling authority*; *to resist or defy an authority* or a generally accepted convention; *to feel or express strong unwillingness* or repugnance" (italics added).

The words I put in italics are some we can use to think about spiritual rebellion. God is certainly a "ruling authority"—no argument there. And if we act toward Him with any of the expressions I put in italics—refuse allegiance, resist, defy, feel or express unwillingness—then we have acted in rebellion toward Him.

Therefore, we've all rebelled against God (see Romans 3:10–18). If He is the authority and we are subject to Him, whenever we think contrary to His thoughts or act contrary to His desires, we're in rebellion. I talked about Adam and Eve in the previous chapter, and that's where rebellion in the human race began. God said, "Don't eat that," and Eve ate anyway, joined by Adam. Rebellion is in the water in the human gene pool, spiritually speaking.

The great A. W. Tozer had a way of stating things plainly and succinctly, and his thought on rebellion doesn't disappoint: "The essence of sin is rebellion against divine authority." And Charles Colson said the same thing a different way: "Sin is essentially rebellion against the rule of God." The great Reformer, Martin Luther, parsed the definition even finer: "What greater rebellion, impiety, or insult to God can there be than not to believe His promises?"

Every human being, and every Christian, qualifies as a rebel under one or more of those definitions—even if all we did was not believe one of God's promises, according to Martin Luther. But surely all acts of rebellion are not the same in God's sight—are they? Yes, in that they all are acts that can break our connection with God. And no, in that some acts of rebellion, such as Saul's, have far-wider-ranging consequences than others.

Now that we've defined rebellion, I want to focus on the kind of rebellion I have seen be most destructive in individuals' lives—the kind they usually regret long after it happens. And that is the tantrum-like act where, on the basis of some great disappointment in life, we decide that waiting on God, or obeying Him when it is difficult, is not worth it. We break off our relationship with God, feeling we just don't have the strength to continue, and we are (mistakenly) sure that He won't notice our absence.

I haven't seen many people reach that level of disappointment after committing a minor act of disrespect or disobedience toward God. Usually we can say, "God, I'm sorry. Please forgive me," and feel sure that we have been restored to our place of fellowship with Him on the basis of promises like 1 John 1:9. But I have seen people "throw such a tantrum" that they have a hard time recovering and finding their way back to God. They are consumed with guilt—especially if they've thrown this tantrum more than once—and feel sure that God is tired of their antics and has rolled up the welcome mat.

I have found it very helpful in my own life, and have seen it help in others', to realize this: when I am angry at God—when I rebel against Him—I'm really angry at something else and taking it out on Him. (After all, doesn't God get blamed for most of the bad things in this world? Who else are we going to blame?) The challenge then becomes discovering the real object of my anger or rebellion.

A dear friend, Dr. Ron Jensen, has developed a suite of spiritual tools and inventories designed to help people do just that. *Spiritual Growth: A Workbook for Group Study*[1] is a 350-page resource that acts as an "onion peeler" (my words) in individuals' lives. Working through this resource in a group setting, folks learn how to peel back the accumulated layers of life and get to the core issues that account for undesirable and unprofitable spiritual or emotional behaviors—like rebellion.

Sometimes people discover that their rebellion against God is actually rebellion against a parent or other authority figure with whom they have unresolved issues. Or perhaps rebellion is an expression of fear—an inability to trust God with what He desires them to do. Or there may be a child in an adult's body who never reached emotional maturity, never learned to "put away childish things" (1 Corinthians 13:11 NKJV) and climb the upward path to spiritual and emotional adulthood. Or any number of other issues could lie at the core of our rebellion against God and His standards and direction for our lives.

Because we all have "issues" in life—baggage from the past—I believe such exercises hold great value. They certainly have for me and for many in our church who have worked through Dr. Jensen's materials. But there is a bottom line that must be reached on this issue regardless of the cause of our rebellion (disobedience, disaffection, lack of respect) toward God: What do we do about it? How do we get reconnected to God if we find ourselves on the distant end of a rebellious tantrum that has separated us from Him?

First, we need to resolve Saul's case: he was never restored to God, as best we can tell from Scripture. Not because God closed the door, but because Saul allowed bitterness and anger over being removed as king of Israel to fester into a psychotic state of rage and anger toward God and his (Saul's) appointed successor, David. Saul died a defeated and disconnected man—indeed, he apparently took his own life. But it wasn't because God shut the door on their relationship. It was because Saul didn't know how to accept God's discipline for his sin of rebellion (the loss of his throne) and move on with his life in fellowship with God.

If you find yourself estranged from God—you feel completely disconnected—because of guilt over an act of rebellion in your life, don't take the path Saul took! Yes, you sinned against God, and yes, sin breaks your fellowship with God. But it doesn't matter whether your act of rebellion against Him was "small" (you had an impure thought) or "large" (you committed a vile or immoral act and are now consumed with guilt) or somewhere in between—it's all the same to God. He takes as much pleasure (perhaps even more) in forgiving your angriest act of rebellion as He does your smallest misstep in the course of a hectic day. God has not, and will not, shut the door of access to His love and forgiveness. "God is love" (1 John 4:8, 16), and love "keeps no record of wrongs" (1 Corinthians 13:5). Indeed, God's love never fails to embrace those who need it most. And He will not fail to embrace you if you return to Him.

Go to God and tell Him what you have done. Ask for His forgiveness through the shed blood of Christ, and you will have it. You will be reconnected with the God who keeps no records of our wrongs.

Questions for Reflection and Discussion

1. Sometimes we disconnect from God in rebellion by disobeying Him. Sometimes we rebel by living a life of indifference. Which type of rebellion is more apt to be true of you? Explain.

2. Describe a time when you decided that waiting on God, or obeying Him when it was difficult, simply was not worth it. What was the outcome of your decision?

3. At times, rebellion against God is actually an act or show of defiance against a parent or another authority figure with whom we have unsolved issues. Can you think of any ways in which you've done this in the past or maybe are even doing it in your life now?

4. God takes as much pleasure in forgiving our angriest act of rebellion as He does in forgiving our smallest missteps in the course of a busy day. Do you believe this is true? Describe a time when you experienced it in your life.

5. Romans 2:4 tells us that it is God's kindness that leads us to repentance. How have you experienced this in your life? When has God's kindness led you to turn away from your rebellion and back to Him?

4. Accepting Mercy When Weighed Down by Regrets

ALTHOUGH HE PLAYED his last game of professional baseball in 1969, many of his records still stand: the most World Series home runs, runs batted in, runs scored, walks, extra-base hits, and total bases. It's no wonder his World Series records have never been beaten—he played in twelve of them and was on the winning team, the New York Yankees, seven times. During his entire eighteen-year career, he never wore any team's uniform except that of his beloved Yankees. The first year he was eligible to be inducted into the Major League Baseball Hall of Fame, 1974, he made it. To this day he is one of the stars in the galaxy of baseball's greatest players, right up there with Babe Ruth, Lou Gehrig, and Joe DiMaggio, all of whom wore a Yankees uniform before him.

But in spite of being one of baseball's most adored icons, Mickey Mantle lived and died with many regrets. In a press conference in 1995, just a month before he died, Mantle observed that many people looked to him as a role model in life. "This is a role model," he said. "Don't be like me."

For most of his adult life Mickey Mantle battled alcoholism. And after a liver transplant necessitated by years of drinking, liver cancer took his life a year later. He tried to rally near the end—he checked himself into a famous rehab center in 1994 after his doctor told him, "Your next drink might be your last." But it was too little, too late.

Alcohol robbed Mantle of his mind: "I could be talking to you and just completely forget my train of thought.... I'd forget what day it was, what month it was, what city I was in."

Alcohol robbed him of his peace: "I had...bad anxiety attacks. There were times when I locked myself in my bedroom to feel safe."

Alcohol stole his body: "The doctor...said, 'Before long you're just going to have one big scab for a liver. Eventually you'll need a new liver....'"

Alcohol shortened his career: "[Legendary Yankees manager Casey Stengel] had said when I came up, 'This guy's going to be better than Joe DiMaggio and Babe Ruth.' It didn't happen. God gave me a great body to play with, and I didn't take care of it."

Alcohol robbed him of his family: "One of the things I really screwed up, besides baseball, was being a father. I wasn't a good family man. I was always out, running around with the guys."

Under pressure from a domineering father, Mickey Mantle married a girl he didn't love and fathered four sons. His wife and all his sons became alcoholics. Though they all received treatment, their battles with substance abuse became yet another regretful chapter in the story of Mickey Mantle's life. One son died at age thirty-six of heart disease, another at age forty-seven of liver cancer. Another battled prostate cancer. Mickey spent the last fifteen years of his life separated from his wife.

But Mickey Mantle found a way to respond to his regrets near the end of his life. Through the influence of a former teammate, he found a saving relationship with Christ and worked at making amends for many of the mistakes he had made. Along with other charitable endeavors, he established the Mickey Mantle Foundation to raise awareness of the need for organ donations for transplants.

At Mantle's funeral, sportscaster Bob Costas remembered him as "a fragile hero." He concluded by saying, "In the last year of his life, Mickey Mantle, always so hard on himself, finally came to accept and appreciate the distinction between a role model and a hero. The first, he often was not. The second, he always will be."[1]

Just considering those words makes my heart hurt for a man who brought so much pleasure and excitement to sports fans for so many years. And I recount Mickey Mantle's troubled life—and the redemptive end to his life—not to focus on his regrets and remorse, but to make us realize that he is us. Mickey Mantle is Everyman.

Who among us cannot identify with him? I certainly can—no, not in the particulars of his life, but in the ability to look back and wish I had done some things differently. Regrets and remorse are part of the fabric of life, and if we don't learn how to evaluate them and think about them we can find ourselves playing the "woulda-coulda-shoulda" game for the rest of our lives.

Some people have had such large regrets in life that they have concluded God can never forgive them. They think God feels the same way they do about the mistakes they have made. They settle for a second-class quality of life due to their inability to go back in time and erase the events that give them so much regret. They spend the balance of their lives convinced that there is no making up for what they did; no way to exchange debilitating regret for *incorporated regret*, which is regret that has been addressed and incorporated into life as a positive message going forward.

There seems to be little clarity concerning the origin of our English word *regret*, but one source says it may mean to "weep over again." The English word was borrowed from the Old French *regreter*, which may have been based on a German root, *gretan*—to weep.[2] So we weep when something bad happens, then we "re-weep" with regret and remorse for the rest of our lives, never able to find rest. And one of the reasons people can't live with rest instead of regret is because they think God stays sorry (meaning "unforgiving") about what they did.

You don't know me as a famous vocal recording artist—because I'm not! But when I was in college I was a vocal performance major, thinking that I wanted to use music as a ministry and a source of livelihood. But I changed my major to ancient civilizations because it seemed easier than other alternatives—and I regretted having to make that switch. But fast-forward a few years, and you would have found me in seminary being eternally grateful for my knowledge of ancient history and civilizations. It was a perfect backdrop for understanding the world of the Bible and the relationships between the Jews and their neighbors.

And what about music? Do I regret not having majored in music and pursuing a vocal career? Not in the least! I still love music and enjoy it in many different ways in my life, especially when it comes to appreciating the role of the worship ministry in the church I lead today. But looking back, I can see God's hand at work. What I regretted for a moment in time as a college student became an area in which I now rest in God's perfect guidance in my life.

Here's another decision I made, this one being not so clear-cut and easy to see looking back: after seminary, as I was entering the pastoral ministry, I considered joining the U.S. Navy Reserve as a chaplain. It would not have been a full-time responsibility, but it would have allowed me to consistently interface with a much different segment of our society—to get outside my "safe zone" and gain exposure to the spiritual needs of a different part of the human tapestry. Besides the fact that I have always loved the ocean, it would have been an opportunity to serve my country. It seemed like a perfect fit.

But I was the only one who thought so. I sought the counsel of several godly people and got mostly wrinkled brows and quizzical stares when I presented my plan. You know—the "You want to do what?" kind of look. Nobody doubted my motives or the fact that I would gain valuable insights that might help me in my ministry. But it boiled down to (in others' eyes) something *good* being the enemy of the *best*. No one thought it was the best use of my gifts and abilities or the best response to what seemed to be God's direction in my life.

So I gave up the idea—regretfully. Was that the right decision? It remains a bit of a gray area for me in the same way that some of your life choices are gray areas for you. *Did I take the right job? Move to the right city? Have the right number of children? Enter the right vocation?* And on and on. We all have gray areas of life that are impossible for us to judge with exactness in retrospect. I know now that if I had become a Navy Reserve chaplain, by missing one weekend per month during the twenty-year Reserve commitment, I would have missed 25 percent of Sunday worship services at my church—which is a lot. I would have missed that same amount of time with my family, and even more due to additional annual weeks of active-duty service. But by not being a chaplain, I missed out on a wealth of new relationships and experiences that might have broadened my perspectives on life and how God meets the needs of people I am not normally around.

But do I worry about (regret) the decision I made? Not for a minute. Even though it remains a gray area in terms of my understanding, I believe God incorporated that decision into my life and simply expanded my opportunities and service based on the choice I made. I believe that's what God does—uses the events in our lives to conform us to the image of His Son, Jesus Christ (see Romans 8:29). And because that's my ultimate goal in life, I am totally comfortable with His ability to make that happen regardless of the choices I have made.

Now—I can hear what you're thinking: "Robert, those are nice illustrations, but they are marshmallows compared to the hardballs I've been thrown in life. Come on—choosing a college major and choosing whether to add a second successful part-time career to an already blossoming one. Those aren't exactly life-threatening choices. If you knew the regrets I have, the stuff I think about at night before drifting into a fitful sleep... I'm not sure if you, or God, can relate to what I regret."

As I said, I hear you. But remember—unless you are bouncing from chapter to chapter in this book, you read in the introduction about my failed first marriage. That is something I will regret for the rest of my life. So I have eaten at your table. I have drunk from the same bitter cup as you have. But I am here to tell you that it is not a paralyzing regret in my life. It is a regret that I believe God has incorporated into my life to make me wiser, humbler, more realistic, more grateful for the wife and family I now have, more grateful for His redemptive grace, and more empathetic toward the events and regrets in the lives of other people.

When I speak to people today who have been divorced or who are struggling in their marriages, I know how they feel. When I hug a parent whose child is clinging to life in a hospital, I know how he or she feels. (We came "that close" to losing a child of ours.) When I listen to men who are struggling to get a business off the ground, I can identify. When I hear young people confess how they wish they'd lived part of their teenage years differently, those aren't strange words to me.

I may not have been exactly where you are today, but I may have been close. The details are not really what's important. It's our responses to our regrets—and God's response—that matter at the end of the day. Our responses to God's response are what will either set us free or keep us frozen for the rest of our lives. And here is God's response to our regrets: He covers them with His mercy.

I titled this chapter "Accepting Mercy When Weighed Down by Regrets" because that represents a challenge for all of us. First, here's how to think about God's mercy as opposed to His love or grace:

- Mercy is not receiving a negative response we deserve.

- Grace is receiving a positive response we don't reserve.

Please—don't rush by these definitions; they are the key to your moving past your regrets in life. First, when we do something that violates God's standards in life, we deserve to be reprimanded, judged, disciplined, or held to account for it. But God's mercy says that He sets aside the judgment—He *doesn't* give us what we deserve. That doesn't mean we get a "free pass" for our sins and choices. It means that . . .

1. Christ died for our sins, mistakes, and hurtful and bad choices so we can live.

2. Our choices will have consequences, but God will be there to help us work through them and overcome them.

3. God may incorporate discipline into our lives to teach us because He loves us as a father loves a son (see Hebrews 12:5–11).

But God's mercy sets aside everything that makes us believe God is angry with us, that He wants us to live guilt-ridden lives, that He doesn't want us to find success again until we've "learned our lesson." God's mercy says, "Because Christ died for all the frailties of man, I am free to welcome you and help you find new life—to help you incorporate your regrets into your life and become stronger as a result."

Mercy is hard for us to accept when we know we've failed. It's natural to believe that sins and failures need to be punished; it's unnatural to believe that Christ has taken our punishment for us so we can be free from regrets and remorse. The first step toward getting over regrets is accepting the mercy of God in Christ.

In Romans 11:30–32 the apostle Paul mentions God's mercy four times—how we "who were at one time disobedient to God have now received mercy" from Him (verse 30). And then he says in Romans 12:1, "In view of God's mercy, . . . offer your bodies as living sacrifices, holy and pleasing to God."

So instead of our regrets being a reason to be disconnected from God, they should be the very experiences that cause us to offer ourselves afresh to Him. Why? Because of His mercy!

If you have regrets that have caused you to turn away from God, I implore you: in view of God's mercy, offer yourself to Him afresh today. His mercy is the very reality that makes it possible to turn regrets into reasons to rejoice. Indeed, the more regretful you are, the more reasons you have to rejoice in the overflowing mercy of God.

Accept His mercy today, and make your way back to Him.

Questions for Reflection and Discussion

1. Regrets and remorse are part of the fabric of life. Looking back over your life, do you wish you had done anything differently? Make a short list of your regrets.

2. I mention the idea of "incorporated regrets" in this chapter. The idea here is that we learn to address our regrets and make them part of our lives as a positive life-message going forward. Describe one or two "incorporated regrets" that are part of your life.

3. God uses all of the events in our lives to conform us to the image of His Son, Jesus Christ (Romans 8:29). What life events has God used in the past to conform you to the image of His Son? Is there anything happening in your life at present that you may need to apply this truth to?

4. What misperceptions about God have kept you stuck in a world of regret? What truths about God do you need to cling to today to move past your regrets?

5. Understanding and accepting God's mercy is vital to moving through past regrets. Go back to the section in this chapter that talks about God's mercy and apply it to a specific area of regret in your life. Share with your group, or a close friend, the role God's mercy played in helping you overcome that regret.

5. Finding Freedom When Isolated Through Humiliation

AUDREY HECTOR IS MARRIED—a mother and grandmother—and a speaker, writer, and certified lay counselor through the American Association of Christian Counselors. But her life wasn't always that "normal." She spent thirty years reacting to the sexual abuse she suffered as a twelve-year-old child.

Here is part of her story in her own words:

> As a survivor of child sexual abuse, I can personally attest that the effects of abuse touched every aspect of my life—emotional, physical, relational and spiritual. I lived with a victim mentality for over thirty years until I learned to be a survivor.
>
> I was angry with everyone, and afraid to trust anyone. Shame and guilt became my constant companions, convincing me that I somehow encouraged the abusers' advances. I built protective barriers to avoid loving and being loved. . . .
>
> *Because adults betrayed and humiliated me*, I became rebellious, refusing to submit to authority. I kept intimate relationships at bay for fear someone I cared about would learn my secret.
>
> Because some of my abusers were "upstanding" members in the church clergy, I couldn't trust a God who seemed indifferent to my

suffering and who allowed adults to abuse me. I was afraid of that kind of love, so *I rejected God* and the counsel of the church.[1]

Only after decades of inappropriate reactions to her experience did Audrey come to grips with what had happened. She decided to stop abusing herself and learn to forgive those who had hurt her as a child. She reached out to the God she had rejected and experienced His love again, which freed her to, for the first time, love and accept herself and others.

I put two phrases in Audrey Hector's story in italics (go back and read them again in context if you missed them—they're that important) because they form the thesis of this chapter: *"Because adults betrayed and humiliated me . . . I rejected God."*

Sometimes people suffer humiliation so painful they reject God along with themselves and others. In their attempt to hide from the person they think they have become (as a result of someone's humiliating them), they lean away from God. Sometimes rejecting God is an angry, direct reaction: "Why didn't You protect me? Why did You allow this to happen?" But other times it's an indirect result of a person's withdrawing from everyone and everything. One day they realize they've stopped praying, stopped reading their Bible, stopped going to church—they've lost touch with God.

Too often, humiliation is equated with embarrassment, as if humiliation and embarrassment were synonyms. They're not. Humiliation is a *way* deeper form of embarrassment that has elements of anger, rage, pain, and shame all mixed in together. We are momentarily embarrassed when we forget a person's name in a social setting, but we are humiliated when we are the victims of another person's attack. Generally speaking, if we're embarrassed it's because we're guilty of something; if we're humiliated it's because we're innocent victims.

Shame and humiliation are often equated as well, but neither are they (generally speaking) the same. (Radio humorist and author Garrison Keillor speaks of getting the "taste of shame and humiliation out of your mouth" with a piece of rhubarb pie—but that's radio, not real life.[2]) Even the Bible sometimes uses the two words as synonyms: "Do not be afraid; you will not suffer shame. Do not fear disgrace; you will not be humiliated" (Isaiah 54:4). But they really aren't—at least not in experiential terms.

In chapter 2 of this book I defined shame as what we feel about ourselves when we've done something horrendously wrong or sinful—and we know it. We are usually embarrassed but not ashamed after committing a social faux pas. But if we break the law or commit an act of unfaithfulness or immorality, we're ashamed. Shame is the result of legitimate guilt created by our own actions. Humiliation is the result of false guilt heaped upon us by the acts of another.

Let me clear the deck of one more example before we focus on how I'm using humiliation in this chapter: sometimes we deserve the humiliation we endure. Once, in the ministry of Jesus, He healed a woman who had been crippled for eighteen years—and He did it on the Sabbath. The religious leaders criticized Him for breaking the Sabbath laws by healing the woman. Jesus took them to task for their hypocrisy: "Doesn't each of you on the Sabbath untie his ox or donkey from the stall and lead it out to give it water?" In other words, it was okay to take care of an animal on the Sabbath but not a suffering human being. "When [Jesus] said this, all his opponents were humiliated" (Luke 13:15, 17). So sometimes our humiliation at the hands of another is deserved.

But that's rare, and it's not my focus here. I'm concerned with those people who have put themselves in some sort of prison—they have shut down emotionally and spiritually—because of something dreadful that was done to them by another. Someone humiliated them, and instead of turning to God to help them through the situation, they rejected Him. And they don't know how to get back in touch; they don't know how to reconnect with God.

Dr. Evelin Lindner has studied humiliation and loss of dignity in large groups of people who are the victims in armed conflicts. She says that humiliation is "the enforced lowering of a person or group, a process of subjugation that damages or strips away their pride, honor or dignity.... One of the defining characteristics of humiliation as a process is that the victim is forced into passivity, acted upon, made helpless."[3]

Think of all the times this has happened in history to groups of people: the Hebrews (the family and descendants of Jacob) being humiliated by the Egyptians for four hundred years; the Jews being humiliated by the Nazis in Germany prior to and during World War II; the enslavement of Africans against their will in America; the "untouchable" castes in India; and, happening as I write, the systematic persecution of non-Arabs in the Darfur region of Sudan by the Arab-led Sudanese government. In all these cases, the victims of humiliation were "forced into passivity, acted upon, [and] made helpless."

So how does humiliation happen at the individual level? What could happen to you (or to any person) that would force you into a state of passivity—a feeling of helplessness—and cause you to see God as part of the problem rather than the solution?

- You might have been suddenly terminated from a job, throwing you and your family into financial difficulty.

- You might have been divorced by your spouse against your will. Or you might have initiated the divorce due to your spouse's creating an abusive or degrading environment in which you were forced to exist.

- Your reputation might have been ruined as the result of lies or slander spread by someone with a grudge or vendetta against you.

- You might have been the scapegoat for another person's crime. You might have been punished (jail, prison, fines, loss of status in the community) and been powerless to prove your innocence.

- You might have been raped as an adult or sexually abused as a child and become convinced, over time, that it was somehow your fault.

- You might have been born with an embarrassing congenital defect or challenging circumstance inflicted upon you by "nature."

The power of humiliation is hard to understand for those who have never experienced it. The *Chicago Tribune* newspaper carried the sad story of Samuel, a twelve-year-old boy in Fort Lauderdale, Florida. On Monday morning, August 26, 1996, Samuel's two brothers found him dead in the yard of their home, hanging from a tree. Beneath the tree were a step stool and a flashlight.

Did you note the day and date? It was a Monday at the end of August, and Samuel was scheduled to begin the school year at a new school. That's a challenging task for any peer-sensitive twelve-year-old, but for Samuel it was especially challenging. He had a serious weight problem, and he knew he would be teased unmercifully by the kids at school. Not only would he be a newbie, he would be a fat newbie in the eyes of his peers. He was so afraid of the humiliation he was certain he would endure that he sneaked out of his house in the middle of the night and ended his life. For Samuel, the pain of hanging was preferred over the pain of humiliation.[4]

Samuel is not the only person who has made that painful choice. For those who have not been tempted with that choice, it seems hard to believe that humiliation could wield such a sharp sword, but it can. Humiliation can occur as a result of becoming so overwhelmed with the realities of life—drug or substance addiction, rejection by a loved one, dire economic straits, loss of hope—that there seems no way out. Sometimes it happens for people who have not known God, but it can also happen to people who knew Him but lost touch in the midst of their pain.

It seems clear to me that, regardless of the external circumstance, the internal effect of humiliation is a perceived change of identity. The humiliated person sees himself or herself as having lost value, purpose, and a future. It's easy to see how a humiliated person would withdraw from friends and family. Think about how a person who is now a homeless beggar, but who used to be part of the elite segment of society, would feel about attending a high-society charity ball in New York City. Recently humiliated by forces beyond his control, he would not want to be seen by his former friends for fear of what they would think.

And that leads us to the next, harder step—how we get disconnected from God. We transfer what we believe other people think about us to God. We believe that He wants no more to do with our humiliated selves than we believe our friends and family do. In other words, we believe the lie. We start believing that God loves us "because of" instead of loving us "in spite of."

The way to reverse the effects of humiliation, insofar as God is concerned, is to reject the lie and believe the truth. The way to escape the self-imposed solitary confinement of humiliation is to experience the freedom of God's unconditional acceptance.

King David in the Old Testament didn't get everything right, but here's an instance when he did. He sent a group of men as ambassadors to pay respects to the family of a neighboring king who had died, a king who had once shown kindness to David. When David's men arrived at the king's city, the new king's advisers convinced him that David's men were there on a reconnaissance mission, preparing for an attack on their kingdom. So the new king "seized David's men, shaved off half of each man's beard, cut off their garments in the middle at the buttocks, and sent them away" (2 Samuel 10:4).

If it's true that "a man ain't a man without a hat" in Texas, then it was infinitely more true that a man wasn't a man without a beard in the ancient Near East. And remember in the movie *Braveheart* when the Scottish rebels of William Wallace turned around, bent over, and "mooned" the arrayed forces of King (Longshanks) Edward I of England? The sight of a man's bare buttocks in thirteenth-century AD Scotland was the same as in tenth-century BC Israel—highly offensive!

So what the new king of Ammon did to David's men was, to put it mildly, very humiliating: "When David was told about this, he sent messengers to meet the men, for they were greatly humiliated. The king said, 'Stay at Jericho till your beards have grown, and then come back'" (verse 5).

What David did for his men is what God does for us in our day of humiliation: First, He understands how we feel. Second, He defends us against the lies that accompany humiliation by telling us the truth. And third, He makes time and provision for the covering of our humiliation. David sent a sympathetic message of understanding to his men and allowed them to remain in nearby Jericho until their beards grew back before asking them to return to his service.

For us, God says, "Your humiliation is not your fault. You've done nothing wrong. You may be rejected by others, but you will not be rejected by Me. My Son, Jesus, bore His own humiliation, and yours, when He suffered His death on the cross of Calvary. That is the truth—and this truth is what will set you free indeed from your prison of humiliation."

Jesus said, "The truth will set you free" (John 8:32). Those who have been forced into the prison of isolation by their humiliation can be set free by the truth that God's love has not changed and will never change. Here are some reminders of the love God has for you today and how to experience it again:

- "In God I have put my trust; I will not be afraid. What can man do to me?" (Psalm 56:11 NKJV).

- "In my anguish I cried to the LORD, and he answered by setting me free" (Psalm 118:5).

- "I run in the path of your commands, for you have set my heart free" (Psalm 119:32).

- "I will walk about in freedom, for I have sought out your precepts" (Psalm 119:45).

- "The LORD is righteous; he has cut me free from the cords of the wicked" (Psalm 129:4).

- "[The Lord] has sent me to proclaim freedom for the prisoners" (Luke 4:18).

- "I am free and belong to no man" (1 Corinthians 9:19).

- "Why should my freedom be limited by what someone else thinks?" (1 Corinthians 10:29 NLT).

- "Where the Spirit of the Lord is, there is freedom" (2 Corinthians 3:17).

- "It is for freedom that Christ has set us free. Stand firm, then, and do not let yourselves be burdened again by a yoke of slavery. . . . You, my brothers, were called to be free" (Galatians 5:1, 13).

Most of those verses were not written as therapy for humiliation in their original context. But they nonetheless represent the heart of God. Whether one has been humiliated by the Law of Moses ("You're a worthless, guilty sinner!") or by one's enemy ("You're a worthless, guilty sinner!"), the antidote for humiliation is the same: God's truth. If you have been humiliated, the last thing in the world you want to do is disconnect from God and His truth. Indeed, you need to do what Jesus did in the day of His own humiliation—entrust yourself to God: "When they hurled their insults at him, he did not retaliate; when he suffered, he made no threats. Instead, he entrusted himself to him who judges justly" (1 Peter 2:23).

Let today be the day you walk out of the prison cell where humiliation has confined you. If this book is in your hand, you hold the key it contains: God's truth that you are loved, and you always will be.

Questions for Reflection and Discussion

1. Humiliation is not the same thing as embarrassment. Humiliation goes much deeper and has elements of anger, pain, and shame all mixed together. Humiliation is the result of what someone else has done to you. Can you think of anything that happened in the past that today is still a source of humiliation for you? Explain the cause of your humiliation to the degree you are comfortable doing so.

2. One of the defining characteristics of humiliation is that it makes us feel victimized and helpless, and forces us into a position of passivity. As you look out at the world, where do you see this happening today?

3. In this chapter I mention a list of reasons that might cause someone to feel humiliated at a personal level. Which of the things mentioned in the list did you identify with? What else would you add to that list?

4. Sometimes people suffer humiliation so painful they reject God along with themselves and others. Describe a situation where you've seen this happen.

5. The way to reverse the effects of humiliation is to start believing that God loves you "because of" instead of loving you "in spite of" who you are. The book of Psalms is filled with many reminders about the love God has for us. Search Psalms this week and jot down some of the reminders you find there of God's love for you. Be ready to share during your group discussion one or two verses you found especially meaningful.

Part 2

Flexing Your Faith Power

6. Tapping into Faith When Debilitated by Fear

STEVE WAS RAISED IN A nominally religious home—twelve years of perfect attendance pins for not missing Sunday school or church. But when he got to college, he gave himself a long vacation from church.

Long story short—through the influence of some fraternity brothers, Steve eventually realized he was religious, but he wasn't a Christian. That is, Jesus Christ meant little to him personally. But he made a faith commitment to Christ and began to grow in his faith, and his life began to change as well. This caused no end of questions on his part, summarized by this one: *What was I doing in church all my growing-up years if not developing a relationship with Christ, the core figure of Christianity?*

To get an answer to that question, Steve and a friend named Fred, whose spiritual experience had mirrored Steve's, made an appointment with one of the ministers at their denomination's "mother church," which happened to be in their college town. They each told the minister their story: faithful church attendance during growing-up years, falling away from church during college, then discovering what it meant to know Christ personally, and now "really excited," for the first time in their lives, about what it means to be a Christian.

"Why," they asked, "weren't we taught the Bible in our churches growing up? Why weren't we told what it means to have a personal relationship with Jesus Christ? Why wasn't it explained that Christianity is not just a religious exercise but the expression of God's revelation to His creation? And most important, why weren't the temporal and eternal ramifications of our sins explained to us—and how we could be forgiven? To be honest, we feel cheated, spiritually shortchanged."

The minister listened patiently and did not interrupt as the two young men verbalized their frustrations and then their excitement about knowing Christ, studying the Bible, prayer, and the Holy Spirit.

And then he spoke: "I appreciate what you've shared. And I have to tell you that personally, I agree theologically with everything you believe. And historically, our denomination's roots are in that same biblical soil. But when it comes to what I preach and teach from the pulpit of this church, I have to be honest—I have a wife and a family to think about."

The room was silent as the two young zealots digested the minister's last statement. Had he really just told them that he was afraid to be biblically faithful in his ministry for fear of losing his job—putting his wife and children at risk?

Let's not jump to conclusions. Maybe there were other issues going on in that minister's life, his church, or his denomination that complicated the matter. And maybe the two young firebrands were looking for a fight and weren't mature enough to know what it meant to "become all things to all men" (1 Corinthians 9:22) in order to save some.

But this we can say for a fact: fear can cause people to water down their faith, even abandon their faith. Whether it's fear of persecution for being a Christian, or some other kind of fear at a personal level, fear can unravel the heavy-duty cord of faith that connects us to God.

Fear can fray the cord of faith in lots of different ways:

- Fear of death (martyrdom) can lead to apostasy—the denial of Jesus Christ.

- Fear of ridicule and loss of income can lead to watering down the faith.

- Fear of public speaking can keep one from having a ministry of teaching for Christ.

- Fear of failure can prevent one from launching a new business or ministry that would bring honor to Christ.

- Fear of failure can prevent one from marrying and raising a family.

It doesn't matter what kind of fear it is. Fear negates faith. And where faith is negated, our closeness to God is weakened. Therefore, our goal in life is to live fearless lives—that is, faith-full lives in which we are completely connected to God at every point: spiritually, emotionally, physically, vocationally, relationally, and personally.

Think of a heavy-duty electrical cord that is made up of a thousand tiny copper wires. Think of those wires as representing the thousand ways in which our faith keeps us connected to God. Every time one of those tiny wires of faith is replaced by fear, the power in our lives is weakened. The cord might be cut in an instant by an act of apostasy—cutting ourselves off from belief in God altogether. Or it might be weakened over time as fear replaces faith. Either way, fear has the ultimate effect of weakening our relationship with God. Our goal, therefore, is to replace fear with faith.

First, let's establish this fact: the opposite of faith is not unbelief. Lexically, one might say that the opposite of faith is nonfaith, or unbelief. But the Christian life is not an exercise in definitions, it is an exercise in experience. And experientially, Jesus Himself suggested that the opposite of faith is fear.

Everyone knows the story of Jesus and the disciples crossing the Sea of Galilee in a boat when a violent storm arose (see Matthew 8:23–27). Jesus had fallen asleep and didn't see the storm brewing until the disciples woke Him, yelling, "Don't just lay there—do something!" (my paraphrase). Jesus looked at the storm and looked at the disciples and said, "You of little faith, why are you so afraid?" (verse 26). (This question in Mark's version of the story is even more pointed: "Why are you so afraid? Do you still have no faith?" [4:40].)

Notice that Jesus didn't say, "Why are you so unbelieving?" For Him, the opposite of strong faith ("you of little faith") was fear (being afraid). Why? Because life can be defined by how one perceives the future. Whether you are considering something that might happen in the next few moments (like being drowned in a storm at sea) or in the next few years (like not finding a marriage partner) or the next few decades (like not having adequate financial resources or medical support in your latter years)—life is about the future. And there are only two ways to approach the future: with fear or with faith.

If we are beset by fear—of any kind or to any degree—our futures are going to be limited as fear crowds our faith and makes it impossible for us to trust God completely.

Let's be honest: we all have fears—and yours aren't the same as mine. (I say we all have them because I don't know of anyone who exercises perfect faith, all the time.) I recall seeing or reading a Jerry Seinfeld routine in which he was talking about a list of people's "Top Ten Fears." On that particular list, public speaking was the number one fear, ranked even higher than the fear of dying. His observation was that, given the choice at a funeral, people would rather be in the casket than at the podium delivering the eulogy! Since I grew up deathly afraid of public speaking, that's one I can really identify with.

Or you may be beset as an adult with childhood fears you never got over: fear of thunder, spiders, the dark, being alone, or heights. One list I have seen contains more than 350 cataloged fears along with their bizarre names—something for everyone.[1] Many of the fears are peculiar and rare, unknown except to the people who live with them.

But there are plenty of adult-size fears that most of us face at one time or another: fear of being rejected or unloved; fear of being criticized by others; fear of the collapse of our health, finances, or social networks; fear of new places and challenges; fear of failure; fear of being alone in life; even the fear of success subconsciously immobilizes some people.

We laugh and joke about people's fears, but they can be deadly serious. Fears can become larger than life. During the January 17, 1994, Northridge/Los Angeles earthquake, more than one hundred Californians literally died of fright, according to Robert Kloner, cardiologist at the Good Samaritan Hospital in Los Angeles. In another study in Cleveland, coroners studied the hearts of fifteen assault victims who died even though their assault wounds were not serious enough to have caused death. It was determined that eleven of the fifteen had torn fibers and lesions in their heart muscles most likely caused by mortal fear.[2]

The same thing happened in 1991 during the Gulf War when Iraq sent Scud missiles into Israel. The vast majority of Israelis who died on the first day of the Iraqi attacks did not die from the missiles but from heart failure brought on by fear and stress. As soon as it was realized that the Iraqi missiles were causing little harm, the death rate during the seventeen attacks dropped rapidly to a level considered normal for Israeli society.[3]

An August 14, 1989, *Time* magazine article reported the story of a Michigan man who spent a good bit of time in the outdoors. He had been bitten by ticks a number of times over the years and became obsessed with the probability that he had contracted Lyme disease and passed it to his wife. Despite tests showing he didn't have Lyme disease and assurances that, even if he did it was incommunicable, the man's fears of the disease drove him to take his wife's life and then his own.

Some people who read these stories will shake their heads in unbelief. Others will nod their heads in affirmation, knowing just how strong fear can be. Even if our fears are not life threatening in a physical sense, they certainly can be in a spiritual sense. Past failures in marriage, relationships, business ventures, spiritual growth, finding a church home, correcting personal problems—all these and more can make us fearful of ever finding success. And when that happens, we pull away from the ultimate source of all our success, God Himself. When we allow fear to crowd our faith, our relationship with God is weakened or destroyed.

I was amazed to learn that fear is such a prevalent theme in the Bible. Various forms of the terms "fear" and "afraid" occur more than 520 times (some of those are references to the healthy "fear of the Lord"). We are exhorted more than one hundred times, "Do not be afraid," "Do not fear," and "Fear not." Given that the Bible is an accurate reflector of human experience, it's clear that fear has been plaguing humans forever.

In fact, fear was so common in Jesus' day that the presence (or absence) of faith amazed Him—literally. The only places I can find in the New Testament that document Jesus' being amazed at something was in connection with faith or its absence. For instance, a Roman centurion sent some Jewish elders to Jesus to ask Him to come and heal the centurion's servant. When Jesus was on His way to the centurion's house He was met by friends of the centurion with a message: Jesus didn't need to physically come. The centurion believed that if Jesus spoke a healing word the servant would be healed. "When Jesus heard this, he was amazed at him, and turning to the crowd following him, he said, 'I tell you, I have not found such great faith even in Israel'" (Luke 7:9).

The other time Jesus was amazed was in Nazareth, His hometown. People there knew Him as "the carpenter," the son of Mary; they knew His brothers and sisters. They didn't believe He was anything special. As a result, "he could not do any miracles there, except lay his hands on a few sick people and heal them. And he was amazed at their lack of faith" (Mark 6:5–6).

I don't think we realize how important faith and fear are to God. They are so important that Jesus was amazed by them: the presence of faith or its absence (the presence of fear). Why are they so important? *Because fear is a statement about the character and power of God.* If we have fear, we say that there is something bigger and more powerful than God Himself—something outside His control. It's a denial of who He is and what He desires for us: "'I know the plans I have for you,' declares the LORD, 'plans to prosper you and not to harm you, plans to give you hope and a future'" (Jeremiah 29:11).

I'm not talking here about getting over our childhood fears. We can have true love for and trust in God and still be haunted by things buried deep in our psyches. For those fears, some "peeling back of the onion" in a therapeutic context—removing layer after layer of experience until we find the root of the fear—will be helpful. What I'm talking about is the kinds of fears that immobilize us, that keep us from trusting God, that freeze our feet to the floor when it comes to exercising faith. Those are the fears we need to give up and get over because they strike at the heart of who we think God is and who He wants to be in our lives.

Ironically enough, the way we get over our human fears is by replacing one kind of fear with another. When we fear the Lord, fear equals honor, respect, trust, and joyful obedience. In a logical sense, it's impossible for us to fear (trust) the Lord and fear anything else at the same time:

> The LORD is my light and my salvation—
>> whom shall I fear?
> The LORD is the stronghold of my life—
>> of whom shall I be afraid?
>
> (Psalm 27:1)

> When I am afraid,
>> I will trust in you.
> In God, whose word I praise,
>> in God I trust; I will not be afraid.
>> What can mortal man [or anything else] do to me?
>
> (Psalm 56:3–4)

First John 4:18 says that God's "perfect love drives out fear." If you are living in the presence of God and an awareness of His love, there will be no room for fear. And nothing "in all creation, will be able to separate us from the love of God that is in Christ Jesus our Lord" (Romans 8:39).

May I encourage you to amaze Jesus Christ today? Not by the absence of your faith, but by its presence and strength!

Questions for Reflection and Discussion

1. What were some fears you had as a child? Are any of those fears still part of your life today? (Before answering this question too quickly, consider this: Were you afraid of being alone as a child? Do you fear being abandoned as an adult?)

2. In what ways do you identify with the statement "Fear has the ultimate effect of weakening our connection to God"? How have you experienced this in your life?

3. Life is about the future. And there are only two ways to approach the future: with fear or with faith. As you think about the future—either the near future or the more distant future—are you aware of any fears you have concerning it? Identify those fears by name. In what ways have those fears created a separation between you and God?

4. Fear is a statement about how we see the character and power of God. Based on the current "fear factors" in your life, how would you describe the God you believe in at present? What do you need to believe is true of the character and power of God to overcome your fears?

5. What steps can you take to eliminate fear from your life and increase your capacity to trust God in a positive, proactive way?

7. Plugging into Renewed Confidence When Crushed by Disappointment

I F YOU HAVE HAD YOUNG CHILDREN in your home between 1996 and the present time, chances are good you've seen the Walt Disney classic movie *101 Dalmatians*. While the movie was a giant box-office success, it helped to spawn an unforeseen disaster that no one anticipated.

So many people (I'm guessing it was the children) fell in love with the adorable, spotted Dalmatian puppies featured in the movie that there was a run on them all over the country. Pet stores and breeders couldn't make them available fast enough. But within a couple of years, the trend reversed. Many of the same people (this time, the parents) who couldn't wait to be a Dalmatian owner now couldn't wait to be rid of the rambunctious, spotted animals that had taken over their lives. They discovered that watching and laughing at a Dalmatian puppy on the movie screen was nothing like having a young adult Dalmatian in their homes. What they expected was not what they got.

The Associated Press reported that dog shelters across America reported a dramatic rise in the number of Dalmatians being abandoned by their owners. A Florida organization called Dalmatian Rescue took in 130 Dalmatians in the first nine months of 1997, the same number they would normally see over a two- or three-year period.

What went wrong? The people who bought Dalmatians allowed fantasy to replace reality. They created expectations based on their own desires instead of based on knowledge born out of research. They laughed at five-pound puppies on the movie screen and found themselves yelling at seventy-pound, four-legged home-wreckers a few months later.

Dalmatians are large, muscular, energetic dogs that require lots of exercise and "entertainment." They were originally bred as "coach dogs" to run alongside the carriages of their owners and to live in the stables with horses, not indoors with humans. They were capable of running alongside carriages for fifteen to twenty miles in a day.[1] They can become bored, moody, restless, and destructive if they are not given ways of staying busy and burning up energy. They shed all year long and as many as 10 percent of Dalmatians are born deaf.[2]

Would you buy a puppy that might turn into a dog like that? Well, certainly a lot of people do. But I'm betting the people who buy Dalmatian puppies and keep them forever do so on the basis of informed expectations. The people who were disappointed with their purchases and gave up their Dalmatians to an adoption agency or rescue shelter had misplaced expectations to begin with.

I have met no small number of people in my life whose experience mirrored that of the post–101 Dalmatians purchasers of a spotted puppy. But instead of being disappointed in their *dog*, they were disappointed in their *God*. And that kind of disappointment can be far deeper and life changing.

When we expect God to come through in our lives in a certain way, we construct an outcome in our hearts and minds—an expectation—and see God as the only One who can meet our need. In that regard, we are being card-carrying human beings. We're supposed to depend on God to meet our needs. We become like the biblical Job, crying out to God from our sackcloth and ashes. But sometimes, like Job, we get nothing in return. At least nothing that we can recognize at the moment.

When do we cross the line from being disappointed to being disappointed with God? If the mail is late or we burn the toast, we may be disappointed, but we're not disappointed with God. But at some point we cross the line and hold God responsible for not doing what we expected He would. The mail will eventually come. We can make more toast. But when we lose a child to a miscarriage after trying for years to get pregnant...when a three-decade-old marriage comes to an end...when a child chooses a wayward path...all in spite of countless hours of prayer and pleading and deal-making with God, then at that point we are disappointed with Him.

And we've all crossed that line. Haven't you? I know I have. I've been at a place where I asked God for things that He didn't provide, and I was disappointed. Okay, I was disappointed *with Him*. Not yelling and screaming and leaving-the-faith disappointed, but disappointed with Him nonetheless.

Disappointment, at any level, happens when we make an appointment with "the future" and that appointment isn't kept. We keep it—but the other responsible party (often God) fails to show. We make an appointment and get dissed, to use the language of the street. We get rejected, stood up, and blown off. We make an appointment and are dissed. Therefore, we're dis-appointed.

Put another way, we have expectations about the future—what it's going to look and taste and feel like. And when our expectations aren't met, we are let down. We're disappointed. And if that expectation was shaped like a newborn baby, a happy marriage, a big promotion, or the financial payoff from a big investment, then we get seriously disappointed with God. Mail and toast are on our list to handle. But babies, marriages, jobs, and large sums of money—those are on God's list. And we expect Him to come through.

We don't ask Him for much, we think. And we give a lot: church, money, committee time, Little League coaching, family faithfulness. Hey, we do our share. Is it too much to expect God to do His?

Some would say the answer to avoiding disappointment is simple: "No expectations, no disappointments." If we don't set the bar too high, then we won't be disappointed when we aren't able to get over it. But is that really the answer—to live a life of low expectations? Are healthy children, a happy marriage, a successful career, and a joyful life examples of setting the bar too high?

I don't think so. I believe all of those are just a few examples of the wonderfully abundant life God created us to experience. Even when He entered our disabled world, Jesus still said, "I came so they can have real and eternal life, more and better life than they ever dreamed of" (John

10:10 *The Message*). No, the answer to disappointment with God is not lowering our expectations. The answer is dreaming and scheming and seeking all this God-gifted life has to offer, but learning how to respond when our expectations aren't met.

(Caveat: If you are sixty-five years old and your expectation is to be the first person to walk on Mars, I would say you need to lower your expectations. Or, if you want to go for it, more power to you. Just read the rest of this chapter before you apply to astronaut school.)

You can go to your local bookstore and load up on books by gurus and personal coaches about how to set realistic goals (expectations) in life, but as far as I can tell it boils down to this: Make them too low, and you'll live a safe, but passive and boring, life. Make them too high, and you'll live a hyperactive and dangerous life. Either way, you'll end up disappointed and perhaps blame God in the end. On the one hand, you'll be disappointed that life returned little for your conservative, safe efforts. On the other, you'll be disappointed that life returned little for your proactive, over-the-top efforts.

The key is to get to know God and yourself. Discover who God made you to be and learn to conform your expectations to the kinds of things God seems to bless. And don't compare how God meets someone else's expectations with how He meets yours. His plan for your life is unique.

Now—once you've done that, how do you handle disappointments when (not if) they come?

For starters, learn to live by the wisdom of Proverbs 16:9: "In his heart a man plans his course [sets His expectations], but the LORD determines his steps." Set your goals and create your expectations, all the while remembering that God has the final answer. "The LORD works out everything for his own ends" (Proverbs 16:4)—that's the Old Testament version of Romans 8:28: "We know that in all things God works for the good of those who love him, who have been called according to his purpose." (His purpose is explained in the next verse: to conform you to the character of Jesus.)

Sometimes people try to console those who are disappointed by saying, "God does everything for a reason." And disappointed people don't like to hear that. Well, it's not an easy answer, but there are two ways to approach disappointment. If you want to approach it from the Bible's perspective, this is the way: God has reasons for everything. Or you can approach it apart from the Bible and view the universe as a giant pinball machine in which sometimes you win and sometimes you lose.

What we can't do is approach life from the Bible's point of view and then disconnect from God when He doesn't come through—when He doesn't meet our expectations of how God should act.

Here's the New Testament's version of Proverbs 16:9:

> Listen, you who say, "Today or tomorrow we will go to this or that city, spend a year there, carry on business and make money." Why, you do not even know what will happen tomorrow. What is your life? You are a mist that appears for a little while and then vanishes. Instead, you ought to say, "If it is the Lord's will, we will live and do this or that." As it is, you boast and brag. All such boasting is evil. Anyone, then, who knows the good he ought to do and doesn't do it, sins.
> (James 4:13–17)

The apostle James, who wrote those words, is not known for dancing around the point, and he doesn't here. The people in his parable had an expectation of going into a city, setting up a business, and a year later having a healthy profit to show for their efforts. That scenario has been repeated countless times by others—plans, dreams, expectations. If they are God-fearing people and make their profit, hopefully they give God thanks. But if they fail in their efforts, they run a big risk of being disappointed with God.

James's solution is the way, as Christians, we manage expectations: We say, "If it is the Lord's will," then we'll do so-and-so. We work hard, do the best we can (that's our part), and leave the results to God.

I can hear someone saying, "What a cop-out!" Here's why that's not a cop-out for the person who fears the Lord: you can't thank God for letting you start the business and make a profit and then curse God if the business fails. If you're going to include God in your life when things are good, you have to include Him when things are bad. It's that simple.

And it's not that simple—because we cannot understand the ways of God: "The secret things belong to the LORD our God" (Deuteronomy 29:29); "It is not for you to know the times or dates the Father has set by his own authority" (Acts 1:7). There were things about God that not even Jesus knew or understood (see Matthew 24:36). So we ask Him for

His involvement in our lives and then leave it to Him to shape how that involvement looks in the end.

But (I can hear someone saying) doesn't the Bible say that God will give us the desires of our hearts? Here's the verse often quoted by those who are disappointed with Him: "Delight yourself in the LORD and he will give you the desires of your heart" (Psalm 37:4). Sounds like a carte blanche, doesn't it—a promise to prevent all future disappointments? Sounds like it, but it isn't.

The context of that verse is persecution by evil, unjust men (see Psalm 37:1–2). The psalmist's advice is to delight in the Lord (verse 4) and trust in the Lord (verse 5), and the desire of your heart will be realized. And what is that desire? To have your righteousness vindicated (verse 6). Therefore, rather than being a promise that God will give you anything your heart desires, this passage is an exhortation on what to do when you are persecuted unjustly: "Be still ... wait patiently ... do not fret ... refrain from anger" (verses 7–8). Sadly, this great verse (verse 4) has been mis-quoted and taken out of context so often that it has become a setup for disappointment. When we don't get the desires of our hearts, we think God has failed us.

The Bible says the only way to avoid disappointment is to put your hope in God: "Those who hope in [God] will not be disappointed" (Isaiah 49:23); "Hope does not disappoint us, because God has poured out his love into our hearts by the Holy Spirit, whom he has given us" (Romans 5:5).

Often when we are disappointed in life we are embarrassed or ashamed of ourselves: "I can't get pregnant—what's wrong with me?" "I lost the great job I had." "Our engagement was broken off." Psalm 25:3 says, "No one whose hope is in [God] will ever be put to shame." Why? Because you are trusting Him with the outcome of your expectations! You can right-fully say, "He knows best. I trust my expectations to Him."

If you have been disappointed to the extent that you have lost faith in God's love for you, don't let the weakness of your faith keep you from reconnecting with Him. Again, hope in the Lord: "Those who hope in the LORD will renew their strength" (Isaiah 40:31). The word *renew* in Hebrew means to exchange, like changing one's clothes (see Genesis 35:2; Judges 14:12).[3] If you are disappointed and weak in faith, take off your weakness and put on God's strength today. Man's highest expecta-tion and hope—being perfectly loved by God—is yours if you will.

Questions for Reflection and Discussion

1. Disappointment is what lies between our expectations and unfulfilled realities. Describe a time recently when you experienced a deep sense of disappointment.

2. How do you handle disappointment when it comes?

3. How can we learn to set expectations that are neither too high nor too low?

4. How do you respond to someone who disappoints you? How do you respond when you feel God doesn't come through for you or meet your expectations?

5. Isaiah 49:23 tells us that "those who hope in [God] will not be disappointed." Why do you think this is true? When have you experienced this in your life?

8. Claiming Courage When Derailed by Anxiety

FROM THE TIME LUCINDA BASSETT was a child, she had been anxious. She lived in dread of almost every circumstance in life. The daughter of an alcoholic father, she grew up in a home where insecurity and anxiety were the norm. As a result of living in a situation in which there was little peace, she grew up without peace in her own life.

Panic attacks started at age seven and an eating disorder developed at age twelve. By age fifteen the eating disorder had become IBS—irritable bowel syndrome—and she eventually became an agoraphobic, a person who lived in fear of leaving home and interacting with normal social situations: shopping, work, recreation. Looking back, she describes herself as living like a duck as an adolescent and young adult. On the surface she appeared to float along normally in life, but beneath the surface her emotional feet were paddling ninety miles an hour trying to maintain balance and make some kind of progress in life.

Here's Lucinda's own description of her life as a young adult:

> I worried constantly—about *everything*! I worried about being liked. I worried that something bad was going to happen to my family. I worried about my health—fearing I had this disease or that illness.
>
> It was around my twenties when my world became most limited and intolerable. I was having panic attacks on a daily basis. It wasn't long before I began limiting my activities to avoid these attacks. I had difficulty driving, flying, socializing—even sitting in closed-

door meetings at work. I was an emotional roller coaster, frustrating everyone around me with my obsessiveness and negative, irrational thinking.

I visited doctor after doctor, saw specialists, psychiatrists and had just about every medical test known to man at the time. I literally spent a small fortune over 10 years looking for answers and relief from my heart palpitations, headaches, stomach problems and other symptoms. Yet, I wasn't getting any answers.

But within twenty-four hours she got an answer that began the process of her transformation *From Panic to Power*[1]—and it began with a prayer. Lying on her sofa one night, head in hands and crying in despair, she prayed a simple prayer: "God, please show me one person that has survived what I have, that hasn't gone crazy or died. And I promise I will help You for the rest of my life." By her own admission, she didn't know exactly what the last part of that prayer meant. She only knew she didn't want to "go crazy or die." So she cried out to the only person she thought could help.

The next morning, while Lucinda was preparing for work, a television morning show was on in the background, and she heard a woman's voice describing the same kind of symptoms she had experienced all her life. The woman used terms like "anxiety and panic attacks" and "agoraphobia" with which Lucinda was unfamiliar. But she was definitely familiar with the symptoms. *That's exactly what I have*, she thought.

Lucinda's anxiety-filled life had disconnected her from almost everyone and everything in her life, including God:

> I always felt like I wasn't good enough for anybody including God. I felt like God had kind of given up on me. We went to church when I was younger and yet I felt like, How could a God let my father be an alcoholic? You know, How could God let my family feel so much pain? How could God not be here for me and my family? And so I guess I maybe even blamed God.

It was when she prayed her desperation prayer that God's answer, delivered through a woman unknown to her via a television program the next morning, put her on the road to recovery. At last, her anxiety and fear had names. She spent the next six months in the library and bookstores reading everything she could find about panic and anxiety attacks and agoraphobia. Over twenty years later, Linda says:

> That was the beginning of my path to recovery. And the funny thing is, God has constantly been there just pushing me along, I went looking for my healing through God and God would bring things to me that would help me heal; would constantly and consistently show me things. It was then up to me to take them and make them work in my life.

Not only was her life restored to spiritual, physical, and emotional health through God's answer to her prayer, she has helped countless others through her books, tapes, and as cofounder of the Midwest Center for Stress and Anxiety.[2]

Although she didn't know it at the time, Lucinda was applying to her anxiety a very simple biblical premise: "You do not have, because you do not ask God" (James 4:2). The Bible pictures God as a heavenly Father. And what do children say to their earthly fathers when they have a need? "Father, would you please give me"—and they name what they need. But somehow we have a hard time with that when it comes to God. First, because He's God. It seems too much to think that He would stop and attend to our needs. And second, in the case of needs like freedom from anxiety, when we're anxious we're not thinking right. We're too anxious to sit down quietly and pray for peace!

Jesus Himself must have sensed this reluctance in people to ask God for help in their lives. With a bit of first-century Jewish humor (as I imagine it to have been), here's what He said: "Which of you fathers, if your son asks for a fish, will give him a snake instead? Or if he asks for an egg, will give him a scorpion?" (Luke 11:11–12).

Jesus' point is obviously this: God is a loving Father who will give to His children what meets their needs. If they need fish, they'll get fish. If they need eggs, they'll get eggs. And if they need peace, they'll get peace.

We're used to seeing bumper stickers that read "Pray for Peace" and think it's a good thing for the world. But when it comes to ourselves and our anxieties we find it hard to be as believing. After all, fish and eggs are "things" that we can touch and feel and eat. We know when our prayers for them have been answered. But peace? Peace is a feeling, a state of mind, a way of thinking that manifests itself in how we live and act. How do we know when we have peace and when our anxiety has been displaced—and how long our peace will last?

Here's how we know we *can* have it. The last statement Jesus made as part of His reproof to His listeners (and to us) about prayer was this: "If you then, though you are evil, know how to give good gifts to your children, how much more will your Father in heaven give the Holy Spirit to those who ask him!" (Luke 11:13). Even human fathers, who are not perfect, know how to meet their children's needs. How much more will God the Father do the same? Especially by giving "the Holy Spirit to those who ask him." And do you know what the Holy Spirit gives to those who have Him? Peace, freedom from anxiety. The fruit of the Holy Spirit is peace (see Galatians 5:22).

The common element in the verse from James and these words of Jesus is a tiny one, on which your peace of heart and mind may depend: ask. Peace is ours for the asking. There is more to it than asking—but let's start there with this illustration from Haddon Robinson, one of America's best preachers and trainers of preachers.

In one of his own sermons on prayer, Robinson recounted a game he played with his children when they were very young. He would put a few coins in his hand and close his fist over them. His children's job was then to pry open his fingers, one at a time, until they gained access to the coins. When they had them all they would squeal with delight and run off with their treasures.

"Sometimes," Robinson wrote, "when we come to God, we come for the pennies in His hand. 'Lord, I need a passing grade. Help me to study.' 'Lord, I need a job.' 'Lord, my mother is ill.' We reach for the pennies. When God grants the request, we push the hand away."[3]

In other words, we are more interested in the gift than the Giver. When we feel anxious, we pray for peace and run back to our lives when we get it. But if we would simply stay close to God's open hand, from which flows peace like a river, peace would be ours all the time.

The most important passage in the whole Bible on praying for peace, and receiving it, is Philippians 4:6–7: "Do not be anxious about anything, but in everything, by prayer and petition, with thanksgiving, present your requests to God. And the peace of God, which transcends all understanding, will guard your hearts and your minds in Christ Jesus."

I've set these two verses apart for a reason because they represent a common biblical way of thinking about how our provision comes from God—even the provision of peace when we are consumed with anxiety. You'll notice that prayer is mentioned in verse 6 and peace is mentioned in verse 7. That is, the experience of peace follows the practice of prayer. It's another expression of James's way of looking at things that we discussed earlier: you have not because you ask not. *If* we will pray and ask God, *then* we will receive peace from Him.

The *if-then* formula was common in the Old Testament (see Deuteronomy 28:1–2; 2 Chronicles 7:14; Proverbs 2:1–5). It was an expression of the covenant relationship God had with His people. God was the King, and He was responsible for their welfare. If they would follow God's direction as Lord, then every need they had would be met. "If you..., then I...," God said.

This relationship didn't apply just to things like rain for their crops or victory in battle (the equivalent of the fish and eggs Jesus referred to—the tangible stuff of life); it also referred to what we're talking about in this chapter: freedom from anxiety. Consider this verse from the tumultuous, war-torn days of life in the Old Testament: "You will keep in perfect peace him whose mind is steadfast, because he trusts in you" (Isaiah 26:3).

The two verses that precede Isaiah 26:3 talk about strong cities with walls and ramparts, so there is an element of physical peace involved—peace from harm by Israel's neighbors. But in the Old Testament, physical and spiritual/emotional peace were inseparable. The Hebrew concept of *shalom* encompassed peace and well-being in all dimensions of life.

Restated in the if-then framework, Isaiah 26:3 would read like this: "If your mind is steadfast, trusting in God, then He will keep you in perfect peace." "If you..., then He..." It's life lived in covenant with God. We make Him the focus of our faith, attention, and trust, and He keeps us in perfect peace.

I'm going to show you how Jesus brought this Old Testament idea into His own teachings, but first let me give you another human illustration of the idea. In fact, I wonder if Jesus was using a conversation between Jonathan and David as a model for the promise He made to His own disciples (and to us).

Jonathan, the son of King Saul, and his best friend, David, who had been anointed to succeed Saul as king, made a covenant of protection between themselves. Saul was jealous of his young successor, and Jonathan promised to protect David any way he could. At one point, when it became obvious that Saul was seeking to take David's life, Jonathan said to his covenant-friend, David, "Whatever you want me to do, I'll do for you" (1 Samuel 20:4).

Have you ever had a friend like that? "Tell me what you need. I'll do anything you ask." The reason Jonathan made such an offer was because of his and David's covenant love for one another (see 1 Samuel 18:1–4). They had already done the "if . . . then" thing with each other, and now Jonathan was making good on the "then" part: "Tell me what you need, and I'll do it."

That's an amazing promise for anyone to make, isn't it? You may not know it, but Jesus has made the same promise to you—and included in it is freedom from anxiety.

When talking with His disciples shortly before He was to leave them and return to heaven, Jesus said this (note the "if . . . then" formula): "If you remain in me and my words remain in you, [then] ask whatever you wish, and it will be given you" (John 15:7). There are elements of Isaiah's verse and Jonathan's words here: "*If* you will stay steadfastly focused on Me, *then* you can ask whatever you wish." If you need freedom from anxiety in your life, you can receive it if you will steadfastly stay focused on God.

Which brings us back to Lucinda's desperate prayer and how God showed her the path to peace through faith in Christ. In Philippians 4:6 the apostle Paul said that, instead of being anxious, we should commit everything in prayer to God. ("Whatever you need, including personal peace, just ask Me.") That's the "if"—our part. God's part is the "then": "The peace of God, which transcends all understanding, will guard your hearts and your minds in Christ Jesus" (verse 7). Lucinda asked God to show her someone who had survived the anxiety she had lived with all her life and He did. He restored her relationship with Himself and taught her how to keep her heart and mind guarded "in Christ Jesus."

And there was more—the promise of Ephesians 3:20 was fulfilled as well. That verse says God "is able to do immeasurably more than all we ask or imagine, according to his power that is at work within us." Lucinda wanted freedom from anxiety, and she got it. But she also received insights that have helped hundreds of thousands of people around the world—insights now used in the top medical and academic institutions in

America. She never dreamed that a simple prayer, in a desperate moment, would result in a peace that surpassed all her understanding.

But Lucinda is not unique. She was an anxious person who called out to God and was reconnected with Him by faith, and peace was the result. It can be your result as well if you will call on Him.

Questions for Reflection and Discussion

1. All of us worry or feel anxious from time to time. The dictionary defines *anxiety* as "a state of uneasiness and apprehension." Think back over the past couple of weeks. What things have you worried about or felt uneasy or apprehensive about? Is there anything you worry about repeatedly?

2. What has been the impact of anxiety on your life physically? Spiritually? Socially? Relationally?

3. Philippians 4:6 tells us: "Don't worry about anything; instead, pray about everything." For many of us this command in Scripture is easier said than done. Why do you think that is? What is at the heart of worry?

4. The experience of peace follows the practice of prayer. Describe a time when you found this to be true of your experience.

5. Is there any area of concern in your life right now where you need to see God do "immeasurably more than anything you could ask or imagine"? What steps will you take to guard your heart and mind against worry while you wait for God to act?

9. Finding Direction When Lost and Confused

ROBERT ROBINSON WAS BORN into poverty in England in 1735 and reborn into a relationship with God in 1752. But he did not come easily into the kingdom.

History indicates that Robert's mother was a godly woman with high aspirations for her son. But the death of her husband when Robert was young left the family in dire straits. Her inability to control his wanton behavior, along with a lack of resources to provide him an education, caused her to place Robert in an indentured apprenticeship with a barber and hairdresser in London at age fifteen. There he fell in with a crowd who spent most of their time drinking and carousing.

One night he and his friends plied a Gypsy fortune-teller with alcohol in an attempt to have their fortunes told for free. But the prophecy Robinson received from the woman—that he would live a long life and see his children and grandchildren—scared him into serious reflection about the state of his life. Not long after, he went to hear the famous English evangelist George Whitefield, who preached on the wrath that was to come upon sinners who did not repent.

That apparently did it for the young carouser. In a note inscribed on a blank page of one of his books, he recorded that he was born again under the powerful preaching of Whitefield in May 1752, then came to a full satisfaction of his faith in Christ three years, seven months later in December 1755. That almost-four-year period was dark and fearful as he labored over the condition of his soul. But when he found peace in Christ in 1755, he knew what he wanted to do.

He entered a period of his life in which he studied, pastored several nonconformist (Methodist, Baptist) churches, and wrote a number of widely praised volumes of theology. But today, Robert Robinson is best known for the words to a hymn he wrote when he was only twenty-two years old: "Come, Thou Fount of Every Blessing."

Solidly biblical in its wording, two references in the hymn would speak prophetically to Robinson's own spiritual condition in his latter years. In the third verse (of the original five) Robinson wrote,

> Jesus sought me when a stranger,
> Wandering from the fold of God;
> He, to rescue me from danger,
> Interposed His precious blood.

And in the fourth verse he touched on the wandering theme again:

> Let Thy goodness, like a fetter,
> Bind my wandering heart to Thee.
> Prone to wander, Lord, I feel it,
> Prone to leave the God I love;
> Here's my heart, O take and seal it,
> Seal it for Thy courts above.

At twenty-two years of age, Robert Robinson remembered well his years of youthful debauchery. He knew he had wandered from the faith his mother apparently possessed, and he recognized the tendency of the human heart—at least *his* human heart—to be prone to wander: "Lord, I feel it." He asks God to seal his own heart, to preserve it for heaven alone. He knew he ran the risk of wandering again.

While the details of Robinson's latter years are sparse, we do know that he remained impulsive and unstable, changing ecclesiastical affiliations at least three times. And it was his association with a teacher in London, a man who denied the deity of Jesus Christ, that raised the question of whether he had wandered yet again in his final years. While hard to document, a story about Robinson lends some support to the notion that he had wandered—at least in his own estimation.

Riding in the same stagecoach with Robinson was a woman passenger he didn't know. The woman was reading a hymnbook, and eventually, as they conversed together, she asked Robinson what he thought of the hymn she was reading and humming to herself, "Come Thou Fount of Every Blessing." The story goes that Robinson burst into tears and exclaimed, "Madam, I am the poor unhappy man who wrote that hymn many years ago, and I would give a thousand worlds, if I had them, to enjoy the feelings I had then."[1]

Whether those are the actual words of Robert Robinson or not, we will likely never know. But if they weren't his, they have surely been the words of many tormented souls who have found themselves far from the God they once loved with all their hearts, souls, and minds—and who are wondering how to reconnect with Him.

We're familiar with wandering into "lostness" by the many accounts of hikers who have to be rescued in the wilderness every year. They set out with the best of intentions and suddenly find themselves in unfamiliar territory. They knew where they were when they set out but have no idea how to return to that place. And that doesn't happen just to serious trekkers who go on extended stays in ultra-rugged and isolated wilderness. It can happen to hikers who set out for an afternoon hike around what they thought was a simple area. Fog rolls in, or a violent snowstorm, and suddenly they're in whiteout conditions, unable to see the trail or anything familiar. They have no warm clothes or provisions since they hadn't planned on being out long, and they find themselves spending the night in freezing temperatures with no protection.

Wandering into unfamiliar territory does not happen all at once. It happens one step at a time, the same way cows find themselves outside their pasture. They graze along, heads down, moving from one juicy clump of grass to the next until they find themselves next to a break in the fence. They just keep moseying along, following the food supply until they are rounded up by the farmer and brought back to the pasture.

But they also act more willfully, based on the philosophy of "The grass is greener on the other side of the fence." During the summers I spent on my uncle's farm as a child, it was not unusual for the cows to get out of their pasture. They would spy greener grass on the other side of the fence and force their way through, leaving tufts of hair on the barbed wire and uprooted fence posts.

Yes, getting disconnected from God can happen suddenly as the result of a traumatic event in life. But wandering away is, by definition, a process, not an event. This chapter is for those who find themselves disconnected from God as a result of wandering—and for those who haven't. Robert Robinson's words apply to all: "Prone to wander, Lord, I feel it. . . . Here's my heart, O take and seal it." Those words are like the provision every hiker should make before setting out. One never knows when the path home might become hard to follow.

I have a friend whose family played a valuable game when he was a child. His mom would pile the kids into the car and then drive until they were lost! That's right—the goal was to purposely get lost so that they had no idea where they were or how to get home. As they drove through the streets of Southern California, the children would continually ask with glee, "Are we lost yet?" The game started when Mom would respond, "Now we're lost!" And that became the learning exercise for the children. What do you do when you're lost? How do you find your way home?

There were two valuable lessons he learned from the Lost Game. First, the skills for finding one's way home: maps, asking directions, calling home for help, being prepared for emergencies when you leave home, and others. Second (and perhaps even more important), the game took the fear out of being lost. And if there is no fear in being lost, then there is also no fear in exploring and taking risks.

Just as people never intend to get lost when they go hiking, people never intend to get lost spiritually—but it happens. We can draw a few lessons from the Lost Game to help us think about how to find our way back home.

First, prepare to be lost. In the northwest corner of the state of Alabama sits the 180,000-acre Bankhead National Forest. Part of that forest is the Sipsey Wilderness, 25,000 acres of canyons, cliffs, towering trees, and more than 100 waterfalls. Motorized vehicles are not allowed in the Sipsey, and there are no directional signs posted. In other words, you enter at your own risk.

District ranger Glen Gaines describes the danger:

> It's like a maze of canyons and ridgetops, especially in the
> summertime when you can't see very far. It's very easy to get
> [lost]. . . . [People] think it's a real serene national forest and they

can walk around and see nature. But nothing is certain in the wilderness area. . . . They approach it like they're going to a city park or a walk around the block. Many times they don't have an adequate supply of water. Typically, they don't have any kind of map and won't have a compass.[2]

There are a lot of spiritual hikers in this world who are similarly naive about preparedness, and many of them get lost—disconnected from God. Know this: the wilderness of this world is conspiring against you to help you lose your way. To be forewarned is to be forearmed.

Second, admit it when you're lost. The worst thing to do in the wilderness is to deny reality—to deny that you are lost—and go into fast-forward as though nothing is wrong. If you are spiritually lost, it will do no good to say, "Fine!" when someone asks how you are. If you won't admit you're lost, the idea of being found will have no meaning to you or to those people who surround you daily. They may have an idea that you're lost by observing your life, but without your admission their hands are tied.

Here's the lesson: spiritually speaking, the wrong road never turns into the right road. To get reconnected with God, you must return to the fork in the road where your wrong decision occurred and take the better path. The Bible calls that process *repentance*. The original Greek word for repentance is a compound word, made up of two words that mean "after" and "to perceive, or think."[3] So it means to consider something after the fact; to change one's mind. Before repentance ever gets to the stage of "sackcloth and ashes" that we usually think of, change has to begin in the mind and the heart.

If you are going to find your way back to God, you'll have to change your mind about having wandered away.

Third, go back to the last place you remember being "not lost." When we lose something like our car keys, someone inevitably will ask, "Where's the last place you remember having them?" That's a good question, spiritually speaking, as well. The last place you might remember being "not lost" could be when you were in a relationship with a spiritual mentor, a Bible study or church you attended, or a time just before a crisis event in your life. Recalling the patterns and events of that "not lost" time may be a good place to look for healthy patterns going forward.

In the hymn he wrote, Robert Robinson said, "Here I raise my Ebenezer; here by Thy great help I've come." He was referring to 1 Samuel 7:12, where the prophet Samuel set up a large stone as a memorial to how God gave Israel victory over an attacking enemy: "He named it Ebenezer [Hebrew for "stone of help"], saying, 'Thus far has the LORD helped us.'" Perhaps Robinson saw his hymn as an Ebenezer—a testimony to how God had delivered him from his wandering ways.

What are the Ebenezers in your life? Going forward, mark the times, places, and ways God has helped you. They may become a beacon of hope for you in a future day when you have lost your way.

Fourth, be willing to ask for directions. In this day of GPS units in our cars and on our mobile phones, the idea of asking for directions is almost a thing of the past. But we still need to ask for spiritual guidance if we intend to reconnect with God. In the words of Proverbs 2:9, we need to find the "good path" and avoid those "who leave the straight paths to walk in dark ways" (verse 13). And here is how verses 1–5 say we find that path—by asking:

> My son, if you accept my words
>   and store up my commands within you,
> turning your ear to wisdom
>   and applying your heart to understanding,
> and if you call out for insight
>   and cry aloud for understanding,
> and if you look for it as for silver
>   and search for it as for hidden treasure,
> then you will understand the fear of the LORD
>   and find the knowledge of God.

Notice: "turning your ear . . . applying your heart . . . call out for insight . . . cry aloud for understanding . . . look for it as for silver . . . search for it as for hidden treasure." Those words describe the person who wants to be found; to gain "knowledge and understanding" (verse 6). That person will not be lost for long. God promises to respond and give the help needed.

Fifth, look for landmarks. Imagine being completely lost in a wilderness forest. You're following a trail when you come to a Y, or a crossroads, and you have no idea which path to take. Hikers lost in the woods have been known to climb a tall tree to see if they can spot a familiar landmark by which to reckon their new direction.

When I was younger, my father and I built a small cabin in the California mountains where our family would retreat as often as possible. I could sit on the porch of the cabin and look out at a particular mountain peak that loomed over the surrounding area—and one day I decided to climb that mountain. From the cabin porch, it looked as if I could go straight up the side of the mountain. But once I started climbing I realized the mountain was actually a series of peaks and valleys. Whenever I was in a valley, I lost sight of the cabin and experienced that eerie "lost" feeling. But then, on the next peak, I could look back and see the cabin and maintain my bearings. The cabin was my landmark. Only by keeping it periodically in view did I keep from becoming seriously lost.

At a time when the nation of Israel was wandering, disconnected from God, the prophet Jeremiah gave her this advice from the Lord: "Stand at the crossroads and look; ask for the ancient paths, ask where the good way is, and walk in it, and you will find rest for your souls" (Jeremiah 6:16). Yes, new paths can be profitable, but it's the ancient, established paths, the ones that brought you to God to begin with, that will lead you back to Him.

Think about the "ancient" paths, the established paths, in your life—the paths you took to God before being disconnected. If you will return to those paths, you will return to Him.

Finally, be assured: regardless of how far you have wandered or for how long, your heavenly Father is looking for your return. That is one of the lessons in the Bible's greatest story about a lost person coming home, Jesus' parable of the prodigal son (Luke 15:11–32). Humanly speaking, the father in that story had every reason to close the door when his son returned and asked to be readmitted to the family. Not so: "While [the son] was still a long way off, his father saw him and was filled with compassion for him; he ran to his son, threw his arms around him and kissed him" (verse 20).

That is exactly how God will greet you when you return to Him—if you will. You won't need to explain. You simply need to say what the son in the parable said: "Father, I want to come home." You will find the loving arms of God embracing your lonely heart without another word. Set your sights on the heart of God today and return to Him.

Questions for Reflection and Discussion

1. Have you ever been so lost you couldn't find your way back to the place from which you started? What emotions do you associate with being lost?

2. For some of us, being separated from God happens suddenly as a result of a traumatic event in life. For others, we disconnect from God as a result of wandering—it's more of a process than an event. Describe a time in your life when you experienced either kind of spiritual separation from God. Try to identify the point at which the distance began.

3. It's not until we admit that we're spiritually lost that we begin to find our way back to God. This is what the Bible calls *repentance*—"to change one's mind." If we're going to find our way back to God, we have to change our minds about having wandered away from Him in the first place. What has kept you from admitting you were lost in the past? From repenting and reconnecting with God?

4. Where do you turn for help when you feel spiritually lost or disconnected from God? Why do you turn there for help?

5. Jesus' parable of the prodigal son (Luke 15:11–32) shows us the tender heart of God and the eagerness with which He waits for us to "come home" when we've wandered away. What are some reasons people run away from God? What keeps people from heading back to God? Have you ever been like the prodigal son? What made you return home to the Father?

10. Exercising Blind Belief When Weakened by Trials

GROWING UP IN COASTAL CALIFORNIA, I had a recreational focus on the West: beaches and the Pacific Ocean—and still do to this day. But one of my sisters gravitated eastward to the snow-covered mountains. She became an expert snow skier and provided my first introduction to the sport. She kept me from looking foolish on the slopes, dressing me appropriately and serving as my guide in my tentative first efforts on the bunny trails. I quickly learned the value of exercising faith in someone who loved me, had my best interests in mind, and was an expert.

And I learned something else while learning to ski: you don't have to be able to see. I had no idea it was possible for visually impaired people—even those who are totally blind—to ski. I discovered that such programs arose in post–World War II Europe, where snow skiing is part of the culture. Many veterans who were blinded in the war had grown up skiing in Europe, and they refused to let a simple thing like not being able to see keep them off the slopes. So techniques developed, guides were trained, and the movement spread.

A half-century later, blind American veterans of the war in Iraq are regaining some of their prewar confidence by learning to ski and ice-skate in spite of their visual handicap. For example, in Sun Valley, Idaho, the Sun Valley Adaptive Sports organization furnishes guides and trainers who lead the vets down the slopes and across the ice—even some who had never skied or skated before.

"We want them to try things that they have *never tried before* or *try things again that they used to do*," explained Tom Iselin, the executive director of the Sun Valley program. From the vets' perspective, "*it's a leap of faith*"—the words of John Crabtree, a senior naval petty officer blinded in Iraq. "The trust that you put into those that are helping you and instructing you—*that's already taken care of.* The challenge is more to *concentrate on what they're telling me.*"

The key to skiing blind is to heed the admonition of one of the instructors: "*Follow my voice.*"[1]

The portions of the quotes that I italicized jumped out at me as I read them because of their relevance to the subject of this chapter—especially when the director of the ski program said that they wanted to get people to do things they'd never done before or to get people to try things they had once done but had stopped doing. That's a perfect description of people who are disconnected from God: either they have never known Him (never had a reltionship with Him), or they knew Him and have somehow leaned away from Him. To use the metaphor of blindness, either their eyes have never been open to seeing God, or their eyes are presently shut after once seeing Him.

And how does one come to the place of spiritual blindness after having "seen" God by faith? It sometimes happens in the spiritual world the same way it happened to the blinded veterans returning from war: as the result of a trial or a difficulty. To call being blinded in a war "a trial or a difficulty" is an understatement, and I don't mean to trivialize such a terrible event. But my point is this: being a member of the military doesn't result in physical blindness, but being the victim of a bullet, bomb, mortar, or some other injury can.

Just so, being a Christian doesn't make one lose sight of God, but sometimes a difficult trial or period of suffering can. During such an event one might feel abandoned by God and gradually lose sight of Him: *If God had been here, or cared about me, this never would have happened.* When such a trial occurs, the challenge is to regain spiritual sight, to get reconnected with God.

John Crabtree, the blind naval officer I quoted, even used spiritual language to talk about learning to ski: "It's a leap of faith." That phrase has been used by critics of Christianity to imply that believing in God defies logic and reason. The term "leap of faith" is usually (and incorrectly) attributed to a nineteenth-century Danish theologian named Søren Kierkegaard. Kierkegaard did use the words *leap* and *faith*, but he spoke of a "leap *to* faith," not a "leap *of* faith."[2] "Leap *to* faith" suggests that evidence is in hand and faith is exercised on the basis of that evidence, whereas "leap *of* faith" suggests a *blind leap*—a sort of hope against hope. That is certainly not in view when it comes to Christianity.

The phrase "leap of faith" has been weakened even more by the addition of the word *blind*—a "blind leap of faith." That suggests a person closes his eyes to the real evidence about God (or lack of evidence) and chooses to believe anyway. Again, this is definitely not how faith is defined in the New Testament.

So, why did I use "blind belief" in the title of this chapter if it doesn't actually describe Christian faith? I'm using it in the same sense the naval officer used it when learning to ski without sight: "The trust that you put into those that are helping you and instructing you—*that's already taken care of.* The challenge is more to *concentrate on what they're telling me.*" He was willing to take a leap of faith on the ski slope because his trust was a settled issue: "That's already taken care of."

Think of all the things that could happen on a ski slope: running into other skiers, hitting a tree or boulder, going over a ledge or cliff, skiing into a dangerous off-limits area—the possibilities are endless and potentially life-ending. In order not to worry about those possibilities, the skier puts his absolute, total trust in his trained ski guide. The danger factor is then off the table—the trust issue "is already taken care of." With total trust in the guide's ability to protect the skier from harm, the blind skier can concentrate on keeping his balance, perfecting his skills, and making it safely to the bottom of the run. He replaces worry about danger with "concentrating on what [the guide] is telling me." Or, to use the words of the guide I quoted, it's all about "following [the guide's] voice."

I'm sure you see the spiritual parallels to the challenge of walking by faith. I'm using the term "blind belief" in this chapter in the context of the spiritual guide we have—One in whom we place our implicit trust as we try to maneuver over, around, and through the dangers of this life. Our belief is "blind" just as the skier's is in that we cannot physically see our divine guide, God Himself. Yet with the assurance of His presence, we step out in faith and follow His lead. We have enough evidence and experience with Him to know that our trust is warranted.

Yet faith is still required! It requires no faith on my part to believe that my computer keyboard is right in front of me. I see it, touch it, and hear its sounds. But it does take faith for me to believe that the person of Jesus Christ is even nearer to me than my keyboard. Faith is not blind in the sense that I have the records of eyewitnesses who experienced Christ with their five senses both before (see Luke 1:2; 24:39; John 1:14; 1 John 1:1–2) and after (see 1 Corinthians 15:3–8) His resurrection. Plus, there are the accounts of life-changing experiences of people (including me) through the ages to testify of the reality of Christ.

But those evidences, for me today, are good only up to a point. I still must believe—exercise faith in what I cannot comprehend with my senses. So after a certain point—after I've seen what I can see and examined what evidence I have—my faith is blind belief. My experience, and that of millions of other believers, is that described by the apostle Peter: "Though you have not seen him, you love him; and even though you do not see him now, you believe in him and are filled with an inexpressible and glorious joy" (1 Peter 1:8).

The Bible's own definition of faith fits the context I'm discussing in this chapter: "Faith is being sure of what we hope for and certain of what we do not see" (Hebrews 11:1). In the words of the blind skier, "That's been taken care of." He is sure and certain of what he cannot see—that his ski guide is going to lead him safely to the bottom of the mountain even though he can't see him. The same reasoning applies to one who, through some trial or tribulation, has lost sight of God. *Just because you cannot see God in the midst of, or after, your troubles does not mean He is not there.*

No insistence on our part that God reveal Himself will change anything. He is not obligated to prove His existence to us by making Himself visible whenever our faith wavers. If He did, the Christian life would cease being a walk of faith, which is what the Bible says it is: "We live by faith, not by sight" (2 Corinthians 5:7). Paul says that, in our present circumstances, "we groan and are burdened," wishing to be free of the trials of this life (verse 4). And we will be free one day. But for the moment, "we live by faith, not by sight."

In another place, Paul writes, "We fix our eyes not on what is seen, but on what is unseen. For what is seen is temporary, but what is unseen is eternal" (2 Corinthians 4:18). Everything you and I can see with our eyes is temporal and will one day pass away. The only "thing" that matters—God Himself—is unseen. We can see Him only with eyes of faith—eyes of blind belief. We let go of the security that our eyes bring us and, like a blind skier, trust our Guide to see us safely past all that might harm us.

So what should we do when we, like a soldier on a battlefield, are blind-sided with an event that takes away our sight—our ability to trust God for what He allowed to happen in our lives? We could do what some have done and disconnect from God. And while that may satisfy a natural desire to strike back and regain a measure of power in a powerless situation, ultimately it is not the right choice. It's not even a good choice. For disconnecting from God relegates you to the conclusion that you are a pinball in the cosmic machine I mentioned in a previous chapter, being swatted to and fro by forces beyond your control.

Instead, I would suggest a lesson from a man who was like the blinded war veterans—a man who had no physical sight. But unlike the blinded soldiers, this man had been blind all his life. We find his story in the New Testament in John 9—Jesus' disciples inquired as to the cause of the man's blindness, assuming he was being punished by God for someone's sins, either his or his parents'. Jesus said neither, that the man was born blind "so that the work of God might be displayed in his life" (verse 3).

Though the man was unlike the soldiers, he responded just as they did: with settled trust. Jesus told the man to go and wash his eyes in a pool of water, and when he did, he could see (verse 7). The man didn't debate with Jesus about why he was born blind, nor did he debate about the rather unusual healing remedy Jesus employed. He put His trust in Jesus so he could "concentrate on what his guide was telling him to do"—just as the soldiers did.

I believe that is what any of us must do when we find we have lost our spiritual sight, and especially if the loss was so traumatic that it caused us to disconnect from God. Debating the whys and wherefores of God's working is an exercise in futility: "As the heavens are higher than the earth, so are [His] ways higher than [our] ways and [His] thoughts than [our] thoughts" (Isaiah 55:9).

We are far wiser to take the evidence we have for God's trustworthiness and exercise our faith in Him. Just because something difficult has happened in your life does not mean God is not trustworthy. It does not mean God does not love you. It just means that you will need to exercise blind faith—the faith that steps beyond what you can see and touch of God—and trust Him.

It is our feelings that make us want to disconnect, not our faith. It is our feelings that challenge the worthiness of God, not our trust. It is our feelings that make us want to pull back our hands from our Guide, not our commitment. The ironic thing about feelings is that they are the first to surface but the last in terms of credibility. Feelings are the last thing on which we should make a decision in the realm of faith.

The little booklet titled "Have You Heard of the Four Spiritual Laws?" written by the late Dr. Bill Bright, the founder of Campus Crusade for Christ, contains a helpful diagram on the last page.[3] It pictures the silhouette of a train: a locomotive, a coal car, and a caboose. The locomotive is labeled "Fact," the coal car is labeled "Faith," and the caboose is labeled "Feelings." The implication is obvious: "Fact," not "Feelings," drives the train. "Faith" is the fuel we spend on the "Fact" of God's character and His promises. Just as the caboose on a train goes wherever the engine takes it, so our feelings will follow the faith that we invest in the facts (the evidence) we believe about God.

If you have never connected with God but would like to, the place to begin is not with your feelings but with the facts about Him as revealed in the Bible and in creation (see Psalm 19:1–6; Romans 1:18–20). If you have been connected with God in the past but have followed your feelings into a dark place, ask yourself whether the facts about God that you once believed have changed. Your feelings may have changed, but God hasn't: "Jesus Christ is the same yesterday and today and forever" (Hebrews 13:8).

Your fears of trusting Him while in a difficult place are the same as those of a blind soldier standing at the top of a ski run. Like the soldier, if you will settle the trust factor with your faith, you will move safely ahead—and back into the light of His presence.

Questions for Reflection and Discussion

1. Think of a time when you had to put "blind belief" in someone else. Tell why the situation called for blind belief, whether or not you decided to put your trust in that person, and what the outcome of your experience was.

2. When it comes to trusting God as your spiritual guide, is there anything about the concept of "blind belief" that bothers you? How do you see blind belief being played out in your life day to day? Is blind belief something that comes easy for you or something with which you struggle at times? Explain.

3. Describe a time when you were blindsided with an event that challenged your ability to trust God.

4. "Just because you cannot see God in the midst of, or after, your troubles, doesn't mean He's not there." How do you know this statement is true? What evidence do you have for the trustworthiness of God?

5. According to Hebrews 11:1, the essence of faith "is being sure of what we hope for and certain of what we do not see." Where in your life do you need to apply this definition of faith right now? What is it you hope for but can't be certain of?

Part 3

Allowing God
to Heal Your
Soul Wound

11. Finding Wholeness Through Prayer When Debilitated by Brokenness

ON JULY 11-12, 2008, Tracey Bailey was the keynote speaker at the Florida Institute of Technology's Department of Science and Mathematics Education's fiftieth-anniversary reunion celebration. Bailey earned his bachelor's degree in science education from the school twenty years prior and had gone on to distinguish himself as an outstanding high school teacher. So outstanding, in fact, that he found himself in the Rose Garden of the White House in 1993 receiving the National Teacher of the Year award from President Bill Clinton and Secretary of Education Richard Riley.

Before receiving the traditional "Crystal Apple" at the White House, Bailey was invited to work with Florida governor Jeb Bush and Florida Commissioner of Education Frank Brogan to create and implement Florida's new charter school law. And today he serves as the director of education policy for the Association of American Educators in Washington, D.C.

As a high school science teacher, Tracey Bailey had a burden for the at-risk students who filled many of the seats in his classes: "I am thrilled that my classes reached more than just high ability students and helped all students become excited about learning! I am a firm believer that nearly every student will rise to the level of expectations placed on her or him, and my students continue to confirm this." He says that in the heart of every teenager is a void, a search for something worthy of commitment—and his job is to help them find that "something."

Tracey Bailey sounds like a model student who became a model teacher.

Actually, nothing could be further from the truth. Some fifteen years before he stood in the Rose Garden with President Clinton, a teenage Bailey stood before a county judge in an Indiana courtroom to be sentenced to jail. He had gone on a drunken rampage with some friends and vandalized a high school building. But getting caught and being sentenced to an Indiana juvenile detention center for five years wasn't enough to break him. As he stood before the judge, all he could think about were the words of his high school wrestling coach: "Don't you ever hang your head. Don't admit defeat. The minute you do, it's over."

Bailey entered the detention facility with his pride in place, but it wasn't long before he was a broken young man. Sitting one day in his solitary confinement cell containing nothing but a cot, a sink, and a toilet, the reality of what a mess he had made of his life began to sink in. Through his tears he began to pray: "God, I need help. I am defeated without You."

That prayer marked a turning point in Tracey Bailey's life. He joined a prison Bible study and began taking college correspondence courses. Due to the changes in his life, he was released on probation after fourteen months of incarceration. He continued to pursue his college degree and became a high school teacher in Florida...and a consultant to the governor...a Teacher of the Year...a keynote speaker at his college.

The teenager who broke into a high school became a broken young man, but in his own words, Tracey Bailey "bowed his head and tasted victory."[1]

Tracey Bailey is not the only person whose response to brokenness has been prayer. While he, as a desperate young man, probably prayed out of a sense of desperation and hopelessness (which is fine), he was actually doing exactly what God wants us to do when we find ourselves in similar circumstances. Even a spiritual giant like the apostle Paul found himself in such a frustrating place that he called out to the Lord to be delivered from his place of torment. Three times he prayed and asked

God to remove the affliction he was experiencing. The short answer from God was "No"—but the long answer was better: "My grace is sufficient for you, for my power is made perfect in weakness" (2 Corinthians 12:9).

My father wrote this outline when talking with people who are praying for God to deliver them from a hard place but who aren't getting the answer they want:

- If the request is wrong, God says "No."

- If the timing is wrong, God says "Slow."

- If you are wrong, God says "Grow."

- But if the request is right, the timing is right, and you are right, God says "Go!"[2]

Oswald Chambers wrote,

> The point of prayer is not to get answers from God, but to have perfect and complete oneness with Him. If we pray only because we want answers, we will become irritated and angry with God. We receive an answer every time we pray, but it does not always come in the way we expect, and our spiritual irritation shows our refusal to identify ourselves truly with our Lord in prayer. We are not here to prove that God answers prayer, but to be living trophies of God's grace. . . . When you seem to have no answer, there is always a reason—God uses these times to give you deep personal instruction, and it is not for anyone else but you.[3]

When it comes to prayer, we pray best when we are weakest. God doesn't mind if we cry out to Him from our place of desperation. As a father, He longs to hear the call of His child who needs Him. Anthony Bloom, a Russian Orthodox monk, captured beautifully the reason why brokenness and weakness are the proper postures for prayer:

> Weakness is not the kind of weakness which we show by sinning and forgetting God, but the kind of weakness which means being completely supple, completely transparent, completely abandoned in the hands of God. We usually try to be strong and we prevent God from manifesting His power.

> You remember how you were taught to write when you were small. Your mother put a pencil in your hand, took your hand in hers, and began to move it. Since you did not know at all what she meant to do, you left your hand completely free in hers. This is what I mean by the power of God being manifest in weakness.[4]

When a child is learning the alphabet, she doesn't know what the letters should look like. She doesn't know whether the pencil should be moved up or down, right or left. So she relaxes her hand completely in her mother's and allows her to write the letters—write the story of that moment—for the child. Our problem is that we think we know how to write the story—especially the end of the story—when we are in a place of brokenness. And it's always the same: healing and wholeness now! Because we think we know how to write the letters and the story, we find ourselves struggling against God as He tries to write the story with us in His hand. Our prayers are a large part of our attempts to write the story: "Lord, please restore me now." And if wholeness doesn't come, we find ourselves wrestling with God. We want to move up when He wants to move us down. We try to push the prayer-pencil left when He is moving it right.

But why should we be so bold as to think we know how our story will end? We have never been in this particular place before in our lives. In that regard we are like a child confronting the alphabet for the first time; like an English-speaking adult confronting the Chinese alphabet for the first time. If we are going to write God's story instead of ours in our time of brokenness, we will have to relax in His hands and let Him move us as He will. We must let *His* strength be manifested in *our* weakness.

How do we do that in prayer? Perhaps the way Jesus did it in His hour of brokenness is a good place to begin. Did Jesus know how the story of His betrayal, arrest, and suffering at the hands of others would end? With some degree of exactness, He must have since He told His disciples that He was going to be "handed over to be crucified" (Matthew 26:2). But even if He knew the final end, He did not know with precise detail the steps leading to it. He had never walked that particular path before in His life, just as we have not walked any path of brokenness ourselves. It was new territory for Him; it is new territory for us.

But He knew enough to be in a place of brokenness at the prospect:

"Being in anguish, he prayed more earnestly, and his sweat was like drops of blood falling to the ground" (Luke 22:44). So what did He do—what did He pray?

He prayed what any person would pray in a broken place: "Going a little farther, he fell with his face to the ground and prayed, 'My Father, if it is possible, may this cup be taken from me'" (Matthew 26:39). Even Jesus Christ had a preferred ending to the story of His own brokenness; a way He would write it given the intensity of the pain He was experiencing.

Yet the way He finished that prayer reveals where His heart was: "Yet not as I will, but as you will" (verse 39). Jesus allowed the hand of the Father to wrap around His hand and move the pencil without opposition. More than anything, Jesus wanted the Father's story to be written in and through His life. He had never lived out that story before so He didn't know the script—the words to write. So He yielded His pen in prayer to the Father and allowed the story that would unfold to be His story: "Yet not as I will, but as you will."

That is how we should pray in our time of brokenness as well: "Father, I have never been in this broken place before. I have never been to this time in my life before. I know how I would write the story if I were in Your place. But I am not. You are God and I am not. More than anything, I want my story to be Your story. I yield up the pencil in my hand to You. I ask You to take my hand in Yours and write what You will, what will glorify You and be best for me, as You see fit: 'Not as I will, but as You will.'"

Why can the child of God pray that prayer? Because, like Jesus, we know how the story ends. Jesus knew that after three days He would rise again (see Mark 8:31). He knew that His brokenness in the Garden of Gethsemane was not the final chapter in the story God was writing through His life. So He was willing to yield the pencil to God and allow Him to fill in the details.

The child of God who knows his Bible also knows how his own story ends. Our final chapter is the same as Jesus': resurrection! Paul wrote in 1 Corinthians 15:

> I declare to you, brothers, that flesh and blood cannot inherit the kingdom of God, nor does the perishable inherit the imperishable. Listen, I tell you a mystery: We will not all sleep, but we will all be changed—in a flash, in the twinkling of an eye, at the last trumpet.

> For the trumpet will sound, the dead will be raised imperishable, and we will be changed.
>
> (verses 50–52)

I hope you remember to tell yourself, when you are in a broken place, that that place is not the end of your story. If you've embraced God's offer to you of eternal life through Christ, then your broken place is only a temporary one. Indeed, Paul closed his words to the Corinthians about their coming wholeness this way: "Therefore, my dear brothers, stand firm. Let nothing move you. Always give yourselves fully to the work of the Lord, because you know that your labor in the Lord is not in vain" (verse 58).

"Work of the Lord" certainly means ministry for Christ, but there is other work of the Lord as well: "Being confident of this, that he who began a good work in you will carry it on to completion until the day of Christ Jesus" (Philippians 1:6). The work God is doing in you is a work in which you are called to participate—to give yourself "fully." And that means not resisting God's work when you find yourself in a broken place, not trying to write the story ahead of Him.

Rather, we are called to prayer—to submit ourselves "fully" to the work God is doing in us: "Not as I will, but as You will." Assuredly, that is not an easy prayer to pray since it means giving up control. It means that the story could even get worse before it gets better! ("It may be that the answer to prayer will come in a shape that seems a refusal. It may come even in an increase of that from which we seek deliverance."[5]) But in prayer, we talk it out and reaffirm what we believe: "Lord, I know You are with me. I know You love me. I know You have promised never to leave or forsake me. I know Your goal is to conform me to the image of Jesus, and if I have to follow Him through this broken place in my life in order to become like Him in spirit, then I will do it. I will let You write this chapter in the story of my life."

Don't forget that "although [Jesus] was a son, he learned obedience from what he suffered" (Hebrews 5:8). He learned it on His knees and then lived it with His hands and feet. And we must do the same. George MacDonald, from whose literary and spiritual well C. S. Lewis drank deeply, wrote, "Because we easily imagine ourselves in want, we imagine God ready to forsake us."[6]

But He is not! In fact, it was Jesus Himself who taught us that prayer is how we should call on God daily. And when it comes to praying from our broken places, here is the key phrase in the disciples' prayer: "Your kingdom come, your will be done on earth as it is in heaven" (Matthew 6:10). That was the very prayer that Jesus prayed when He said, "Not as I will, but as You will."

Praying for God's kingdom—His glory and His will—is hard when we are broken and hurting. But if we will pray that way, God's grace will be sufficient and His power will be made perfect. Sometimes it is difficult to know what to pray in those broken places. If your heart is empty, follow the pattern of the prayer Jesus taught the disciples: "We cannot easily err when we have our pattern before us."[7]

You may not be in a jail cell as Tracey Bailey was, but you may be in a place that feels the same. He prayed a simple, heartfelt prayer, and God led him through his broken place to a place of victory. God will do the same for you if you will pray. He is your Father, and He wants you to call out to Him.

Questions for Reflection and Discussion

1. When was the last time you prayed out of a sense of desperation and hopelessness? What brought you to your knees? What happened in your life as the result of praying that desperate prayer?

2. God works best in our weakness—the kind of weakness that means being completely pliable, completely transparent, completely abandoned in the hands of God. How easy do you find it to be "weak" as it's described here? Why?

3. Jesus modeled for us in His hours of betrayal, arrest, and suffering at the hands of others what it means to let the Father write His story in and through our lives, to say, "Father, not as I will, but as You will." Is there anything you are currently facing where you want to pray that prayer but are having a difficult time doing so? Why do you think that is?

4. The work God is doing in you is a work in which you are called to participate—to give yourself to "fully." That means not resisting God's work when you find yourself in a broken place; not trying to write the story ahead of Him. How difficult is it for you to let go of control? Control has some very subtle disguises. What might that control look like in your life?

5. Write a simple, heartfelt prayer asking God to lead you through your broken place to a place of victory. Share your prayer with a friend or your small group if you feel comfortable doing so.

12. Receiving Spiritual Health Through Praise When Disabled by Dis-ease

THE PITCH HEARD round the world" was thrown by Dave Dravecky, an All-Star pitcher for the San Francisco Giants, on August 10, 1989. The sound heard throughout the stadium was his pitching arm snapping in two.

It was the second game Dravecky pitched after making a comeback from radical cancer surgery on the muscle and bone in his left arm—his pitching arm. But the comeback was short-lived. In the sixth inning of the game, his arm snapped so loud the fans in the stadium could hear it. He obviously pitched no more that season, and in an X-ray toward the end of the year a doctor noticed a mass in his arm. The cancer had returned. He retired from baseball and began yet more treatments on his cancerous arm, but the treatments were not enough. His left arm, shoulder blade, and part of his collarbone were amputated in an attempt to keep the cancer from spreading and taking his life.

Fortunately, God had bigger plans for Dave Dravecky than playing baseball. As an in-demand motivational speaker and author of numerous books, he has spent the years since his retirement and amputation encouraging those who are battling difficult circumstances. He had to learn that sickness and suffering do not mean an end to significance, nor do they mean that God has turned His back. Indeed, for Dave Dravecky, God has never been so close. His new life message is that God is just as worthy of praise in times of ease as He is in times of dis-ease:

> Looking back, [my wife] Jan and I have learned that the wilderness is part of the landscape of faith, and every bit as essential as the mountaintop. On the mountaintop we are overwhelmed by God's presence. In the wilderness we are overwhelmed by his absence. Both places should bring us to our knees; the one, in utter awe; the other, in utter dependence.[1]

Beginning with Job in the Old Testament, mankind has played a Q & A game with God when it comes to the subject of dis-ease, or physical suffering. We don't like it and wonder why God has allowed it to happen. Job was convinced, in spite of his three friends' protestations to the contrary, that he had done nothing wrong, nothing to deserve the calamities and plagues he was experiencing. He believed God was just—that God didn't allow affliction to come upon any except the unrighteous. And since he wasn't unrighteous, he demanded an explanation of God.

We often hear reference made to "the patience of Job." But truth be told, Job wasn't all that patient. He didn't like his lot in life and wanted to know why it had changed. In a matter of days he had gone from being the healthiest, wealthiest man around to being the poorest and the sickest; from sitting at his table surrounded by his wife and children to sitting on a pile of ashes scraping his boils and sores with a piece of pottery, mourning the deaths of his children and listening to his wife's criticism.

But we have to give credit to Job for furnishing us with the theme of this chapter: how to experience relief from dis-ease through the practice of praise. Shortly after experiencing his calamities, Job fell to the ground in worship and prayed, "Naked I came from my mother's womb, and naked I will depart. The LORD gave and the LORD has taken away; may the name of the LORD be praised" (Job 1:21).

Job didn't get well as a result of that prayer of praise, and he became somewhat less full of praise as his saga developed. But by the end of his story, Job's praise was more profound than at the beginning. Though it was a struggle, Job kept the faith through his entire dis-eased experience:

> Job answered the LORD:
> "I am unworthy—how can I reply to you?

I put my hand over my mouth.
I spoke once, but I have no answer—
    twice, but I will say no more....
I know that you can do all things;
    no plan of yours can be thwarted....
Surely I spoke of things I did not understand,
    things too wonderful for me to know."
(Job 40:3–5; 42:2–3)

I keep using the word *dis-ease* instead of *disease* in this chapter—for a reason. We think of sickness when we think of disease, but I don't want to focus totally on physical illness as an experience in which we ought to praise God. Rather, I'd like to broaden the term "disease" to include the whole range of mental, emotional, and physical discomfort that we all experience from time to time. And that, in some people's lives, has been so intense as to cause them to lose their faith and hope in the God they once praised and loved..

The prefix "dis-" simply means the absence of or opposite of. By hyphenating "dis-ease," I'm emphasizing the times in our lives—especially sickness—in which we experience dis-ease—the absence or opposite of ease. And I want to suggest that, contrary to human nature, those are the times in which we should praise God.

Contrary is right! The longer we live in the kingdom of God, the more we realize that life is the opposite of living in the kingdom of man. In the world, we grasp in order to have, but in the kingdom of heaven we give in order to have (see Malachi 3:10). In the world, we struggle to live, but in the kingdom of God we die in order to live (see John 12:24). In the world, we fight to become the greatest, but in the kingdom of God we become the least in order to become great (see Luke 9:48). In the kingdom of man, we take the first seat, but in the kingdom of God we take the last (see Luke 14:8–11). And in the world, we rejoice when things are going well, but in the kingdom of God we rejoice at all times (1 Thessalonians 5:16–18).

Sometimes when people first read verses like 1 Thessalonians 5:18—"Give thanks in all circumstances, for this is God's will for you in Christ Jesus"—they are totally put off: "I can see giving God thanks when I'm healthy, but are you saying I should give Him thanks and praise when I'm sick?" I'm not saying it, but the Bible is. The larger context of the words Paul wrote is this: "Be joyful always; pray continually; ... Do not put out the Spirit's fire" (verses 16–17, 19).

In other words, being joyful and full of praise for God has less to do with specific circumstances than with living a life that is controlled by the Holy Spirit. Paul says in Ephesians 5:18 to "be filled with the Spirit." And in Romans 14:17 he says, "The kingdom of God is not a matter of [arguing about] eating and drinking [practices], but of righteousness, peace and joy in the Holy Spirit."

If your loved one's life is tragically taken by a careless driver, or your child's life is cut short by a disease, we are not exhorted to praise God for those specific events. How foolish that would be! "Father, I praise You that my wife was killed by a drunk driver." Or "Father, we praise You that our child's life was taken by cancer." No normal human being, nor any mature follower of Jesus, would be thankful for experiencing such terrible events.

So how is it possible that praise can erupt from within us when we are in the midst of pain and dis-ease? First, by noticing that Paul said to give thanks *in* every circumstance, not *for* every circumstance. We are able to give thanks to God in those circumstances for *Him* even when we are being torn apart by the circumstances: "Father, I thank You that You are bigger than my dis-ease. I praise You because You are good, loyal, faithful, loving, all-knowing, and all-powerful. Even though I don't understand the reasons for this situation, I praise You that You do. I praise You that nothing escapes your attention; that nothing is too small for You to care about, including this situation I am in. Because I am more committed to your glory being manifested through my life than I am to my comfort and ease, I will continue to praise and proclaim Your name because I know that You are love. I want to praise Your loving character to others, not complain about why You didn't protect me from this situation."

I encourage you to open your Bible to Psalm 107 and read this most amazing song, probably composed for use by the Israelites in one of their worship settings. The psalmist identifies four classes of people whose lives reflected some state of dis-ease and exhorted each to praise the Lord: the lost had no purpose in life (verses 4–9), the rebellious found themselves in prison (verses 10–16), the foolish had become sick (verses 17–22), and the proud were in danger of shipwreck at sea (verses 23–32). In each case, "they cried out to the LORD" (verses 6, 13, 19, 28) and were given the same prescription: "Let them give thanks to the LORD for his unfailing love" (verses 8, 15, 21, 31).

Even when we find ourselves in a state of dis-ease by our own hands, we should call out to the Lord and give thanks and praise to Him "for his unfailing love." One can imagine Israelite worshipers representing each of these (and other) groups coming forward to sing these four testimonies and to give praise to God, the entire congregation receiving this final exhortation: "Whoever is wise, let him heed these things and consider the great love of the LORD" (verse 43)—a sort of ancient version of the modern "whole body worship" concept now practiced in many churches.

Understanding the meaning of *worship* helps us understand the necessity of praise in our dis-eased condition. Our English word *worship* derives from an Old English word for "worthiness." Indeed, *worthship* was the original, nonreligious word that conveyed a sense of "credit" or "dignity," then "respect" and "reverence." By the thirteenth century in England, "worthship" began to be used with regard to God to express His credibility and worthiness. And "worthship" eventually became "worship."[2]

We praise God because we believe He is worthy of our praise. Said another way, we praise God because of His worth to us. That which we value highly, we express praise for. In fact, according to C. S. Lewis, it is almost impossible not to praise that which excites us, that which we value:

> It is not out of compliment that lovers keep on telling one another
> how beautiful they are; the delight is incomplete till it is expressed.
> It is frustrating to have discovered a new author and not be able
> to tell anyone how good he is; to come suddenly, at the turn of the
> road, upon some mountain valley of unexpected grandeur and then
> to have to keep silent because the people with you care for it no
> more than for a tin can in the ditch; to hear a good joke and find no
> one to share it with.[3]

Can you imagine a football stadium filled with fifty thousand people who sit silently throughout an entire nail-biting championship game? Of course not! They value their teams, their favorite players, the schools or towns represented by their teams—and they value the experience. So what do they do? They praise at the top of their lungs! They jump out of their seats, hug one another, high-five complete strangers—all because of the worth they have assigned to the teams, players, and experience.

I know sports is not the best analogy—fans can stop praising when the team stops winning. But it serves the point: we praise that which is valuable to us. Therefore, we praise God for His value to us, not for our circumstances. If we fail to praise God "in everything," we are no different from fair-weather fans who praise their team only when it's winning. In another place, C. S. Lewis said, "Praise is boasting about what you enjoy."[4] Refining his words just a bit, we can say, "Praise of God is boasting about *whom* you enjoy."

It is said that when Robert Kennedy visited the Amazon jungles on one occasion, he conversed with a Brazilian Indian. Unknown to Kennedy, the Indian had recently made a profession of faith in Christ through the ministry of missionaries. Using a translator, Kennedy asked the Indian what his favorite pastime was, expecting an answer like hunting in the jungle or fishing in the Amazon River. But the Indian gave the American visitor a surprising answer: "Being occupied with God." Feeling sure the Indian had misunderstood the question, Kennedy asked the translator to repeat the question—which he did, but the Indian's answer was the same: his main avocation in life was being "occupied with God."[5]

That's an excellent way to think about living a life of praise to God—a life in which we give thanks *in* (not *for*) everything. Our natural inclination in times of dis-ease is to be occupied with self—our pain, our needs, our return to normalcy, and our questions of "Why me?" But a life of praise is a life that is occupied with God, even in times of dis-ease: God's purposes, God's comfort, God's provision, and our questions, such as "What can I learn about my relationship with God, and about life, through this experience?"

William E. Sangster was a widely appreciated British minister who died in 1960. In the mid-1950s he began noticing a degree of dis-ease in his legs and throat, only to discover that he had an incurable disease that would result in progressive muscular atrophy. His muscles would waste away, he would lose his voice, and he would eventually be unable to swallow.

Sangster pleaded with God for a ministry that would fit his diminishing physical abilities. He devoted himself to writing, praying, and organizing prayer cells throughout England. Gradually, he lost the use of his legs and his voice. But while he could still write, just a few weeks before he died, he wrote a letter to his daughter. In it, he illustrated how praise can remain a sign of spiritual health even when physical health is taken from us: "It is terrible to wake up on Easter morning and have no voice to shout, 'He is risen!' But it would be still more terrible to have a voice and not want to shout."[6]

There are many who have lost their voice of praise because of some dis-eased experience in their lives. God's value to them has been diminished because He allowed them to experience a difficult situation. They have lost the relationship they once had with God.

But praise can be a bridge back to God. The quickest way to gain a clear vision of God again is to praise Him, for, as Psalm 22:3 says, God is "enthroned upon the praises of Israel" (NASB). Build Him a throne, one praise at a time, in the center of your heart. In due time you will see Him the same way Isaiah did, in the midst of Israel's dis-ease: "I saw the Lord seated on a throne, high and exalted, and the train of his robe filled the temple" (Isaiah 6:1).

To see Him in your praises is to see Him for who He is: the God who loves you and is reaching out to you, reconnecting with you, putting His arms of comfort and care around you.

Questions for Reflection and Discussion

1. We have all had "mountaintop" experiences as well as "wilderness" experiences. Name one or two of your mountaintop experiences. What did you learn about God from those experiences? What are one or two "wilderness" experiences you've endured? What did you learn about God through them?

2. The Old Testament character of Job gives us a picture of pain and suffering. Do you know anyone whose life parallels Job's? How did he or she deal with their pain? How do you deal with pain?

3. How is it possible for praise to erupt from within us when we are in the midst of pain and dis-ease? Cite a time when you, or someone you know, experienced this. What are some of the positive benefits of praising God when you are in pain?

4. Our natural inclination in times of dis-ease is to be occupied with self. Where does a preoccupation with self lead? When have you seen praise provide a tangible cure for dis-ease?

5. Worship is about praising God for His value to us. Make a list of reasons you highly value God. You might begin your list with something like: "God, You are good, loving, all-knowing and all-powerful. You...."

13. Rediscovering Joy When Overcome by Grief

APTAIN CLELAND, ALONG WITH TWO other soldiers, was ferried by helicopter to a barren hilltop in Vietnam to set up a communication outpost. After setting up the equipment, he and the other soldiers were preparing to reboard the helicopter when he looked down on the ground and saw a live hand grenade of the type normally hooked onto the flak jackets of soldiers in a combat zone. Assuming it was one of his grenades that had fallen off, Captain Cleland reached down to pick it up—when it exploded.

The twenty-five-year-old captain's life changed forever on April 8, 1968. His flak jacket protected his vital organs, but both his legs were eventually amputated above the knee, as was one arm. After healing from his wounds, he made a conscious choice not to let the loss of his limbs dictate the kind of life he would live or the contribution he would make.

Max Cleland went on to serve in the Georgia state senate, serve as a member of a U.S. senator's staff, serve as the administrator of the Veterans Administration, as secretary of state in Georgia, and as a United States senator from Georgia. He also authored and coauthored several books along the way. The hand grenade in Vietnam took part of his body, but none of his heart, soul, or mind.

In spite of his obvious success in life, Max Cleland was not a free man. For more than thirty years he had beaten himself up over the notion that a careless mistake—allowing an unsecured hand grenade to fall from his vest—had so radically disfigured him and injured the other soldiers with him. He had grieved over that incident for decades and thought less of himself as a person. It was the one thing the doctors had not been able to repair. Somehow, he hadn't been able to forgive himself for his costly mistake—until he received a phone call in 1999.

While appearing on a television interview program on the History Channel, he had occasion to repeat the story from Vietnam that resulted in his losing his limbs. It so happened that a man named David Lloyd saw that program and heard Cleland's story—and knew that the former army captain had the facts wrong. He made contact with Cleland by telephone as soon as he could to set the record straight.

Lloyd was a nineteen-year-old U.S. Marine, part of a mortar battery on the hilltop where Cleland's helicopter landed. When he heard the grenade explode he and others ran to help the wounded men. On the phone, Lloyd told Cleland that he had heard one of the other wounded soldiers crying out, "It was mine—it was my grenade." The grenade that exploded had not been Captain Cleland's at all. But somehow, in the confusion of the moment, Cleland had never been told whose grenade it was. He had assumed for three decades that it was his.

The other soldier was a young recruit who had not learned the tricks of the battlefield trade, which included always bending or taping the pin on a grenade so it could not accidentally fall or be pulled out, activating the grenade. The grenade must have fallen off the soldier's vest as they regrouped after their mission, dislodging the pin and exploding.

When Max Cleland told this story to my father, Robert H. Schuller, on *The Hour of Power* television program (November 14, 1999, not long after that life-changing phone call), he summarized it this way: "There's a funny thing about human nature: We tend to blame ourselves. The challenge for us all is to see ourselves as God sees us instead of carrying around all the baggage. When I was relieved of that baggage it made a powerful difference in my life, publicly and self-consciously....We need to know that things don't eventually work themselves out in life, but God works out things."

The edge had been taken off Max Cleland's self-confidence, self-esteem, and joy for more than thirty years because of his grief over something that wasn't even his fault.

Have you ever gone thirty-plus years with what seemed like a leak in your emotional or spiritual bucket? Grief can be caused by so many things: accidents, bad choices, things others have done to us, "acts of God" or nature, lost relationships, missed opportunities—the list is as endless and unique as individuals themselves. And we can use other words to describe what I am calling "grief": *sadness, regret, guilt, despair, heartache*—you get the idea.

In my experience, the greatest effect of grief in an individual's life is that it puts a damper on joy. When I was in junior high school, I played in a bell choir. We met at church every week for practice and would perform in the services five or six times a year. One of the skills we had to learn was to quiet the bell. With gloves on our hands, we could make the bells loud, soft, or quiet depending on how much pressure we placed on the outside of the bell. Grief is like someone putting his hands on the outside of a brass bell, muting the tone. We expect a brass bell to ring with clarity and brightness, with a sound that radiates far beyond the bell itself. But if the bell is muted, there is only a hushed sound or a dull clank.

The sad thing is that, the longer we live with grief, and the more joy is muted in our lives, the easier it is to forget what a joyful life really is. We get so used to looking at life through gray-colored glasses that we forget the color and beauty of joy.

And what is joy? It is not just laughter or a positive outlook, though those can be manifestations of joy. Joy is deeper. While laughter is dependent on circumstances at the moment, joy is present regardless of circumstances. One can have joy in the midst of death or disaster or demanding days. Joy is the foundation of all emotions; the deep-seated certainty that purpose and meaning in life are dependent on something more serious than circumstances.

Grief can deflate and mute joy because it is almost always caused by an event—a circumstance. And if we don't have the right perspective on life's circumstances in general, and joy in particular, we can allow an event to steal our joy. Until we correct the perspective we had on the event it is almost impossible not to be preoccupied with it—even for decades, as in the case of Max Cleland, or longer.

The late Dr. Elisabeth Kübler-Ross, a Swiss psychiatrist, set forth the "Five Stages of Grief" in her 1969 book, *On Death and Dying*. Note how they progress—from "Denial" to "Acceptance." And note the potential for getting stuck along the way and never reaching that final stage:

- Stage 1: Denial ("I'm fine. Nothing's wrong.")

- Stage 2: Anger ("Why me? This is not fair!")

- Stage 3: Bargaining ("Please, give me just a little more time!")

- Stage 4: Depression ("There's no hope. What's the point?")

- Stage 5: Acceptance ("What has happened is okay. I can accept it.")[1]

Acceptance of the circumstances in our lives is the goal, but we probably all know people who are stuck in denial, anger, bargaining, or depression. What Kübler-Ross has documented, as a medical scientist, is what she has observed in the lives of the grief-stricken. Generally speaking, she has documented the stages of grief in what the Bible calls the "natural man," or "the man without the Spirit" (1 Corinthians 2:14)—those who respond to grief out of their own natural, human resources. It's easy to see how individuals' personal emotional resources might not be sufficient to carry them all the way to the stage of acceptance.

With all due respect to Dr. Kübler-Ross, I want to suggest that we can learn to live lives of joy by embracing and accepting those events in our lives that are potentially grief-inducing. I don't mean that it's easy or instant. But there is a process, fueled by deep-seated joy, that will allow healing to take place over time. Without even delineating the specific stages, we can move through them with confidence to the final stage of Acceptance, embracing the pain and allowing it to do its complete work in our lives.

Embrace the pain? Absolutely. You've no doubt heard the quote by the German philosopher Friedrich Nietzsche: "That which does not kill us makes us stronger." That's one way of saying "Embrace the pain," but let's look for a better, and more biblical, way.

Think of how athletes train strenuously, especially with weights, to build up muscle tissue in their bodies. It's common knowledge that strenuous exercise actually results in micro-tears (think *pain*) in existing muscle tissue. But following such an episode of exercise, rest and proper nutrition allow the muscle tissue to repair itself at a level of density higher than before. So the pain–rest/nutrition cycle over time increases strength and muscle mass. That's why athletes embrace the pain in their training regimens—because they are looking for the end result. The same is true with severe momentary pain, such as a broken bone. Usually such a bone is stronger after it is healed than it was before the break.

But such healing (of muscle and bone tissue) takes time. During that time the athlete or individual is already at the place of acceptance, embracing the process. He or she knows that the ultimate purpose of the pain is to produce greater strength, even if times of rest (or sitting on the sideline) are part of the process.

Jesus presented a similar scenario to His disciples before leaving this earth—not in athletic terms, of course, but using a common metaphor of His day: pruning. It was common then, and still is today, for vineyard workers to prune back the grapevines after the harvest each year so they would put forth new and more abundant growth the following season: "Every branch that does bear fruit he prunes so that it will be even more fruitful" (John 15:2).

The lesson, of course, is that God is the Gardener. His goal is for every branch to bear "much fruit" (verse 5). So He reserves the right to prune back the branches to make them more fruitful in their next season of growth. But pruning takes time. It begins after the harvest, then the vines lie dormant for months until the warmth of spring and sun and rain coax new growth. But if the vines could speak, they would say that they embrace their pain, their grief, knowing that more abundant fruit will be the result.

I find it fascinating to trace Jesus' line of thought in these lessons He taught His disciples:

- John 15:1–8: Accept God's pruning and remain in Jesus, the true Vine.

- John 15:9–10: Live your life centered in God's love.

And then the key for our thoughts in this chapter:

- John 15:11: "I have told you this so that my joy may be in you and that your joy may be complete."

Do you see the connection between the pruning accomplished by the Gardener and the completeness of the joy of the branches? If we are faithful to embrace life's difficulties and trust the work of God in our lives, our joy will be complete *in spite of the pain we may experience in the process.* Indeed, living a life of joy—living a life of centeredness in the love and goodness of God—is the best defense against getting stuck in the steps of grief and never making it all the way to acceptance.

On Sunday, March 18, 1979, a twin-engine light plane took off from Aspen, Colorado, and crashed shortly after becoming airborne. At that moment, Stephanie May lost her husband, John Edward, her son, David, her daughter, Karla, and her son-in-law, Richard. For the next two months she kept a diary in which she recorded her process through the valley of grief. These are her entries for May 7 and 8:

> My burden is heavy, but I don't walk alone. My pain is unrelenting, but I thank God for every moment that He blessed me with. I pray that my life will be used for His glory, that I might carry my burden with Christian dignity, and that out of my devastation, may His kingdom become apparent to someone lost and in pain. I close this diary, and with it goes all my known ability and capacity for love. I must climb to a different plane and search for a different life. I cannot replace or compare my loss. It is my loss. I am not strong. I am not brave. I am a Christian with a burden to carry and a message to share. I have been severely tested, but my faith has survived, and I have been strengthened in my love and devotion to the Lord. Oh, God, my life is Yours—comfort me in Your arms and direct my life. I have walked in hell, but now I walk with God in peace. John Edward, David, Karla, and Richard are in God's hands. I am in God's arms and His love surrounds me. This rose will bloom again.[2]

Stephanie May's words tell me that she did not wait for grief to strike before living a life of joy and contentment in God. No one could sustain such a horrific loss and, overnight, marshal the resources necessary to gain such a deep and contented perspective. No doubt her grief and pain were hellacious, as she herself wrote. Yet she believed that both she and the family members she lost were in God's hands, surrounded by His love.

Stephanie May would have found a kindred spirit in the psalmist David. Consider these words, written from an Old Testament perspective, and see how they parallel hers:

> I will bless the LORD who guides me;
>> even at night my heart instructs me.
> I know the LORD is always with me.
>> I will not be shaken, for he is right beside me.

No wonder my heart is filled with joy,
 and my mouth shouts his praises!
 My body rests in safety.
For you will not leave my soul among the dead
 or allow your godly one to rot in the grave.
You will show me the way of life,
 granting me *the joy of your presence*
 and the pleasures of living with you forever.
(Psalm 16:7–11 NLT, italics added)

David was writing about the ultimate kind of grief that many people spend their whole lives afraid of: death (see Hebrews 2:15). But it held no fear for him! The two lines I put in italics reflect his thinking about the present ("my heart is filled with joy") and the future ("You will ... [grant] me the joy of your presence ... forever). Joy now and joy forever, even in the face of death, the ultimate enemy in life.

Old Testament saints didn't have near the detailed view of heaven and eternal life that we gain from the New Testament, but they understood this: *joy is a result of living in the presence of God, both now and forever!*

I don't know the kind of grief you may have suffered in the past or may be experiencing today, but it need not drain away the joy of living wholly connected to God. "The fruit of the Spirit is ... joy" (Galatians 5:22), and if you will dwell in His presence—stay connected to Him—His joy will be your shield against whatever life may bring.

Questions for Reflection and Discussion

1. There are many causes of grief in life: accidents, bad choices, things others have done to us, "acts of God" or nature, lost relationships, missed opportunities. What have been some causes of grief in your life? Is there anything you are grieving in your life right now?

2. What are some ways you've observed people deal with grief? How do you deal with grief?

3. Working through grief is a process. What have you learned about the process of grief as the result of walking through it yourself?

How has walking through your own grief prepared you to walk with others through theirs?

4. What are some common misperceptions of what it means to experience joy in the midst of grief? Describe what you think real joy looks like in the life of someone who is walking through grief. Can you think of an instance when you experienced the kind of joy you just described?

5. Read and reflect on John 15:1–11 this week. Picture the idea of "pruning" the writer describes here first in physical terms as it relates to a bush or tree and then as it relates to life. Looking back at the losses and the resulting grief you've experienced in your life, what would you say God was "pruning" from your life? Would you say that your joy was made more complete as the result of the grief you experienced? Why?

14. Learning to Forgive When Gripped by Bitterness

IVE DAYS BEFORE CHRISTMAS, ten-year-old Christopher Carrier was outside his south Florida home when he was approached by a stranger who said he was a friend of Chris's dad. "I want to buy him a gift, and I need your help," the man said. Thinking there was a nice Christmas gift being planned for his father, Chris eagerly went with the man and entered his motor home, parked up the street.

The man said they needed to drive a ways to pick out the gift but ended up parking in a remote field. Claiming to be lost, he spread out a map and asked Chris to help him figure out how to find the way home. As the young boy leaned over the map he suddenly felt a sharp pain in the back of his neck. The "friend of Chris's father" had stabbed the boy with an ice pick. From there, the man drove farther into the Florida Everglades, shot Chris in the left temple, and left him for dead in the alligator-infested swamp.

For six days, Chris Carrier lay unconscious until someone driving through the swamp spotted his body. Miraculously, he survived his wounds, though he was blind in his left eye. Since he was not able to give the police an adequate description of the man, no arrest was ever made.

For three years Chris lived in fear, despite police protection and surveillance of the Carriers' home. But when he turned thirteen, at a church youth function he felt compelled to turn his fears over to Jesus Christ, asking Him to become the Lord of his life. At age fifteen, he shared his story for the first time publicly and eventually went into full-time ministry to help others find the peace he had discovered in Christ.

In 1996, now with a family of his own, Chris received a phone call from a police detective saying that a man had confessed to assaulting Chris when he was ten years old. Chris arranged to visit the now seventy-seven-year-old man, feeble, blind, and broken, in the nursing home where he lived. But before visiting his attacker, Chris learned what had motivated the attack: the man had once been employed by Chris's father, who had fired him for drinking on the job. The attack on Chris had been a senseless act of revenge for the firing.

When Chris met the man, he initially denied knowing anything about the kidnapping and attack. But after hearing the story of Chris's life he softened and eventually apologized for what he had done. "What you meant for evil, God has turned into a wonderful blessing," Chris told him, explaining how God had used his story through the years to open doors for sharing the gospel. God had prepared Chris to forgive his attacker long before the two ever met.

Following that first meeting, Chris, along with his wife and children, began almost daily visits to the nursing home to minister to the man. And one Sunday afternoon, the man confessed his sins to God and gave his heart to Christ in the presence of the man he had tried to kill as a child. Having received forgiveness from man and God, the forgiven sinner, now a saint, died peacefully in his sleep a few days later.[1]

How does an innocent victim of kidnapping and attempted murder find the ability to forgive? The long answer is dependent on each circumstance and the mysterious grace of God at work in the heart of the offended party. That is not a formula that can be written down. The work God did in the heart of a young teenager to enable him to forgive a vengeful attacker is not, in detail, the exact same work God would do in you or in me to help us come to grips with the need to forgive.

But the short answer is easier to write down: "Be kind and compassionate to one another, forgiving each other, just as in Christ God forgave you" (Ephesians 4:32). The principle of Christian forgiveness is based in the act of divine forgiveness. We can even go further and say that human forgiveness, not just Christian forgiveness, is based on God's initiative to offer forgiveness to the whole world (see John 3:16). For a person who has received the unmerited forgiveness of God through the death of Jesus Christ on the cross not to offer that same forgiveness to others can lead to a loss of fellowship with God Himself.

This book is about leaning into God—restoring power to our relationship with Him when that relationship has been disconnected for one reason or another. And failing to forgive those who have hurt us can lead to such a disconnect. The relationship between our forgiving others and God's forgiving us is found in Jesus' words in Matthew 6:14–15: "If you forgive men when they sin against you, your heavenly Father will also forgive you. But if you do not forgive men their sins, your Father will not forgive your sins."

These words of Jesus have caused some confusion among readers regarding one's relationship with God. Since the forgiveness of our sins is the basis for our being reconciled to God for eternity, does Jesus mean our salvation is placed in limbo while we struggle to forgive another person? No, that is not what Jesus meant. Jesus is referring to our fellowship with God—our clear and consistent communication and intimacy with Him—not our salvation.

But that shouldn't be a cause for relief. Losing our intimacy with God on a temporal basis should not be viewed as a less-threatening prospect than losing the same intimacy for eternity. For the Jesus-follower, eternal life has already begun (see John 17:3)! We should be relating to God now just as we plan to for eternity in heaven.

To get a better idea of the meaning of Jesus' words, think of them this way: if you maintain a transparent and forgiving relationship with others, you will enjoy that same kind of relationship with God. But if you fail to live in a forgiving and open way with others, you can expect your intimacy with God to suffer. The focus is on connecting with others and connecting with God, not on salvation.

I wonder if Jesus had this verse in the Psalms in mind when He spoke His own words: "If I had cherished sin in my heart, the Lord would not have listened; but God has surely listened and heard my voice in prayer" (66:18–19). It is a sin not to forgive others. If we cherish the sin of unforgiveness in our hearts, we block our reception connectors to see, hear, or feel the blessings God has for us.

Another way of getting the meaning of Jesus' words in Matthew 6:14–15—the connection between human forgiveness and divine intimacy—is to meditate on Eugene Peterson's paraphrase of these verses from *The Message*. He relates Jesus' words on forgiveness to the teaching on prayer that He had just given (Matthew 6:5–13): "In prayer there is a connection between what God does and what you do. You can't get forgiveness from God, for instance, without also forgiving others. If you refuse to do your part, you cut yourself off from God's part" (verses 14–15).

Jesus had just taught the disciples to pray, "Forgive us our debts, as we also have forgiven our debtors" (verse 12), and then He reminds them: don't ask God to forgive you if you haven't forgiven others first.

The most powerful illustration of this principle is in the parable Jesus told in Matthew 18:21–35 in response to Peter's question: "Lord, how many times shall I forgive my brother when he sins against me? Up to seven times?" (verse 21). Jesus' answer was (my paraphrase), "If you're counting, you're not forgiving"—and told this story to illustrate the point:

A king's servant owed the king a massive amount of money—call it a zillion dollars. When the king called for the account to be settled and discovered that the servant couldn't pay, he ordered the servant's family and property be sold to pay the debt. The servant begged for the king's patience, promising he would pay back the money. Suddenly, the king had compassion on the servant's bankrupt condition and canceled the entire debt, setting the servant and his family free.

But then the servant encountered one of his friends who owed him a dollar—and the servant demanded repayment on the spot. The friend didn't have the dollar and begged for the servant's patience. "No way," the servant said, and he had his friend thrown into prison for failure to pay the dollar debt. So, the servant had been forgiven a zillion-dollar debt by the king but then had failed to forgive a one-dollar debt owed him by his friend.

When the king heard about this he was not happy:

> The [king] called the servant in. "You wicked servant," he said, "I canceled all that debt of yours because you begged me to. Shouldn't you have had mercy on your fellow servant just as I had on you?" In anger [the king] turned him over to the jailers to be tortured, until he should pay back all he owed.
> (Matthew 18:32–34)

Jesus added, "This is how my heavenly Father will treat each of you unless you forgive your brother from your heart" (verse 35).

Do you think Peter got his question answered? That and more! Jesus' story illustrated the principle of divine-human reciprocity: what God has done for us, He expects us to do for others. Choosing not to do for others (forgive) what God has done for us (forgiven) results in a power disconnect between us and God. Conversely, the way to restore the power connection is to make sure we keep short accounts when it comes to forgiveness. So short, in fact, that Paul puts our responsibility in terms of hours: "Do not let the sun go down while you are still angry" (Ephesians 4:26). Why? Because to do so is to "give the devil a foothold" (verse 27). Not to forgive is to issue an engraved invitation to the enemy of your soul to take up residence and begin complicating and troubling your life. (Paul's exhortation to settle spiritual and emotional accounts by the end of the day comes from the requirement under the Old Testament law, stated in Deuteronomy 24:11–13, to do the same regarding physical goods held as a pledge on a loan.)

We know what God expects us to do—now it's time to face the truth of the matter: forgiveness isn't easy! Forgiveness is covered by the old saying "If it was easy, everybody would do it." And we all know (perhaps from personal experience) that everyone isn't forgiving.

So why is forgiveness so difficult? It's because there is a price to pay. In the story Jesus told about forgiveness, what did it cost the king to forgive his servant? A zillion dollars. What would it have cost the servant to forgive his friend? A single dollar. (It's easy to see why the king was so angry, given the comparison.)

Whether the price is big or small, forgiveness is never free. The price God paid to forgive human beings for our sin was watching (and feeling) the torture and death of His own Son, Jesus. The price God paid adds another dimension to Paul's words in Ephesians 4:32: "...forgiving each other, just as in Christ God forgave you." If we are to forgive others as God forgave us, there will be a price to pay.

While we can never say, "I forgive you," too quickly, sometimes we may say it without counting the cost. If we don't consider the cost of forgiveness and write the full check when we say the words, a forgiveness "relapse" can occur down the road. It's like buying something on credit—the bill is going to eventually come due. As the man on the old TV commercial used to say, "You can pay me now, or you can pay me later." If we "forgive" without writing the check on the spot, resentment can set in when we realize the bill is due and we discover we didn't really forgive after all.

For instance, your spouse says something that deeply offends you. Realizing you are hurt, he says, "I'm very sorry for hurting you. Would you forgive me?" You may say, "Yes, I forgive you" right away—and mean it. If so, all is well. But let's say you verbalize your forgiveness without counting the cost. A few minutes later when the spouse who just hurt you comes into the room with an amorous look in his eye and gets the cold shoulder from you, he is going to wonder what's going on.

"I thought you forgave me. Are you still upset?" he asks.

"I thought I did, too," you reply. "But maybe I didn't. I think this is going to take a little longer than I imagined." In other words, you checked the balance in your Forgiveness Account and discovered you were overdrawn. You were writing forgiveness checks that you couldn't cover when it came time to move forward with life.

Pastor Glenn Schaeffer was delivering a children's sermon to the kids in his congregation one Sunday morning when he held up an "ugly" (his words) summer shirt that he occasionally wore around the house. He explained to the children that a friend of his had actually told him the shirt was so ugly that he ought to throw it away.

"That really hurt me," he said. "I'm having trouble forgiving the person who said those mean things. Do you think I should forgive that person?"

His six-year-old daughter was part of the group listening to the sermon, and she immediately raised her hand. "Yes, you should," she said without a moment's hesitation.

"But why?" the pastor said. "That person really hurt my feelings."

Came the answer from the mouth of the six-year-old: "Because you're married to her!"[2]

The little girl knew the theory perfectly. It's ironic that the people we love most in life are the ones we know the best—and therefore the ones it is sometimes hardest to forgive. We are immediately forced back into a face-to-face life with that person—and we have to live and love as if he or she were totally innocent! (Which they are if we have forgiven them.)

We resent the fact that they get to sin one minute and be free from the consequences of sin the next. But that's the price of forgiveness. If your child knocks over a valuable vase and you watch it shatter into a thousand pieces, the price of your forgiveness is the cost of the vase plus giving up your anger and resentment. But because most relational hurt in life doesn't involve physical objects, it's harder to determine the cost of giving up resentment, bitterness, anger, frustration, and the desire for vengeance.

However you do the math, you have to count the cost and be prepared to live with the person you have forgiven as if he or she had never done anything wrong—which is exactly how God forgives us, which is exactly how we are required to forgive (see Ephesians 4:32).

But—there is an exception to this rule: *forgiving* is not a synonym for *reconciling*. For instance, if a woman and her children have suffered from a physically and emotionally abusive spouse and father, such that they've had to leave the home (and perhaps the relationship) for their own protection, they are not required by God to put themselves back into danger by reconciling with the abuser every time he says "I'm sorry" or asks for forgiveness. In that case, reconciling might enable the same behavior to continue. Forgiveness "up to seventy times seven" (Matthew 18:22) should never be a means of enabling sin. Are we required by God to forgive? Yes. But we are not required to enable another's sin by acting as if it had never happened.

Not only is forgiveness pricey, it is risky. In Saint Patrick's Cathedral in Dublin, Ireland, an ancient wooden door, known as the "Door of Reconciliation," is on display. This door, which has a rectangular hole cut in the middle, opened into the chapter house (meeting room) that was part of the cathedral, a room that served as a refuge place in 1492 for Black James, nephew of the Earl of Ormond, and his men. They had sought protection in the chapter house from Gerald Fitzgerald, Earl of Kildare, with whom James's family had conducted a lengthy feud.

Even though Fitzgerald had Black James cornered and surrounded, as Ireland's leading earl he wanted to bring the long-standing bitterness between the two families to an end. For a long time, Fitzgerald pleaded with James to give up: to unbolt the door and come out and be reconciled. Fearing a trick, Black James refused to open the door and exit the chapter house.

So Fitzgerald went on the offensive, having his men chop a hole in the center of the door. Through that hole he thrust his arm, begging for Black James to take his hand and be reconciled. It was a risky move—one of Black James's men could easily have hacked off the earl's arm. Instead, thankfully, James grasped the extended hand of Fitzgerald and agreed to forgive all.

The Irish have an expression today—"chancing one's arm"—that some say is linked to this event (though scholars disagree). Whether the historical reference is correct or not, the point is well made: there is risk in taking the initiative when it comes to forgiveness and reconciliation. You may have your head or your heart handed to you by the very person you are willing and ready to forgive.[3]

Examine your connectedness to God and the status of your forgiveness of others. If you see a correlation between unforgiveness and a lack of intimacy with God, you now know what to do in order to restore that intimacy. No price, no risk, and no delay is worth being out of fellowship with—disconnected from—the God who has already forgiven you.

Questions for Reflection and Discussion

1. Having read this chapter on forgiveness, what concepts or ideas make you most uneasy or do you find most challenging to act on in life? Why?

2. In doing a quick inventory of your own life, is there anyone in your life you feel you simply cannot forgive? What has a lack of forgiveness "cost" you—emotionally, spiritually, relationally?

3. Where have you seen God turn something that was meant for evil into a wonderful blessing in life? Have you had this happen in your own life? When?

4. What does it mean to "count the cost of forgiveness"? Come up with some examples from your life that show either how you've effectively done this or how you miscalculated the "cost" only to discover that you really didn't forgive someone after all.

5. What are the risks in taking the initiative when it comes to forgiveness and reconciliation? Is there anyone in your life you want to risk forgiving now or in the future? What steps might you need to take to get ready to do that?

15. Seeking Restoration When Shattered by Rejection

D R. HUDSON ARMERDING was president of Wheaton College (Illinois) from 1965 to 1982. At one point during his tenure as president, a particular crisis arose at the college based on prejudice—and he was faced with the decision of how it should be handled. Such a problem would be a challenge for any college president, but this one presented long-term ramifications of a financial nature.

It seems that some of the college's largest financial supporters had been visiting the campus and noticed that some of the male students were wearing their hair unusually long—and some even had facial hair. This presented such a breach of Christian decorum (in the minds of the donors) that they made it known to Dr. Armerding that, unless the "problem" was corrected, they would consider withdrawing their financial support from the college, as some had already done.

This news had circulated among the student body, and Dr. Armerding made plans to address the situation at a meeting of the student body in the college chapel. After explaining the problem to the students, Dr. Armerding looked out over the student body, his eyes falling on a young man whom he knew by name. He called the student by name and said, "I want you to come and join me on the platform," which the student did with not a small degree of reluctance. The two stood together—the distinguished president and the bearded, long-haired student.

"Young man," Dr. Armerding said to the student, "you have long hair and a long beard. You represent the very thing that these supporters of the school are against. I want you to know that the administration of this school does not feel as they do. We accept you and we love you. We believe you are here to seek and to find the truth as it is in the Lord Jesus Christ."

The president then stretched out his arms and wrapped them around the young man, drawing him close to himself. And the student body jumped to its feet with shouts and applause for a college president, from a different generation, who refused to reject his students at any price.[1]

That potential case of rejection turned out well for a group of students, thanks to the unconditional love of a godly college president. The students were not faced with what would have been a painful "either/or" decision: either you get your hair cut and shave your beards, or leave the college.

But not all "either/or" situations turn out so harmoniously. Almost everyone has faced the possibility of rejection—and many have experienced it—because of seemingly trivial matters. And there is perhaps no pain more personal than the pain of rejection, especially if you are the "innocent party." By that I mean you might be experiencing the pain of rejection even though you did nothing to deserve it. Those who violate the law are rejected by society and incarcerated. A marriage partner who seriously abuses his or her spouse might suffer the pain of rejection when the abused spouse files for a divorce for the sake of protection. People sometimes suffer rejection when, in fact, it is their behavior that is being rejected. But to reject the behavior sometimes means, in extreme cases, rejecting the person.

In this chapter I'm talking about the kind of rejection that is undeserved. To use marriage as an example again, a spouse might be the "innocent party" in a divorce proceeding. A teenager might be rejected by his or her peers because of not measuring up to some arbitrary social standard. An entire social class of people might be rejected for racial, cultural, religious, or ethnic reasons. An individual might suffer the pain of rejection after being fired by a company to which she or he had given years of loyal service.

Realizing that no one is 100 percent innocent in this life, there are situations in which rejection is decidedly undeserved. Jesus of Nazareth comes to mind, of course. Isaiah spoke prophetically about Jesus hundreds of years before He came on the scene: "He was despised and rejected by men, a man of sorrows, and familiar with suffering. Like one from whom men hide their faces he was despised, and we esteemed him not" (Isaiah 53:3).

That is a perfect illustration of the experience of rejection: being despised and rejected leads to sorrow and suffering; people hide their faces from us and we lose our self-esteem. They despise us and so we despise ourselves. Jesus did not despise Himself, of course, but that is often the result of rejection. Rejection by others (or what we perceive as rejection) leads to self-loathing, and self-loathing leads to pain.

The very successful actress Sigourney Weaver told the London *Daily Telegraph* in an interview:

> I was teased at school for being a too-tall beanpole and I yearned to be the pretty one. When I was about [eight years old] I asked my mom if I was pretty. She said, "No dear, you're just plain." That was, well, hard. My mother meant well; she was worried her kids would grow up conceited. She said it for the best of reasons. But I became a really awkward teenager. I thought, "Gosh, if my mother doesn't think I'm pretty, I had better crawl under the couch."

Things didn't get any better when Weaver studied drama at Yale. There, her teachers told her she would never find work. She concluded, "Well, if my teachers don't think I have any talent then I mustn't have any talent." It took "lots and lots of therapy" for Weaver to emerge from the rejection she felt growing up—and to prove her teachers wrong.[2]

If the cycle of pain from rejection is not interrupted, it can lead to a dark place—so dark, in fact, that we cannot even see God. We conclude that He has rejected us, too. And the pain doesn't even have to be the result of a big rejection. The Christian philosopher and counselor Henri Nouwen has said that the many small rejections of every day—a sarcastic smile, a flippant remark, a brisk denial, or a bitter silence—might all be quite innocent and hardly worth our attention if they did not constantly arouse our basic fear of being totally alone with "darkness as our one companion left."[3]

G. Campbell Morgan (1863–1945) was one of England's most famous preachers. Crowds flocked to hear him preach the Bible at Westminster Chapel in London, as well as in the United States when he visited here. So clear was his calling, and so abundant his gifts, that he preached his first sermon at the age of thirteen. But he was not always so widely accepted.

In 1888, Morgan was one of a group of 150 young men who sought to be licensed as preaching ministers in the Wesleyan tradition in England. He passed the doctrinal examination without problem. But the preaching exam proved to be more than the twenty-five-year-old could handle, in spite of his dozen years of preaching experience. He walked onto the stage of a cavernous auditorium that had a thousand seats, only about seventy-five of which were filled with three examining ministers and others who came to listen.

Two weeks later, Morgan's name appeared on a list of 105 candidates who were rejected for the ministry that year. He knew his rejection was because of how he preached that day. Morgan sent a one-word wire to his father: "Rejected." He wrote in his diary later that day, "Very dark everything seems. Still, He knoweth best." A reply from Morgan's father arrived quickly: "Rejected on earth. Accepted in heaven. Dad."[4]

That is the darkness of which Henri Nouwen spoke. Rejection cuts so deeply that we believe darkness is our only companion. It is so easy, even for a spiritually mature person like G. Campbell Morgan, to think like this: *People have rejected me, therefore God must have rejected me as well.* We make this mistake for one fundamental reason: *we have created God in the image of man!*

Without intervening truth and information, it is natural for us to think of God the way we would the highest earthly authority we can imagine: better, higher, more reasonable, yet still human. So when we feel that "everyone" has rejected us, we believe God has rejected us as well. The next step, of course, is to blame God for the pain of the rejection we are experiencing. If God was truly God—loving and powerful—He would have saved us from the debilitating pain of rejection.

C. S. Lewis stated this argument in his classic book *The Problem of Pain*: "If God were good, he would wish to make his creatures perfectly happy, and if God were almighty he would be able to do as he wished. But the creatures are not happy. Therefore God lacks either goodness, or power, or both. This is the problem of pain in its simplest form."[5]

The argument Lewis summarized relates to all kinds of pain and suffering in the world, not just the pain of rejection. But it certainly applies to this discussion. Why does God allow us to be rejected when we don't deserve it? Is He not loving? (That is, does He not care about me?) And is He not all-powerful? (That is, is He not able to protect me?) The assumption is that because we experience pain in the world, God must not be who the Bible says He is: loving and powerful.

Indeed, a noted theologian has recently described his own disconnection from the biblical God of his youth based on the problem of pain. He simply cannot reconcile the person of God with the problem of pain in the world.[6] And more than twenty years ago, in *When Bad Things Happen to Good People*, the Jewish rabbi Harold Kushner came to the same impasse after a debilitating illness took the life of his young son.[7]

I would not attempt to expound on and try to resolve something that spiritual giants like C. S. Lewis have already addressed. But I can say this: God is loving (see John 3:16; 1 John 4:8, 16), and nothing is impossible for Him (see Jeremiah 32:27; Mark 10:27). If it was God's purpose for human beings to experience no pain, He would arrange it. In fact, He has already said that a day is coming when "he will wipe every tear from [our] eyes. There will be no more death or mourning or crying or pain, for the old order of things has passed away" (Revelation 21:4).

But that is not God's purpose for us *now*. He has clearly stated what His purpose is in Romans 8:29: "to be conformed to the likeness of his Son." If God did not protect His own Son from the pain of rejection, why should we expect that He would protect us from that same pain? God uses our pain—yes, even the severe pain of rejection—to conform us "to the image of His Son" (Romans 8:29 NKJV).

When we are rejected we must remember that God is not a man. It is not He who is rejecting us. We must separate the actions *caused* by men from the actions *allowed* by God. At the very same time that men are *rejecting* us, God is *accepting* us! God even accepts us when our faith is weak (see Romans 14:3). In fact, His acceptance of us, in spite of our weaknesses, is the model for our acceptance of others (see Romans 15:7). My favorite passage of all about God's acceptance is Ephesians 1:3–6: "Blessed be the God and Father of our Lord Jesus Christ, who has blessed us...chose[n] us...predestined us...to the praise of the glory of His grace, by which He made us accepted in the Beloved" (NKJV).

If you are a follower of Jesus Christ, you can be rejected by every person on the face of this earth, and you will still be accepted by God. The Bible says again and again that God will "never leave you nor forsake you" (Deuteronomy 31:6, 8; Joshua 1:5; 1 Kings 8:57; Hebrews 13:5).

But human rejection happens and we still feel the pain. And to compound matters, we often feel that others' rejection is our fault. The younger we are, the more we carry false guilt for having been rejected. But even mature saints can struggle with this false notion of being responsible for rejection. The famous (and late) novelist Madeleine L'Engle once wrote,

> One time I was talking to Canon Tallis, who is my spiritual [mentor] as well as my friend, and I was deeply grieved about something, and I kept telling him how woefully I had failed someone I love, failed totally; otherwise that person couldn't have done the wrong that was so destructive. Finally, he looked at me and said calmly, "Who are you to think you are better than our Lord? After all, he was singularly unsuccessful with a great many people."[8]

I noted at the beginning of this chapter that sometimes we are responsible for being rejected. But that is not the kind of rejection about which I am talking. I'm talking about the kind that Madeleine L'Engle wrote about—the day-to-day, garden-variety kind, as well as the major life event kind. We are not responsible for others' actions. If they choose to reject us for whatever reason, that is their choice. Our responsibility is not to feel guilty for being rejected, but to love even our enemies—even those who have acted unkindly toward us (see Matthew 5:44).

Our other responsibility is to trust God in the midst of our rejection, to not let man's rejection separate us from the God who accepts us. Even if we are smashed into a million pieces, God will show us how to put the pieces back together again.

History records how Shah Abbas the Great of Iran's seventeenth-century Safavid dynasty heard of the beautiful mirrors being made by the artisans in Venice. He reportedly commissioned twenty huge mirrors to be made for his palaces. When the mirrors arrived in Isfahan, Iran's capital in that day, and were unpacked, it was discovered that the mirrors had been shattered into thousands of tiny pieces. Being an avid lover of the arts, the shah asked his own artists to see if they could create something beautiful from the innumerable fragments. What they did gave rise to the art form known today as Persian stucco mirror art. They took the tiny pieces of the shattered mirrors and cut them into ornamental Persian patterns, gluing them to the walls and ceilings of palaces, mosques, and other buildings. The reflection of the light of candles and chandeliers created a beautiful effect that never would have been known had not the mirrors been shattered.[9]

When something shatters beyond recognition, often the pieces can become something new and different, every bit as beautiful as (or more beautiful than) the original—beautiful in a new, different, and unexpected way. It may not be immediately apparent what the new creation should be, but time will tell.

If you have been shattered by the pain of rejection, you must let God be the artisan of your soul. You must embrace the conviction that your shattering is not the end of something beautiful. And you must wait patiently to see what God will do. Don't be quick to assume that God is finished. Give Him time to pick up the pieces and begin to craft something new and beautiful in your life. If you will allow Him freedom to work, you will remain connected to Him.

Questions for Reflection and Discussion

1. What are some ways people today deal with the pain of rejection? Cite one or two examples where you've seen the negative effects of rejection in someone's life.

2. Rejection is very often undeserved. Have you ever felt rejected? Why did you feel rejected and what was your response to it?

3. The philosopher and counselor Henri Nouwen mentions "the many small rejections of every day"—a sarcastic smile, a flippant remark, a brisk denial, or a bitter silence. What other "small rejections" would you add to Nouwen's list? What small rejections have you experienced in life?

4. At the very same time man is *rejecting* us, God is *accepting* us. What are some truths you see in Scripture or experiences you've

had in life that remind you how much God loves you and accepts you as you are?

5. God can take the pieces of your soul that have been shattered by rejection and begin to craft something new and beautiful in your life. Are you aware of any ways in which He might be doing that right now? What has been your response to the work He is doing in you?

Part 4

Holding On—
Hoping in God

16. In Whom Do You Trust? Getting to Know Your Power Source

T WAS 1978, and a civil war was raging in Nicaragua. But that didn't stop Arthur Blessitt from going there. Arthur Blessitt has carried his twelve-foot wooden cross into various dangerous hot spots around the world in order to tell people about Jesus. In fact, he has carried his cross into 315 countries (52 of the countries were at war), walking 38,102 miles and being arrested or jailed 24 times (not for crimes), since 1968.

Nicaragua was definitely a dangerous place to go in 1978. The Sandanista guerrillas were at war with the Somoza government dictatorship; death and destruction were everywhere. But Arthur Blessitt walked down the Pan American Highway through the middle of the nation, talking to anyone who would listen about the good news of the gospel. His two friends were riding in a pickup truck full of supplies and pulling a small travel trailer that they slept in at night. The natives warned them to keep moving—not to spend the night in the area because of the danger of roving bands of soldiers. But they stayed and pulled off the road to sleep.

In the middle of the night, Blessitt was awakened by someone banging loudly on their trailer door, shouting, *"Narcotica policia!"* He looked out the small window to find a gun aimed back at him. He opened the door and several men with guns rushed into the trailer. The leader motioned with his pistol for Blessitt to go outside, which he did—but not before telling his friend, "Pray, Mike. Pray."

Blessitt didn't know who the men were, but he knew they had guns and were serious. In his broken Spanish, he began to witness to the men, telling them that God loved them and would come into their hearts—to no avail. The men pushed Blessitt up against the side of his truck and then lined up about fifteen feet away. He suddenly realized he was standing in front of a firing squad!

Deciding that if he was going to die, he at least wanted to be shot while distributing God's Word, he turned and opened the door of the truck and reached for a case of Spanish language Bibles, setting it on the ground. The men rushed toward him, shouting, "No! No!" while he knelt on the ground trying to break the tape that sealed the box of Bibles.

At this point in the story, Arthur Blessitt would say later, he doesn't know what happened. He looked up from the ground to find the armed men sprawled on the ground all around him. The leader of the band was actually lying inside the door of the trailer with his feet sticking out. All the men were dazed and confused. Blessitt tried to offer them water and a Bible, but they all got up and ran off into the night.

When he returned to the trailer, his friends were amazed to see Blessitt alive. One of them said they heard the sound of flesh on flesh and thought the armed men were beating their friend. But no one else had been there. Blessitt was unharmed, and the armed men had been knocked to the ground by an unseen force. The next day, native people from nearby houses said, "We saw a bright light. God was there and the gunmen fell to the ground."[1]

Have you ever stood before a firing squad with your very life on the line? Neither have I. But you may have been in situations that felt as dire. And there is only one question that matters at times like that: whom do you trust? Or, to put it more colloquially, "Who ya gonna call?"

A man in the Old Testament was faced with a Blessitt-like situation: King Jehoshaphat of Judah. Jerusalem was surrounded by enemy armies, and the king knew there was no escape. They were doomed, humanly speaking. So he gathered the people together to pray a humble prayer, confessing their trust in God. The last line of Jehoshaphat's prayer is, in my opinion, one of the most beautiful and utterly human in all the Bible: "We do not know what to do, but our eyes are upon you" (2 Chronicles 20:12). And God rescued the people.

We can't relate to King Jehoshaphat's situation any more than we can

Arthur Blessitt's in terms of the actual events. But we can definitely relate when it comes to how it feels to be surrounded by life's circumstances with no hope of escape.

The human dilemma is always the same: "We don't know what to do." I say that respectfully, acknowledging how creative humankind has been, and continues to be, in the face of life's question marks. Man has often been resourceful when faced with life's blank slates and come up with answers.

But the fact never goes away: we often don't know what to do. I dare say that you are asking yourself that question today about some part of your life. "I don't know what to do about health...money...an enemy... a destructive habit...a wayward child or spouse...a relationship...a life-decision...a terrible mistake...." The question is not whether life will present you with "impossible" scenarios today and in the future. The question is, to whom will you turn for answers?

Jehoshaphat concluded his prayer, not with a negative statement "(We do not know what to do"), but with a statement of faith: "But our eyes are upon [God]." Jehoshaphat's words are without parallel in their beautiful simplicity.

Take your eyes off this page for a moment and look straight ahead, directly out in front of where you are sitting. Look at all the things that compete for the attention of your eyes. You can choose any of those things on which to focus—a picture on the wall, a family member across the room, a tree outside a window—but the choice is yours.

Jehoshaphat's view, as he looked out on his world, included many things: allied peoples to whom he could have sent a message for help, an escape route by which he could flee, the armory of Judah and its stockpile of weapons, the temple treasury of gold that might have served as a bribe to his enemies, and the God of his fathers. From his prayer, it is clear what Jehoshaphat chose to focus on when he did not know what to do: "But our eyes are on you." The king chose to focus the eyes of his nation on God Himself.

The Bible says that Jehoshaphat had gathered the people in the courtyard of the temple in Jerusalem (see 2 Chronicles 20:5), and I can imagine him having an Isaiah-like moment: "I saw the Lord seated on a throne, high and exalted, and the train of his robe filled the temple" (Isaiah 6:1). If you and I could see God like that when we "don't know what to do," life would look much different from where we stand in the face of our unanswered questions.

The idea of trusting in God is not new to Americans. Indeed, it's our national motto—you can find it printed or engraved on most of our currency. If you think there's a disconnect between our nation's motto and our nation's mores, you are right. U.S. Supreme Court Justice William Brennan, in a 1984 court decision opinion, noted that "In God We Trust," the nation's motto, has become a form of "ceremonial deism" since it has "lost through rote repetition any significant religious content."[2]

That's a shame since the motto came into existence at a time in America's history not unlike that of King Jehoshaphat of Judah nearly three thousand years earlier: a time when the nation teetered on the edge of destruction. With the rising tensions between North and South over the issue of slavery and states' rights, Christians on both sides urged the Treasury Department to give God a place of greater consciousness in the nation by having Him recognized on U.S. coins. As a result, in 1861 Secretary of the Treasury Salmon Chase sent a letter to the director of the Philadelphia mint instructing him to prepare a motto to be affixed to all U.S. coins:

> Dear Sir:
>
> No nation can be strong except in the strength of God, or safe except in His defense. The trust of our people in God should be declared on our national coins. You will cause a device to be prepared without unnecessary delay with a motto expressing in the fewest and tersest words possible this national recognition.[3]

"In God We Trust" began appearing on coins in 1864 during the height of America's Civil War, and in 1956 an act of Congress made the phrase the nation's official motto.

How did the nation get from "no nation can be strong except in the strength of God" to "ceremonial deism"? I can't answer that question in this chapter except to say that nations don't exist except as a collective of their people—which brings the question down to the individual level. And that's where you and I live. Every time we face an "impossible" question or situation in life, we are faced with whether we are going to believe in "the strength of God" or "ceremonial deism."

Remember—deism as a belief system says God exists but that He takes no active involvement in the affairs of His creation. He wound up the world like a clock and is letting it run on its own, refusing to intervene. When we say we believe in God but refuse to say we *trust* in God, we are participating in *deism*. And when we incorporate that deistic belief into religious rituals, we make it *ceremonial deism*. There is a world of difference between *deism* and *theism*, the latter being the kind of belief exercised by Jehoshaphat.

When Jehoshaphat saw the enemies of his people approaching, did he say, "We don't know what to do and it's all up to us" or did he say, "We don't know what to do, but our eyes are on [God]"? Obviously, as we have seen, he said the latter. Jehoshaphat had a faith in God that incorporated Him intimately into the affairs of his life.

And that doesn't mean Jehoshaphat was passive in his human responsibilities. If you read the whole story in 2 Chronicles 20, you will discover that a prophet of God delivered to Jehoshaphat some specific instructions as to the people's parts in their victory against the enemies. And Jehoshaphat carried out that which was his responsibility: "Listen to me, Judah and people of Jerusalem! Have faith in the LORD your God and you will be upheld; have faith in his prophets and you will be successful" (verse 20).

It would be easy to interpret Jehoshaphat's prayer as being passively irresponsible: "We don't know what to do, but our eyes are on you." In other words, "God, we're not going to do anything. We're going to let You handle our enemies. It's Your name that's at stake since we're Your people, so please do Your thing." Quite the contrary, the king's prayer was intellectually and spiritually responsible. Jehoshaphat knew clearly what was in his power and what wasn't. And he knew that whatever was beyond his power was clearly within God's power.

There was a dear lady in the Crystal Cathedral who wore a rhinestone pin in the shape of the single word, *Believe*. She wore it because it was a great conversation starter—people were not hesitant to ask her, "Believe what?" Once they ask that question, she had an opportunity to convey to them that everybody believes in something, and offer good reasons for why she believed in the God of the Bible through Jesus Christ.

Have you thought about the fact that even atheists believe? They believe there is no God! That is just as strong a belief as the trust of Jehoshaphat in the God of his fathers. We can divide the spectrum of belief into four general categories.

First, some people believe in nothing but science and materialism. They are atheists—they don't believe God exists; that God and religion are "the opiate of the people" as Karl Marx said. Belief in God is just a crutch for people too weak to make it through life on their own. Hard as it is to imagine, there are people who believe this way.

Second, others believe that God exists but that He does not interact with humanity—the deism I described earlier. What is the purpose of believing in a God who wants nothing to do with humanity?

Third, there are those who believe God interacts but only as a judge. God is a cosmic lightning bolt, not a loving and personal Father. This is theism, but with a sour-grape twist.

Finally, there is *Christian* theism, the belief that God exists and wants to be personally involved in the affairs of His creation and the life of those created in His image. He sent His Son, Jesus Christ, into the world to make God's desire and will known and to serve as a bridge between God and man. Though Jehoshaphat lived long before the time of Christ, this is the kind of theism he practiced: trust in a loving, personal God who could be counted on to do the right thing at the right time.

The question for you and me is, what kind of faith do we have? In what kind of God do we believe? That is not an idle question—there are people with all four levels of faith sitting in churches today. Yes, even atheists sometimes attend church purely because of the emotional benefit they derive from participating in a set of religious rituals or beliefs. Atheists often attend churches during religious holidays like Christmas and Easter because of the positive messages associated with those seasonal celebrations.

If the people who fall into the first three of the four categories of belief I just mentioned have faith, it is a faith in faith, not in God. They want to believe in something, so they find or create an object toward which they can direct their belief. But that is not the kind of faith that connects us with God.

Yes, Hebrews 11:6 says, "Without faith it is impossible to please God." But it goes on to say this: "Because anyone who comes to him must believe that he exists and that he rewards those who earnestly seek him." That is the fourth kind of faith I listed above; the kind of faith exercised by Jehoshaphat in Judah 2,850 years ago. And it is the only kind of faith that will provide answers to the impossible questions we face in our lives.

In the first three sections of this book—the first fifteen chapters—I talked about ways people lose their closeness to God. Beginning in this chapter—the second half of this book—we've started to turn the corner and talk more about God Himself and our relationship with Him. Knowing that, you can see why I began the second half of the book with this chapter: your desire, and your ability, to reconnect with God is wholly dependent on how you answer the question: "Who is God?"

If your view of God is so small or unattractive that you have no desire to connect with Him, you likely won't. And if your God is desirable but not powerful, when you do connect with Him, you will likely not call out to Him—because of your assumption that He won't respond.

Based on the last sentence of Jehoshaphat's prayer, how do you think he viewed God? He viewed Him as both personal and powerful, approachable and able, responsive and robust. God has not changed. The New Testament says that God "rewards those who earnestly seek him." God rewarded Jehoshaphat's faith, and He will reward yours. Jehoshaphat expressed his desired outcome to God (deliverance from his enemies), but then put that outcome in God's hands: "Our eyes are upon you." If you will do the same as you earnestly seek Him, God will reward your faith. I can't say how, but I can say that the promise of God's Word is that He will.

Whether you want to connect with God for the first time, or reconnect with Him after an absence, make sure that the God you are seeking is the God who wants to be found by you—the God of the Bible: "You will seek me and find me when you seek me with all your heart" (Jeremiah 29:13).

Questions for Reflection and Discussion

1. There are many times in life when we don't know what to do. Where do you turn for answers when you don't know what the next step is?

2. Everybody believes in something. What are some things people believe in?

3. The words "In God We Trust" are well known to Americans—it's our national motto. Describe the God you trust in. What is the difference between *believing* in God and *trusting* in God?

4. Which of the following four categories best describes the God you believe in?

   a. God does *not* exist; belief in God is a crutch for people too weak to make it through life on their own.
   b. God exists but He doesn't interact with human beings.
   c. God exists and interacts with humans but only as a judge.
   d. God is a loving, personal God who can be counted on to do the right thing at the right time.

   If you answered "d" to the question above, what evidence is in your life that gives credence to what you say you believe?

5. Your desire and ability to connect with God are wholly dependent on how you view God. Describe the God in whom you place your trust. Speak from your heart, not just your head.

17. Turning Wishes into Reality When Dreams Are Dashed

L ISA LOVED HER DAD with a fierce, hero-worship kind of love. Instead of rebelling against her parents when she was a teenager, she actually loved them and got along well with them. She knew her parents loved her and loved each other, and she knew that she was her daddy's girl. She reveled in that security. She feared nothing, knowing her dad would always be there to fix whatever wasn't right.

Lisa's dad was a busy engineer, but he always kept his family as a priority. He arranged his travel and work schedules so as to be there for almost every ball game, birthday party, and school event. And he was loving. He was never shy about showering Lisa's mom with affection, and the kids as well. Even when her parents had disagreements, Lisa knew that they would always be together.

And he was faithful. He had analytical, thoughtful reasons for his faith in Christ. He was a deacon in their church and helped lead a youth program for young boys. And he was in apparent excellent health, in spite of coming from a family where three of his brothers had died in their fifties from various ailments. He was cheerful, never seemed stressed, ate a healthy diet, and was always up for a game of touch football.

But on a routine Thursday morning, Lisa's perfect picture of her father was shattered. He was at his office when he began to experience searing chest pains. He was rushed to a local hospital where the doctors kept him overnight for observation.

The following morning at 5:00 a.m. Lisa's mom got a call from the hospital saying her father had suffered an aortic aneurysm—a small hole in the aorta that was preventing an adequate blood supply from reaching the heart. The aneurysm needed to be repaired immediately, but they needed to transfer Lisa's dad to another hospital for the procedure.

Lisa's mom woke Lisa and her three siblings so they could get ready for school while she went to accompany Lisa's dad to the new hospital. At 6:30, while they gathered as a family to pray, the phone rang again. When Lisa's mom returned from answering the call she said words that Lisa had never imagined hearing: "They tried to move Dad, but it was too late. He died."

Lisa's real-world hero was gone. Twenty-four hours before, her world was peaceful and secure, and that day it fell apart. In the days and weeks ahead, Lisa did what any fifteen-year-old would do, including going through a time of questioning God's love: "Why, God? Why did You allow this to happen? Why did You allow our father to be snatched away in the prime of life? You're supposed to be a good God. Dad was a good man; he was serving You the best he knew how. I still believe in You, but this just doesn't seem fair! Everyone else still has a dad."

Years after those painful days, Lisa would describe how her father's sudden death changed her world: "Yesterday, life had been wonderful. Our family was intact, and I had dreams for a fabulous future, certain to be fulfilled. Now, virtually overnight, life itself became uncertain. I had never felt so vulnerable. The void from Dad's unexpected death seemed impossible to fill."[1]

The best way to sum up how Lisa viewed her life prior to her father's death is to use her own words: "I had dreams for a fabulous future." And she is not alone in that outlook, for we all have dreams for the future. The future might be as short as twenty-four hours from now, or as distant as twenty-four years from now. But all of us have dreams, longings, plans, and expectations.

When we use the word *dreams* instead of the word *plans*, we move into a different mode. We think of plans as less emotional; things on our to-do lists for the day or week or year: get a haircut, pay the bills, go to the ball game Friday night, prepare the Sunday school lesson. But as soon as you put something in the dream category, you're exposing a bit of your vulnerable side. We don't tell our dreams to just anyone, because we don't want to get laughed at: "You want to do what? Are you kidding? Who gets to do that?"

Dreams are emotional. They represent "want to" instead of "have to." They are built with fibers of our own hearts and souls, and so we protect them and reveal them very carefully. And for that very reason, when our dreams come crashing down it is usually a devastating experience. The more secure and possible our dreams feel to us (like Lisa's dreams of her father shepherding her into her future life), the more crushing they are when they crumble.

One of the hardest things to comprehend, digest, and embrace when our dreams disappear is the question of "Why?" We compare the good that might have come out of dreams had they succeeded with the vacuum that exists when they disappear, and we want to know what kind of calculator God used to conclude that "vacuum" is better than "good."

That surely must have been what a young man named Joseph thought when his brothers, out of pure jealousy, sold him into slavery in Egypt from their home in Canaan. Joseph was his father's favorite son, destined for great things (see Genesis 37:1–11). Yet he became a slave, sold to a ruler in Egypt. But even from that lowly position, the hand of God guided Joseph to become the second most powerful man in Egypt. And many years after being betrayed by his own brothers, Joseph was in a position of power that he used to save his family from death by starvation due to a famine in Canaan.

For decades, Joseph probably turned the "Why?" question over in his mind until he finally saw the good that God brought from his misfortunes. When Joseph's brothers discovered that he, whom they had assumed was long since dead, was the one who saved them from starvation, they were mortified and fearful of his revenge. But he told them, "You intended to harm me, but God intended it for good to accomplish what is now being done, the saving of many lives" (Genesis 50:20).

Sarah, the wife of Abraham, no doubt asked the "Why?" question as well. God had given her and her husband the dream of fathering a great nation, but Sarah's womb remained closed for years. She had no son to be an heir of God's promises. Reaching the conclusion that the dream was as dead as her womb, Sarah gave Abraham a son through her own handmaid, Hagar—her carnal attempt to make her dream come true on her schedule. And then, when she was ninety years old, Sarah conceived and bore a son, all in God's time.

Joseph dreamed (literally) of having a place of influence in Jacob's family, saw the dream fail, and then saw it fulfilled. Sarah dreamed of bearing a son to fulfill God's promise of a great nation, saw the dream die, and then saw it be fulfilled.

The hard part of crushed dreams for the child of God is this: What role does God play in the postponing, or canceling, of our dreams? Does He *cause* them to disappear or *allow* them to disappear? Does He *create* the broken pieces or *pick up* the broken pieces—or both? Those are the kinds of hypothetical questions that the apostle Paul gently told his readers in Rome were the wrong questions (see Romans 9:19–21). We must let God be God as to cause and effect. What we do know is that God is more than able to craft dreams that are bigger and better (see Romans 8:28), just as He did for Joseph and Sarah. If God ever takes away (or allows to be taken away) something in our lives, it is only because there is something different (and better—God never moves us from good to not-good) that He is preparing for us.

That is not a cop-out or an attempt to minimize the pain we feel when our dreams come tumbling down. It is simply an acknowledgment that we have to bow before the sovereign will of a God who has demonstrated His love for us: "He who did not spare his own Son, but gave him up for us all—how will he not also, along with [the Son], graciously give us all things?" (Romans 8:32).

Lisa certainly wondered why God allowed the most important person in her life to be taken from her at a time when she needed him most. Little did she know that there were yet more dreams of hers that would crumble. And little did she know that surviving the loss of her father with her faith in God intact was a classroom in which she was prepared for an even greater loss in the years to come.

"Lisa" is Lisa Beamer, wife of Todd Beamer, one of the heroes of Flight 93 who died in the wake of the September 11, 2001, terrorist attacks. He and fellow passengers were trying to wrestle control of their airplane from terrorist hijackers when it crashed, killing all aboard. But their efforts foiled the terrorists' plan of crashing the plane into the White House or the Capitol Building in Washington, D.C.

Lisa's marriage and life with Todd, and the birth of their two sons, had become a replacement dream-life for her. They were like-minded in their faith, their love for each other, and their dreams for their future. It's obvious from these words of Lisa's that the dream that vanished with the death of her father had been replaced by new dreams of happiness with Todd. Look at these excerpts from her book:

> We began our life together with all the hopes, *dreams*, and aspirations typical of most college-educated couples in the mid-1990's. As two goal-oriented, type A people, Todd and I planned every little detail of our lives, including our career courses and our personal lives. We left very little to chance or accident.... Like most young couples just starting out in life, we naively thought we could control our own destiny.[2]

> When [our son] Drew was born, we were in the midst of searching out and buying property, and preparing to build our "*dream* home."[3]

> Todd and I had a lot of other *dreams* we were excited about seeing fulfilled. For instance, we planned to go on a cruise to Alaska for our 10th wedding anniversary in 2004.[4]

> We began building our *dream* house in 2000—well, at least it was a *dream* house to us![5]

You and I could identify with some of her dreams, plus add our own list of similar hopes for the future. It's not likely that many of our dreams will be crushed in as dramatic a fashion as were hers, but some will die. The death of a vision is part of life this side of heaven, and we need to be prepared for it.

(Read this next paragraph carefully—I don't want to be misunderstood.) God is always at work—even in the midst of unfulfilled dreams. Think of the millions of people who have been impacted by Lisa Beamer's story through her book, the movie that was made about Flight 93, and her introduction to the nation by President Bush during the 2002 State of the Union message. Millions—literally—of people have learned that it is possible to live through the devastating collapse of life's most cherished dreams. Would we have preferred that Lisa Beamer not lose her father and her husband? Of course! We would never wish for such heartache in order to achieve a possible, positive result! But the fact is, dreams do get dashed on the rocks of reality in our lives. And when that happens, God is able to pick up the pieces and construct a message of victory and hope.

Some people (not Lisa Beamer) have concluded that it is better not to dream than to dream and suffer disappointment. We could lock ourselves in our houses with the shades drawn and never venture out into the world. But that kind of fortress mentality leads to the atrophy of the imagination. Imagination, from which spring our dreams for the future, is second only to faith in its power to keep alive the human spirit.

Think about it: you have had dreams and desires that no one else in this history of humanity has had. Others have had similar dreams, but no one is like you—no one has a mind's eye like yours. If you have dreams that would be good for you and for those you love, would they not also directly or indirectly benefit others? Of course they would—and that is why you and I should never stop dreaming.

To be honest, you cannot "not dream." The creative impulses God has built into the warp and woof of humanity are unstoppable. Yes, you can quench the sparks, but you cannot keep the flint of your mind from striking the steel of your soul and producing a daily shower of sparks. You need only to nurture and pursue the ones that seem to burn brightest—*with the understanding that no dreams are guaranteed.*

I have referenced this passage once before in this book, but here I'll reproduce it in full because of its relevance to dreaming:

> Listen, you who say, "Today or tomorrow we will go to this or that city, spend a year there, carry on business and make money." Why, you do not even know what will happen tomorrow. What is your life? You are a mist that appears for a little while and then vanishes. Instead, you ought to say, "If it is the Lord's will, we will live and do this or that."
>
> (James 4:13–15)

Notice there is no admonition against dreaming and planning. There is only the admonition to submit all our dreams to God—to ask not only for His help and blessing, but for His grace to endure their dissolution if that is the result.

One of the things I so love about the apostle Paul is that he was a dreamer. There was always more he wanted to do for Jesus Christ. The biggest dream he had (that we know about from his letters) was to take the gospel message to the farthest extent of the Roman Empire—to Spain: "It has always been my [dream] to preach the gospel where Christ was not known, so that I would not be building on someone else's foundation....I plan to [stop in Rome and visit you] when I go to Spain" (Romans 15:20, 24).

Paul had a dream and a plan, but as far as we know he never made it to Spain; he was martyred in Rome. Perhaps he made it and it didn't get recorded. Regardless, Paul didn't limit his dreams by the likelihood of their fulfillment. We know that he dreamed of every one of his Jewish kinsmen becoming followers of Jesus, but that didn't happen (see Romans 9:1–5). He even dreamed about being alive when Jesus returned to earth, and that didn't happen either (see 1 Thessalonians 4:17). Paul just dreamed and left the results to God. And that is exactly what we should do as well.

If you have become disappointed with God and limited your relationship with Him because of a dream that came crashing down in your life, you need not hold that against Him. We are guaranteed only one thing by being God's children: that we will be made into the image of His Son (see Romans 8:29). That is God's dream for you, and it will be fulfilled. If you and I have to suffer the pains of disappointed dreams along the way, so be it.

Even if our temporal dreams don't all come true, our eternal dream will. And that is the best reason we have for staying closely connected to God.

Questions for Reflection and Discussion

1. All of us have dreams, longings, plans, and expectations for the future. What are some of your dreams—past or present? Make a short list. Briefly describe what you hoped and believed would happen and whether or not that dream came to be.

2. Joseph in the Old Testament was called a "dreamer" by his brothers. They ridiculed and resented him for his dreams. And eventually they figured out a way to rid their lives of this annoying dreamer. Have you ever had a similar experience?

3. Have you ever had a dream die only for God to bring that dream to life later on in a bigger and better way than you had originally dreamed? Share your experience.

4. God is always at work—even in the midst of unfulfilled dreams. Where have you seen this in your life? What important lessons about life or yourself have you learned as the result of your unfulfilled dreams?

5. It's easy to believe when our dreams are dashed that it's better not to dream than to dream and suffer disappointment. But you cannot "not dream." God made you to dream. What dreams has God put in you that need to be nurtured and pursued even though there is no guarantee that your dreams will become realities?

18. Living Vigilantly to Keep from Drifting Off Course

JOHN SILVERWOOD HAD BEEN A success in business, but not so much when it came to his personal and family life. He and his wife, Jean, had endured their share of marital struggles; John's bouts with alcohol abuse played no small role in their ups and downs. From their home in San Diego, California, the couple, both experienced sailors, decided to take their four children on a two-year sailing trip around the world as a way to rebuild the unity and harmony their family was lacking.

Predictably, the children, ages five to sixteen, didn't want to leave their comfortable lifestyles and their friends to go sailing around the world. But in due course, the plan began to work. Sailing toward Fiji in the South Pacific, nearly two years after leaving New York's Long Island Sound, Jean reflected on the changes that had occurred:

> We had done what we set out to do two years earlier when we first set sail. Along the way, our children's eyes had opened to the beauty of the world. The kids were very strong characters now, very different from when we began. We loved them in new ways—maybe deeper ways, because we had taken the time to finally get to know them.... Everybody was finally happy to be together—it had taken a few thousand miles, but the family now seemed in sync. I don't mean that it was perfect, but we had learned to live together in a tight space without too much drama.

Whatever tests the Silverwood family had faced prior to their trip, they were nothing compared to what life threw at them that night.

The fifty-five-foot catamaran was sailing on autopilot, and the family was preparing to bed down for the night. Fourteen-year-old Amelia turned over the watch to her sixteen-year-old brother, Ben, and all seemed right with the world as they sailed along more than a mile above the floor of the Pacific. Or so they thought.

The quiet night was suddenly filled with the shrieking sound of the catamaran's twin hulls ripping open on a submerged coral reef—and seconds later the boat slammed to a dead stop on top of the reef. John and Jean looked at each other in horrible disbelief. They were supposed to be sailing in open water across the surface of the Pacific, not sitting on top of a coral reef in a demolished sailboat.

They sprang into action to assess their situation as the boat's cabin areas began filling with water. Luckily, they were atop a coral reef, so they weren't going to sink. But they and the boat were being pounded mercilessly by incoming waves. Putting both the boat's twin engines in full reverse in an attempt to pull the boat off the reef was futile. John had the presence of mind, before the boat lost its electrical power, to broadcast a "Mayday" signal, along with their coordinates from the boat's GPS unit.

After John returned to the deck, the boat's 80-foot-tall, 2,500-pound main mast came crashing down, pinning his left leg and nearly severing it completely. It would be a couple of hours, fighting against the waves, before Jean and Ben were able to free John from the mast's weight and move him into the life raft, a tourniquet on his leg.

The Silverwoods spent the rest of the night huddled together on a coral reef in the South Pacific, far off course, far from home, and far from their destination. In the pale light of the following dawn, Ben popped a flare and waved the tube over his head, attracting the attention of the French navy jet that was searching for them.[1]

I've borrowed from the Silverwoods' gripping tale of survival to make a point for this chapter: without constant vigilance, it's easy to drift off course in life and find ourselves on the edge of disaster. As one who spends as much of his recreational free time as possible on the swells of the Pacific Ocean, I don't fault this family for what happened to them. Even with the best of navigational aids, it's possible to get disoriented in the open sea. But however it happened—poor maps or charts, poor settings in the autopilot's computer, "operator error"—the Silverwoods drifted off course.

What happened to them on the ocean can happen to us in life: without a dead-on accurate way of staying on course, we can drift into mortal and spiritual danger. Without a spiritual anchor or navigational system, we can sail on, blithely unaware that we are on a crash course.

In light of what happened to the Silverwoods, think about the dynamics that are at work when we begin to drift off course:

- We have no reason to think we're off course based on what's happening around us.

- Being off course can appear just as peaceful as being on course.

- Danger, even destruction, can be lurking just inches beneath the surface.

- We are shocked when our off-course direction ends in a crash.

- Remaining on course requires constant vigilance.

- Possessing trustworthy navigational aids, and applying them faithfully, is mandatory to remaining on course.

- The farther we move away from familiar ground, the easier it is to drift off course.

Whether we think of the importance of an anchor that keeps us from drifting, or navigational aids that keep us on course, the lesson is the same: it is possible to drift off course spiritually and find ourselves fighting for survival.

David Wilkerson is the renowned evangelist who took the gospel message into the gritty streets of New York City beginning in 1958. He met a Broadway theater executive with whom he was negotiating to purchase a theater to use as a church. But the man was very standoffish toward Wilkerson—rude, actually. He acted as if he didn't want to be in the same room with him or be seen in public with him. But Wilkerson began to pray for him and ask God to soften the man's heart. I'll let David Wilkerson relate what he discovered:

> One day, as we sat in a restaurant, he began to open his heart to me. And when he did, I was shocked to find out this Broadway

executive had had a powerful experience with Christ when a he was a teenager! The Spirit had come upon him powerfully, and he had broken down, weeping. He had heard the Lord say, "Give Me your life!"—and he received a call to preach the gospel.

After that, he had a caring heart for people and a true love for Jesus. But later, in his early twenties, he began to drift. He didn't turn his back on Jesus; he simply neglected Him. He quit going to church, reading his Bible and talking to the Lord.

He buried himself in work and ended up on Broadway, involved with theater celebrities. Eventually he began to distance himself from his experience with Christ—and he began to drink heavily. His respect for the things of the Lord had lingered; but as he drifted farther away, it became easier for him to curse God and mock other believers.

When I came on the scene years later, invading his world, it brought up all the old memories: of church, God's Word, Jesus, his calling. I was a reminder of what his life should have been—and he resented it!

The last time I saw this man, he had lost his prestigious position—and he was staggering past our church, drunk. I had been a reminder to him and a rebuke—and now, in his need, he couldn't face it.[2]

The great danger in not correcting a drifting course is this: what is a one-inch distance today will be a mile in a matter of days. Anyone who has ever navigated by compass on land or sea knows this all too well. An error of a half-degree at the start of a journey can result in a miles-wide difference between where you are and where you thought you would be. A tiny error, uncorrected over time, *will*—not *may*—result in a huge error in the end.

We have to ask ourselves a serious question about spiritual drifting. Why would the Bible warn us about it if it was not a danger? We have to remember that the Bible was written, for the most part, to people who claimed to be, wanted to be, were trying to be, close to God. It's people who *think they're on the right course* who are repeatedly warned about drifting off course:

- Israel in the Old Testament: "Be careful, and watch yourselves closely so that you do not forget the things your eyes have seen or let them slip from your heart as long as you live" (Deuteronomy 4:9). "My son, preserve sound judgment and discernment, do not let them out of your sight" (Proverbs 3:21).

- To Christians in the New Testament: "We must pay more careful attention, therefore, to what we have heard, so that we do not drift away" (Hebrews 2:1). "If you think you are standing firm, be careful that you don't fall!" (1 Corinthians 10:12).

Drifting, by definition, is a slow process. Sometimes, especially in the spiritual life, it happens so slowly that we don't realize we are no longer where we once were. Consider an auto trip you've taken enough times to get familiar with a number of landmarks. Then one day, you set out to make the trip and discover you're not seeing the familiar landmarks of old. You suddenly realize you must have taken a wrong turn somewhere, and you pull out the map to get your bearings.

So what are the landmarks we should look for that will let us know whether we are drifting off course spiritually? (Note: When I say "you're drifting" in the following paragraphs, my intent is not to be condemning. I'm making the assumption that spiritual direction and health in the New Testament know no neutral ground. We're either on course, following Jesus, or we're drifting off course.)

- *Church attendance.* This is usually one of the first to disappear. If you used to be faithful in church attendance and participation but now you aren't, you're drifting. It has become fashionable today for Christians to say, "I still love Jesus, I just don't like church." The New Testament says that the corporate followers of Jesus are the body of Christ (see 1 Corinthians 12:27) and that participation in worship and fellowship with other followers of Jesus is a sign of spiritual health (see Hebrews 10:24–25).

- *Spiritual disciplines like Bible study.* If you used to make time for regular Bible study but today you don't, you're drifting. The Christian life is a moving-forward experience. And like any journey that involves forward movement, we have to have a map. That is the purpose of the Word of God—to be a "lamp to my feet and a light for my path" (Psalm 119:105). Not to consult that map on a consistent basis is to invite the possibility of drifting off course.

- *And prayer.* In her book *A Slow and Certain Light,* author Elisabeth Elliot tells about a couple of adventurers who asked if she could give them a few phrases with which to communicate with Indians in the South American jungle where she lived. She compared their efforts to how we live the Christian life: "What we really ought to have is the Guide himself. Maps, road signs, a few useful phrases are good things, but infinitely better is Someone who has been there before and knows the way."[3] And that's what prayer is—the opportunity to talk daily, at any moment, with One who has been where you are:

  > We do not have a high priest who is unable to sympathize with our weaknesses, but we have one who has been tempted in every way, just as we are—yet was without sin. Let us then approach the throne of grace [in prayer] with confidence, so that we may receive mercy and find grace to help us in our time of need.
  > (Hebrews 4:15–16)

- *Associations.* With whom do you spend most of your time these days? Don't get me wrong—all Christians should have non-Christian friends to whom they are bearing witness of the life and love of Christ through word and deed. But here I'm talking more about preference and fellowship. Do you find that you have more in common with those who don't belong to Jesus than those who do? If the Holy Spirit is alive in you, then you will (super)naturally be drawn to others in whom that same Spirit dwells. If you are a Christian who enjoys the spirit of non-Christians more than the Spirit of Christians, you are drifting. The word *fellowship* comes from the Greek word known to many, *koinonia,* which means oneness or commonality. Over time, we will gravitate in life to those with whom we have the most in common.

There are other landmarks in the spiritual journey, but these four are certainly important and foundational ones. If you don't pass by them consistently, you know you're off the good path and in danger of drifting even farther off course.

If you are a gardener, you will appreciate the metaphor the apostle Paul uses in Colossians 2:6–7: "Just as you received Christ Jesus as Lord, continue to live in him, rooted and built up in him, strengthened in the faith as you were taught, and overflowing with thankfulness." It's impossible to drift away from Jesus if we are "rooted and built up in him."

It doesn't take long for a tiny oak seedling, sprouted from an acorn, to bury its taproot so deep in the soil that it can't be pulled out of the ground. That seedling, as it grows into a sapling, will *never* drift off course. Why? Because it is rooted so deeply in the medium in which it was intended to grow—an infinite supply of soil—and it will never run out of room for its roots. Just so, the follower of Jesus is to be rooted in the infinite life of Jesus.

In contrast, my friends in the South tell me that the southern white pine is the scourge of neighborhoods in the winter due to its shallow root system. When snow and ice storms hit, the tall, thin trees bow down under the weight and fall on power lines and across roads. And these are trees that have been growing for twenty and thirty years. They simply do not have a root system adequate to keep them anchored.

If the ship of your soul is going to remain safely at rest, the roots of your faith must be anchored deeply in Jesus.

If you have lost your closeness to God because you have drifted off course, I have good news for you. The way back is not hard to find. In fact, Jesus said that He was "the way" (John 14:6). All that's required for you to get back on course is to make your way to Him. Tell Him you have drifted. Tell Him you haven't nourished the roots that were once sunk deeply in Him. That conversation itself is a prayer—one of the landmarks of your spiritual journey. Pick up your Bible and begin to read. Make your way to church or to a Bible study you once attended.

The most important thing to remember about reconnecting with God after drifting off course is that they both happen the same way: one step at a time. If you begin to take those steps today, you will find that what was once familiar to you will become familiar again. Because you know where you are going, the uncertainty you felt while drifting away will be filled with the joy of sweet reunion.

Questions for Reflection and Discussion

1. What things cause us to drift off course spiritually? Have you ever done so? When did you first begin to drift, and where did you eventually end up?

2. What is it about thinking we're on the right course that may actually cause us to drift off course? When have you seen this happen?

3. What does it look like to live vigilantly in your spiritual life?

4. What are the landmarks you should look for that will let you know whether you are drifting off course spiritually? I list four in this chapter. Do a quick inventory of your life. Where do you stand in regard to each of these landmarks right now?

5. If you've drifted off course spiritually, what are one or two steps you can take this week, or even today, to get back on course?

19. Putting Up Sails, Praying for Wind

TOM PERKINS DID NOT REALLY need to make his mark when he set out to build the world's largest privately owned sailing ship. He was already one of the best-known venture capitalists in California's Silicon Valley. As a cofounder of the firm Kleiner Perkins Caufield & Byers, he had made early investments in more than three hundred information technology and biotech firms, including Amazon.com, AOL, Compaq, Genentech, Google, Netscape, and Sun Microsystems—and earned many hundreds of millions of dollars in the process.

Besides being a savvy investor and businessman, Tom Perkins was a hands-on engineer. His electrical engineering degree from MIT and his MBA from Harvard proved a valuable combination as he made his way into the world of high-tech businesses. Along the way, sailing was his passion. He owned, sailed, and raced sailing ships in oceans all over the world. And when he discovered that a Turkish boatbuilder's customer had pulled out of a deal to build the largest sailboat in the world—and the builder was left with the boat's hull, but no buyer—it was just the kind of challenge he wanted.

The ship, christened *Maltese Falcon*, indeed turned out to be gigantic. It was 289 feet long, nearly the length of a football field, had 11,000 square feet of interior living space (multiple times more than most homes), and weighed 1,900 tons. It cost nearly six years to build and was finished in 2006 at a cost of $100 million.

But more than its size, the *Maltese Falcon* had something that no other sailboat in the world had: three carbon-fiber masts from which 15 huge sails, totaling 26,000 square feet, would be automatically unfurled by 75 electric motors. The boat would be able to sail the seas with a crew a fraction of the usual size because the furling and unfurling of the sails would be handled by computer-controlled electric motors. Indeed, as far as the sails themselves, Perkins's design required only one person to push a button.

Here's how Tom Perkins described the experience on the boat's maiden voyage:

> The wind was a mild six knots as we motored away from the coast of Tuzla, Turkey, into the sea of Marmara. I pushed the control screen and, as I had designed, fifteen sails emerged from their housings in the masts and were automatically spread upon eighteen yards high above the deck. In a short space of time, a world record of sail area, some twenty-six thousand square feet, had been set automatically in just under seven minutes. For the first time in history, the vast sails of a square-rigger had been deployed quickly and with no intervention from a single crew member.[1]

I've cited the story of Tom Perkins's amazing sailboat for two reasons: one, it has nothing to do with how we connect with God; and two, it has everything to do with how we connect with God. Confused? Here's the simple explanation: if we don't unfurl the sails in our lives, we will never catch the wind of God's Spirit, which is how we must be moved through this life. But unfurling the sails is not as easy in our lives as it is on Tom Perkins's sailboat. It does not happen via the push of a button.

To explain further, I believe that sails are a wonderful metaphor for the life of prayer that every follower of Jesus is exhorted to embrace. When we enter into prayer with God, we make ourselves available for the powerful wind of His Spirit to fill us and move us forward. I picture the results of prayer as similar to the way God enabled men to record His revelations: "Prophecy never had its origin in the will of man, but men spoke from God as they were carried along by the Holy Spirit" (2 Peter 1:21). Men put up the sails of prayer and faith, and God filled them with His Spirit.

But prayer is not a push-button exercise. It would be nice if it were, but the exact opposite is true. Prayer is a function of time, determination, discipline—and most of all, perseverance. Every large sailboat is also equipped with engines for times when the sea is becalmed—when there is no wind blowing. And there are times in the spiritual life like that, when we unfurl our sails of prayer but there is no Wind filling them. In times like that, perseverance is required. We must continue in prayer until God sends His Spirit to fill our sails.

Jesus described the unpredictable nature of the movement of God's Spirit in His late-night conversation with the Jewish leader Nicodemus: "The wind blows wherever it pleases. You hear its sound, but you cannot tell where it comes from or where it is going. So it is with everyone born of the Spirit" (John 3:8). In other words, the working of the Spirit is as much a mystery as the working of the wind (both words being translations of the same Greek word, *pneuma*). Just as we cannot always predict how the wind will blow, so we cannot always predict how the Spirit will move in our lives. Thus we have to live with our sails of prayer unfurled. We have to stay in a continual attitude of prayer and communication with God so as to be in a place to flow and go with Him when He begins to move us in a given direction.

When we live in the spirit of 1 Thessalonians 5:16–18—"Be joyful always; pray continually; give thanks in all circumstances"—we won't allow ourselves to develop attitudes of negativity and resentment toward what God is or isn't doing in our lives. The simplest way I know to express what it means to "pray continually" is to pray the way Jesus taught the disciples—"Your kingdom come, your will be done on earth as it is in heaven" (Matthew 6:10)—and the way He himself prayed as He waited on the will of God to be revealed for His life—"Nevertheless not My will, but Yours, be done" (Luke 22:42 NKJV).

When we are daily bowing before God the Father and committing ourselves to His timing, His direction, His will, His purpose, His plans—and giving thanks ahead of time—then we will be ready when the wind of His Spirit begins to blow. And by the way, this is not an optional lifestyle for the Christian. Paul's last phrase in 1 Thessalonians 5:16–18 is, "For this is God's will for you in Christ Jesus." It is God's will for us that we rejoice always, pray continually, and live thankful lives.

Prayer is the means for keeping our sails unfurled, keeping ourselves in a place of spiritual readiness, keeping ourselves patient and persevering when life becomes as still as a glass-topped sea, keeping ourselves from thinking that God has left us, never to return and move us where we want or need to go.

Living near the Pacific coastline of Southern California, I've experienced very few times when I've left my home or office and didn't feel a strong wind blowing. If it's not the red-hot Santa Ana winds howling down from the desert hills, it's the continual, prevailing winds blowing in from the ocean. You shouldn't live in Southern California if you don't like the air moving.

But it's not always like that in the spiritual life. There are times when it appears God has left us stalled where we are. And it doesn't happen just to you. One of the most amazing stories in the Bible tells how Daniel, one of the godliest men in Israel's history, prayed for three weeks without an answer from God. And he didn't just pray: "At that time I, Daniel, mourned for three weeks. I ate no choice food; no meat or wine touched my lips; and I used no lotions at all until the three weeks were over" (Daniel 10:2–3). He fasted and humbled himself before God for three weeks, waiting for an answer.

And the answer finally came. The delay was due to some heavenly activity that prevented the angel Michael from reaching him with God's answer. There had been activity in heaven all along concerning the answer to his prayer; it's just that Daniel couldn't see it.

But what if Daniel had taken down his sails on the twentieth day? What if he had given up on prayer a day or a week before the answer came? Annie Dillard, in *The Annie Dillard Reader*, tells how things in heaven can sometimes look completely motionless on earth:

> The Ring Nebula, in the constellation Lyra, looks, through
> binoculars, like a smoke ring. It is a star in the process of exploding.
> Light from its explosion first reached the earth in 1054; it was a
> supernova then, and so bright it shone in the daytime. Now it is not
> so bright, but it is still exploding. It expands at the rate of seventy
> million miles a day. It is interesting to look through binoculars
> at something expanding seventy million miles a day. It does not
> budge. Its apparent size does not increase. Photographs of the Ring
> Nebula taken 15 years ago seem identical to photographs of it taken
> yesterday.[2]

Standing in the vicinity of the Ring Nebula, with dust and gases shrieking by at 2.9 million miles per hour, one would definitely get the impression of motion and activity. But looking at the same scene from planet

Earth, it looks like the same snapshot from week to week—no evidence of motion at all. It's just a matter of perspective. That's why it pays to keep our prayer-sails unfurled at all times. Regardless of how things look when we are on our knees, prayer produces activity in heaven.

A friend related to me a drama he saw performed in a church in Dallas. The pastor was going to preach a message on prayer, and he wanted the congregation to leave being totally impressed with God's ability to hear the prayers of people all over the world at the same time—sometimes people in the same place asking for conflicting things: clear weather for a family reunion and much-needed rain for dry crops. How does God handle it?

The stage was set with tables containing a couple dozen telephones, ostensibly in the office of Saint Peter in heaven, who was responsible for fielding prayer requests as they were "phoned in" from earth. Peter's job was to record the prayer requests and pass them on to God. Phones began to ring slowly and Peter answered them politely, recording each request and thanking the "callers" for their prayer request. But then the pace quickened, and before long Peter looked like a stockbroker in the middle of a market crash—multiple phones cradled on each ear, shouting replies, dropping phones, yelling for someone to "answer that phone," and on and on. At one point, Peter picked up a ringing phone and shouted, *"Hello!"* A second later he was on his feet, standing at attention, saying, "Yes, Lord... no, Lord...right away, Lord.... I'll be more patient, yes, Lord."

For those who were there, it was a hilarious illustration of how humanly impossible it would be for us to be in the place of answering the prayers of humanity. And by contrast, how great our God is—One who can hear and respond to the prayers of all His children.

Sometimes we are reminded of how the prophet Elijah taunted the priests of the idol Baal on top of Mount Carmel when the priests' prayers went unanswered: "'Shout louder!' [Elijah] said. 'Surely [Baal] is a god! Perhaps he is deep in thought, or busy, or traveling. Maybe he is sleeping and must be awakened'" (1 Kings 18:27). Sometimes we wonder if God has been momentarily distracted or is too busy to hear our prayers.

That's what happens when (as I have mentioned previously in this book) we create God in our image. We get tired, we get distracted, we take naps—but God doesn't. We are invited to bring our needs before God's throne at any time, that "we may obtain mercy and find grace to help in time of need" (Hebrews 4:16 NKJV).

I said at the beginning of this chapter that living in an attitude of prayer requires perseverance. Otherwise, if God chooses not to answer our prayers immediately, we'll be tempted to strike the sails and get out of the posture of prayer, believing God is not going to come through.

Do you remember the story Jesus told about the man who had an unexpected visitor arrive in the middle of the night? The man had no food to serve his guest, so he woke up his neighbor and asked for three loaves of bread. The neighbor complained that it was late and his family was sound asleep—he wasn't about to get up and give the man the bread. But the man wouldn't take no for an answer, and Jesus said, "I tell you, though [the neighbor] will not get up and give him the bread because he is his friend, yet because of the man's boldness he will get up and give him as much as he needs" (Luke 11:8).

I like the way *The Amplified Bible* translation renders Jesus' words immediately after telling this parable: "So I say to you, Ask *and keep on asking* and it shall be given you; seek *and keep on seeking* and you shall find; knock *and keep on knocking* and the door shall be opened to you" (verse 9, italics added). The words I put in italics reflect the meaning of the original Greek language and present the idea of perseverance. When we pray and don't immediately get an answer, we are to *keep on asking, seeking, and knocking* until we do. That is, keep the sails of prayer unfurled so you will be prepared to catch the wind of God's Spirit when He comes.

If somewhere along the way you asked God for something and didn't receive an answer, and you shut off your communication with God because of it—you need to unfurl your sails again. But it will take more than the push of a computerized button. You will need to make time to pray, be faithful to pray, pray believing, and pray with perseverance. But if you will remain in that place of prayer with sails at the ready, God will come. Let Him decide the when and where and how. If you're always ready, that won't matter. Prayer is what can keep you connected to God.

Questions for Reflection and Discussion

1. If you were to compare your prayer life to the sails of a ship, what would you say is the position or condition of your sails right now?

2. We never know how the Spirit will move in our lives, so we need

to stay in a continual attitude of prayer. How would you describe a "continual attitude of prayer"? How easy or difficult is it for you to do this?

3. Have you ever felt as if God has momentarily gotten distracted or is too busy to hear your prayers? What do you do when you feel as if you're caught in the doldrums of prayer?

4. The working of the Spirit is as much a mystery as the working of the wind. Describe a time when you experienced the powerful wind of the Spirit during a time of prayer.

5. Based on what you read in this chapter, what is one important idea about prayer you would like to incorporate into your life?

20. The Grand Irony: When Holding On Is Letting Go

THE CAMPSITE THE MILLS FAMILY selected for their weekend outing was chosen for one primary reason: it was situated near the top of a mountain with an unobstructed view facing east. Just a short hike from their campsite was a cliff high above the valley floor—a perfect place for Tom and Sarah to sit with their two kids, Tommy and Megan, and watch the sunrise chase the darkness out of the valley, burn off the morning fog, and paint the cliff walls with the light of day.

After setting up camp on Friday night and cleaning the sticky residue of roasted marshmallows off their fingers, the family turned in early. Forty-five minutes before dawn the alarm on Tom's digital watch began beeping loudly enough to wake him, and fifteen minutes later the family was on the trail leading to the cliff.

The cloud cover, coupled with the thick canopy of trees, made for a dark walk. And it wasn't much brighter when they left the tree line and found themselves on a narrow path along the edge of the cliff. Tommy, six, and Megan, eight, had each held tightly to a parent's hand as they walked silently through the woods, and tightened their grips as they neared the cliff's edge.

But not tight enough. One of the rubber toe-bumpers on Tommy's hiking boots caught a protruding root in the darkness, and Tommy stumbled forward—and over the edge of the cliff. It happened so fast that Tom, whose hand Tommy had been holding, didn't have time to react. One minute

Tommy was holding his hand; the next second his hand was empty and Tommy was gone.

In an instant, Tom overcame his immediate shock and dropped to his stomach and peered over the edge of the cliff, shouting his son's name. Relief flooded him at what he saw. The cliff was not a sheer drop-off but a gradual one, with outcroppings here and there and scrub vegetation rooted in the face. And there, just five feet below him, he saw Tommy's terrified face in the beam of his flashlight: "*Dad!*" Tommy screamed. "Help me!"

Miraculously, Tommy's feet had landed on a small shelf, and his right hand had found the trunk of a shrub growing out of the cliff wall. He was stable—for the moment—but scared to death. His left hand alternated between reaching up toward his dad and clawing for a handhold on the face of the cliff.

"Tommy, you're okay. I need you to calm down and listen to what I'm saying. I can reach my hand down and pull you up. Mom will hold the flashlight so you can see my hand. Can you reach your hand up toward mine?"

Tommy stretched his hand out toward his father's hand and the gap between them closed as Tom edged farther over the cliff, the toes of his own boots dug into the rocky soil. But when Tom's hand got near Tommy's, the boy's survival instinct took over as he tried to grab hold of his father's hand. Tom couldn't grab Tommy's hand because of the boy's frantic efforts to try to secure a grip on his dad's extended hand.

Tom pulled his hand back. "Tommy, listen to me. I don't want you to try to hold my hand. All I want you to do is stick your arm straight up toward me so I can put my hand around your wrist and pull you up. You need to let me do the work, okay? This will only work if you let go of me and let me hold on to you. Can you do that for me, buddy?"

While this story is fictitious, raising four children and spending lots of time hiking in the mountains makes it real enough. Indeed, I've read other first-person accounts of similar types of rescues and know personally how "unhelpful" a child can be when a parent is trying to help him or her.

It's natural, even as adults, for our survival instinct to kick in when we are in trouble. But our survival instinct can sometimes make the situation worse. Lifeguards are trained to keep their distance when they approach someone in danger of drowning because the person's frantic grabbing and clutching can endanger the lifeguard and imperil them both. Somehow, lifeguards have to communicate, in so many words, "You can't save yourself. If you want to survive, you're going to have to let me save you. Your best efforts are only going to make things worse."

There's an irony in that truth. When we are drowning in our own circumstances, we are sure that we have to save ourselves. But more often than not, we have to learn that the best way to hold on is to let go and let God's hand take ours. It's the same dynamic that all parents experience when they instinctively say to their children, "Don't worry, I've got you!" The child has to learn that the parent's grip is stronger, the parent's embrace is more secure, the parent's strength is more dependable.

When a parent and child are walking down a street together hand in hand, their grip is relaxed. But when they are making their way together through a crowd in a shopping mall, the parent's grip takes over completely. It is the parent's strength that keeps the two connected, not the child's.

In 1993 I wrote a bestselling book on the twelve steps entitled *Dump Your Hangups Without Dumping Them on Others*. While the twelve-step, or "recovery," idea was first associated with the Alcoholics Anonymous program, it has been successfully applied to a number of different areas of life. It doesn't matter what one is recovering from—alcoholism or drug dependency, overeating, emotional or physical abuse—people feel weak when they begin the recovery program. They've tried everything in their power to break the destructive cycle they have been in and are often physically, emotionally, and spiritually exhausted.

And that's good—because the first step in recovery, as expressed in the first of the original Twelve Steps of Alcoholics Anonymous, is to admit that one is powerless to correct one's situation by oneself. That's hard to admit for anyone. It's the human way, or at least the American way, to pull ourselves up by our bootstraps and solve our own problems.

And we bring that same mentality into our relationship with God. We believe contradictory things: God can help us, but it's up to us to help God. Somehow we think it's up to us to hold on to God's hand when He stretches it toward us; that if we aren't strong enough and our grip on Him loosens, then it's down into the valley we go. But the truth is, it is God who holds on to us, not we who hold on to Him. No verse in the Bible puts this more clearly than Ephesians 2:8: "By grace you have been saved through faith, *and that not of yourselves*; it is the gift of God" (NKJV, italics added). Not even our faith is "of ourselves." Faith—the ability to look to God for help and to trust in Him—is a gift from God.

When people come into recovery (or when you find yourself disconnected from God), they may be able to do nothing more than whisper, in a barely audible voice, "God, please hold on to me. Please don't let me go." As I read the Bible, that's about all it takes to get God's attention, for Him to extend His arm over the face of the cliff and wrap His hand around our weak wrists and pull us to safety.

You may recall the father whose child Jesus saved from a terrible affliction. When Jesus said, "Everything is possible for him who believes," the father exclaimed, "I do believe; help me overcome my unbelief!" (Mark 9:23–24). He recognized the chasm between the faith he had and the faith he needed and wanted—and he cried out for more. Yet even the little bit he had was enough. Jesus stepped up and delivered the man's son from the afflictions that had nearly taken the child's life.

In the final analysis, the world is divided into those who believe and those who don't. And if you have only enough faith to lift up your hand so God can grab it and pull you to safety, then that's enough.

This idea of letting go in order that you can be held on to by God is an ancient one. In fact, the rescue that most characterizes God's relationship with Israel—the Israelites' rescue from slavery in Egypt—is characterized by their weakness and God's strength. And it can also be seen as the fulfillment of a promise God made to Abraham about his future descendants: "Know for certain that your descendants will be strangers in a country not their own, and they will be enslaved and mistreated for four hundred years. But I will punish the nation they serve as slaves, and afterward they will come out with great possessions" (Genesis 15:13–14).

Those who belong to God need to remember that it is His reputation at stake when it comes to our safety and salvation. When God makes a promise (like "He who began a good work in you will carry it on to completion" [Philippians 1:6]), He always follows through.

My Ethics professor at Fuller Theological Seminary and friend, the late Lewis Smedes, wrote this about promises:

> Yes, somewhere people still make and keep promises. They choose not to quit when the going gets rough because they promised once

to see it through. They stick to lost causes. They hold on to a love grown cold. They stay with people who have become pains in the neck. They still dare to make promises and care enough to keep the promises they make. I want to say to you that if you have a ship you will not desert, if you have people you will not forsake, if you have causes you will not abandon, *then you are like God.*

What a marvelous thing a promise is! When a person makes a promise, she reaches out into an unpredictable future and makes one thing predictable: She will be there even when being there costs her more than she wants to pay. When a person makes a promise, he stretches himself out into circumstances that no one can control and controls at least one thing: He will be there no matter what the circumstances turn out to be. With one simple word of promise, a person creates an island of certainty in a sea of uncertainty.[1]

Yes, Smedes was talking about people who keep their promises. But look whom he used as an example: God. When we keep promises, then *we are like God,* who always keeps His.

Here's how God rescued those who were totally without power to rescue themselves—the Hebrew slaves in Egypt: "The LORD your God carried you, as a father carries his son, all the way you went until you reached [the Promised Land]" (Deuteronomy 1:31). And here's a beautiful description of what it meant for the Hebrew slaves, and for you and me, to be carried by God when we cannot carry ourselves:

> Woe was Moses. He was facing a hot, tired, weary, complaining band of several hundred thousand Hebrew former-slaves. His task? To convince them they would be able to face the sword-swinging, chariot-driving Canaanites and Philistines looming large on the horizon of the Promised Land. The Israelites had just completed a grueling trek through the hot desert sands of the Sinai Peninsula. It was at that point that the perfect analogy for encouragement came to Moses: The Lord your God will carry you to victory "as a father carries his son." *As a father carries his son!*
>
> The Hebrews to whom Moses was speaking had been carrying their small children in their arms. It had all started in the middle of

the night when they fled Egypt during the first Passover. They had carried their little ones the next day over hot Sinai sands, when tiny legs could toddle no further. Then, with walls of water roaring and thrashing on either side, fathers had grabbed up hysterical children and hustled over the floor of the Red Sea to escape Pharaoh's charging chariots. Then, more hot sands...scorpion stings...stone cuts...feet that became pin cushions for desert briars. "As a father carries his son, so God will carry you," Moses assured the weary Israelites.

How does a father carry a son? The timeless way is to come from behind and scoop up the child with a fluid movement that plants him on a shoulder. What child doesn't love that perch? Arms tightly wrapped around Daddy's head, vise-like grip of the father securing his or her safety—from that coveted spot a child knows no fear, sees no obstacles, and is ready to conquer the world. The father's strength becomes the child's as long as he or she is being carried—which is exactly what the father wants the child to feel.

Do you have a promised land to invade—or maybe just a dinner to prepare after working hard all day? Forget your burned, stung and cut feet. Let your Father scoop you up and plant you on his mountain-like shoulders. From there you will see what you couldn't when standing on your own. You'll see things from his perspective.[2]

Sixty-seven-year-old Rowena Duplessis of New Orleans knows the feeling of being carried by God. In 2004, she lost her husband. A year later, she lost her home to Hurricane Katrina. And a year after that, her thirty-eight-year-old son took his own life, which happened just before thieves broke into the trailer she'd been living in since Katrina.

She felt weak from her string of faith-testing events, but her faith in God wasn't shaken: "This is what sustains me: When it is really bad, you put it in [God's] hands. You do what you are able to do and have faith that he can do the rest. *He's carried me on many days when I couldn't walk myself.*"[3]

Rowena's sixty-seven years are proof of the trustworthiness of God and the unchanging nature of His promises:

> Listen to me, O house of Jacob,
>   all you who remain of the house of Israel,

> you whom I have upheld since you were conceived,
>> and have carried since your birth.
> Even to your old age and gray hairs
>> I am he, I am he who will sustain you.
> I have made you and I will carry you;
>> I will sustain you and I will rescue you.
>
> (Isaiah 46:3–4)

God promised to carry His people in the Old Testament and continues that promise in the New. One of the last things Jesus told His disciples was, "I will ask the Father, and he will give you another Counselor to be with you forever" (John 14:16). That's the same promise said a different way—the promise to give us strength and carry us forward when we feel too weak to carry ourselves. Instead of the strength coming from the outside as in the Old Testament, it comes from the inside through the power and strength of the Holy Spirit.

Are you in need of being carried? In need of Someone to reach out and take your hand and pull you through? God is the One who wants to do that; He asks only that you participate in the grand irony of letting go in order to let Him take hold. Nowhere does the Bible say, "Save yourself." But it does tell us to "be saved." Grammatically speaking, it's a passive command. If you will admit your helplessness in the face of a life that can be overwhelming, God will see your admission as a raising of your hand—and He will take your hand in His.

When that happens, you will be leaning into God again.

Questions for Reflection and Discussion

1. It is often difficult to admit our own sense of powerless. We've learned to pull ourselves up by our bootstraps and solve our own problems. It's the American way—to be independent and self-reliant. When can self-reliance be a good thing? When does it become self-defeating and destructive?

2. In what ways has self-reliance crept into your relationship with God? What has your self-reliance cost you? What does it tell you about your view of God?

3. Looking back over your life, what proof do you have that God can and will carry you through the difficult times of life—that He is completely trustworthy?

4. God promises that He will complete the good work in you that He started (Philippians 1:6). Have you ever doubted this promise? Right now, where in your life do you need to believe this is true?

5. Are you at a place in your life where you need to admit your helplessness and let God carry you? What, if anything, keeps you from reaching out and letting Him do that?

Part 5

God's Love Is Forever Love

21. God's Love Burns Bright Forever

T O BE ONE OF THE *Schindlerjuden*, or a descendant of one, is to be a bearer of human gratitude deeper than most people will ever know. There were around 1,200 original *Schindlerjuden*, and there are perhaps 7,000 of their descendants alive today.[1] You saw some of the *Schindlerjuden*—"Schindler's Jews"—and some of their descendants, in the final scenes of the film *Schindler's List*. They were the ones who solemnly filed past the grave of Oskar Schindler in Jerusalem, placing small stones on the gravestone, an Eastern European Jewish tradition—a way of marking one's visit and remembrance of the deceased.

Born in 1908, Oskar Schindler was a German industrialist who spent the early years of his adult life going from one business venture to another, eventually going bankrupt due to the worldwide effects of the Great Depression. In 1939 he became a member of the Nazi Party, using it as a way to profit from the industrialization of the emerging Nazi war machine. Gaining access to a factory through a German bankruptcy court, he was given control of a thousand Jewish slave laborers to work in the factory.

His business prospered, and he became a wealthy member of the German Nazi social and political circuit. But as his lifestyle changed, so did his heart. He began to develop an attachment to the human beings who were being killed by the tens of thousands by the Nazis—and a special attachment to the thousand or more who worked for him.

When it became apparent that the German positions were weakening, Schindler accomplished the impossible: he got permission from Nazi authorities to move his factory, and his eleven hundred Jewish workers, to occupied Czechoslovakia. The names on "Schindler's List" were spared the death sentence of the twenty-five thousand Jews in Plaszow, Germany, where the factory was previously located.

To accomplish this saving task, Schindler bribed and begged everyone he could. And in the days prior to the liberation of Germany by the Allied Forces, he spent every penny he had—even selling his wife's jewels—to provide food, medicine, and clothing for "his children," as he called the Jews in his care. He even persuaded the Gestapo to send him an additional one hundred Belgian, Dutch, and Hungarian Jews, claiming they were necessary for the production of ammunition and bombs for the German war movement.

When Allied forces moved into Czechoslovakia in May 1945, Schindler was able to set "his children" free, admonishing them not to exact revenge on the Germans they would meet as they journeyed home: "Prove yourself worthy of the millions of victims among you and refrain from any individual acts of revenge and terror."[2] His parting from the twelve hundred Jews was tearful and painful. He, a German, had become one with his Jewish children. Though not documented historically, the movie *Schindler's List* portrays Schindler weeping as they parted, saying, "I could have saved more."

He became a German outcast and died penniless in his motherland. But his wish to be buried among "his children" was honored. He is the only member of the Nazi Party ever to be buried at the Catholic cemetery on Mount Zion in Jerusalem.

Could Oskar Schindler have saved even more Jews than he did? Could his sacrificial love have been even deeper? As many do from the perspective of hindsight, he thought he could have done more—yet the whole world has been amazed by what he accomplished.

Oskar Schindler agonized over those who were lost and dying right before his eyes. He and his wife gave up everything to save people they did not know and, at first, did not love. He manifested what we call the supreme attribute of the God of the Bible: redemptive, sacrificial, agonizing love for those who hurt and those who are lost. There is no compelling evidence that Schindler was motivated by religious persuasions, yet what he did clearly reflects the image of God in man.

The love Oskar Schindler demonstrated to twelve hundred Jews was like seeds planted in their hearts. Because they were loved, they passed on that love to others—specifically, the love of forgiveness by not seeking revenge on those who persecuted them and killed so many others.

You have no doubt participated in a candlelight service in your church or other setting. At Rancho Capistrano Church, which I founded in 1981, every Christmas Eve we would take the flame and light from a single candle that eventually lights hundreds more, illuminating an entire building. The light and flame of the original candle is not diminished as it provides the flame for additional candles, nor is any other candle's flame diminished. It is a picture of the infinite love of God. When such love is manifested in one life, it is then passed on to others—only multiplying and growing stronger, never diminishing by having been spread.

Though I have not been privileged to see it in person, one particular candlelight service reminds me of the love of God, of the love of Oskar Schindler for his Jewish children. It takes place at a monastery and retreat center in Taizé, France.

The Taizé Community[3] was founded in 1940 by Brother Roger. It, too, began as a place of refuge for those suffering under and fleeing from the hardships of war in Europe, especially Jews. During a long retreat in the winter of 1952–53, Brother Roger wrote the Rule of Taizé, which said, in part,

> Since my youth, I think that I have never lost the intuition that
> community life could be a sign that God is love, and love alone.
> Gradually the conviction took shape in me that it was essential
> to create a community with men determined to give their whole
> life and who would always try to understand one another and be
> reconciled, a community where kindness of heart and simplicity
> would be at the centre of everything.

Following the war years, the Taizé Community grew and became a place of retreat and counsel for the spiritually needy, especially young people, from all over the world. Today, tens of thousands of young people each year create a river of love, life, and light into and out of the Taizé Community, learning of the biblical love of God and taking it with them back to their own countries and communities. During worship services, the light from a single candle is spread to the thousands gathered in corporate worship of Christ, a beautiful image of the power of God's love to enlighten the whole world.[4]

The Bible is so clear: God is love (see 1 John 4:8). First John 4:16 says, "God is love. Whoever lives in love lives in God, and God in him." There is no love in the world that is not enlivened by the love of God, for He is love. Even when sacrificial love is demonstrated without reference to God, as in the case of Oskar Schindler, that love comes from God. It was God loving the Jews Schindler saved. It is God loving the young people who come seeking Him at Taizé. And it is God who loves you and loves through you.

As to the character of His love, there is no better place to start than 1 Corinthians 13. This chapter in the Bible, often called the "Love Chapter," is usually studied from the perspective of human love. That is, without question, how and why the apostle Paul wrote it. He wanted the Christians in Corinth to know that "the greatest of [all spiritual gifts and traits] is love" (verse 13). He illustrates that fact by describing the nature of love. *Love* is a noun as well as a verb, but Paul presents a list of things love does and does not do—action words to illustrate true love.

Paul's point is broader than just a laundry list of "How to Love." First Corinthians 13 is sandwiched between chapters 12 and 14—two chapters on spiritual gifts. The Corinthians were exercising those gifts of God in decidedly unloving ways in their church. So Paul's point is this: spiritual gifts are given by the Holy Spirit of God and will be manifested only in ways consistent with God's character. God's kind of love, therefore, is the standard by which you (Corinthians) are to act toward one another.

In that light, we can read 1 Corinthians 13 as a description of God and how He loves:

> Love is patient, love is kind. It does not envy, it does not boast,
> it is not proud. It is not rude, it is not self-seeking, it is not easily
> angered, it keeps no record of wrongs. Love does not delight in evil
> but rejoices with the truth. It always protects, always trusts, always
> hopes, always perseveres. Love never fails.
> (verses 4–8)

But there is another side to God's love—a tension, if you will. And the reason it's easy to understand is because we feel it. Compare the following two statements about love:

- "[Love] is not easily angered" (1 Corinthians 13:5).

- "'In your anger do not sin': Do not let the sun go down while you are still angry" (Ephesians 4:26).

Do you see the tension? The apostle Paul says that love is patient, but he doesn't say that love is never angry (emotional). He says that love is not "easily angered" and that anger should never cross the line and become self-serving, that is, sinful.

The only reason we are warned as humans about the danger of righteous anger becoming unrighteous anger is because love is emotional; love *feels*. When the object of our love doesn't respond to our love, our emotions are aroused and our love becomes passionate, and yes, it borders on anger and indignation. It's the kind of angry love that Hosea no doubt felt when his wife, Gomer, was unfaithful to him (see the book of Hosea). It's the kind of angry love God felt when His spiritual children, His chosen people, rejected Him to go after pagan idols. It's the kind of angry love a parent feels when a wayward child repudiates the family's values and brings shame to the family name. It's the kind of angry love that a faithful wife feels when she has been rejected by her husband. It's the kind of angry love for twelve hundred Jews that Oskar Schindler felt when he saw innocent human beings brutalized and killed because of their race.

And it's the kind of love God feels for you if you are not connected intimately with Him. Max Lucado put into words why God's love for you becomes emotional, impatient, and forceful in the face of your disconnectedness:

> One of the sweetest reasons God saved you is because he is fond of you. He likes having you around. He thinks you are the best thing to come down the pike in quite a while.... If God had a refrigerator, your picture would be on it. If he had a wallet, your photo would be in it. He sends you flowers every spring and a sunrise every morning. Whenever you want to talk, he'll listen. He can live anywhere in the universe, and he chose your heart. And the Christmas gift he sent you in Bethlehem? Face it, friend. He's crazy about you![5]

God loves you so much that He wants to be connected with you. He not only loves you, He likes you! And why wouldn't He? He created you.

In the same way Jesus not only loved His disciples, He liked them. They were intimate friends to whom Jesus revealed the secrets of the kingdom of heaven (see John 15:15). When He became disconnected from them following His crucifixion, when they had gone back to being fishermen in Galilee, *He* went to Galilee. He didn't want to be separated from them. He even gave Peter, the one who had publicly denied their friendship three times, a new assignment (see John 21:15–17).

And that's how much God loves you. The greatest illustrations we have of the passionate love of God over the state of His lost and disconnected children come from Jesus' human-divine reactions. On one occasion, "when he looked out over the crowds, his heart broke. So confused and aimless they were, like sheep with no shepherd" (Matthew 9:36 *The Message*). Another time He cried out, "Jerusalem, Jerusalem, killer of prophets, abuser of the messengers of God! How often I've longed to gather your children, gather your children like a hen, her brood safe under her wings—but you refused and turned away!" (Luke 13:34 *The Message*).

The very people who had murdered and abused God's own messengers were the people He loved and longed to be connected with. And it's the same way with us: "God demonstrates his own love for us in this: While we were still sinners, Christ died for us" (Romans 5:8). Think of what you have done, and I have done—and then think about the kind of love it takes to love us still. Yes, God is patient—*but He is patiently seeking a relationship with you.*

John Eldredge and Brent Curtis have posed some questions to make us think about what God has gone through while waiting for us to turn to Him:

- Have you ever had to literally turn a lover over to a mortal enemy to allow her to find out for herself what his intentions toward her really were?

- Have you ever had to lie in bed knowing she was believing his lies and [being intimate] with him every night?

- Have you ever sat helplessly by in a parking lot, while your enemy and his friends took turns [taking advantage of] your lover even as you sat nearby, unable to win her heart enough so she would trust you to rescue her?

- Have you ever called this one you had loved for so long...and asked her if she was ready to come back to you, only to have her say her heart was still captured by your enemy?

- Have you ever watched your lover's beauty slowly diminish and fade in a haze of alcohol, drugs, occult practices, and infant sacrifice until she is no longer recognizable in body or soul?

- Have you ever loved one so much that you even send your only son to talk with her about your love for her, knowing that she will kill him?

  All this and more God has endured because of his refusal to stop loving us.[6]

If you didn't as you were reading, go back through those questions and put yourself in the place of the lover, and God in the place of the one waiting, longing, seeking, and sending after you. That's how much we are loved—so much that He sent His only Son to come to earth to explain His love.

The late Henri Nouwen once explained what it was that gave him the power to say no to worldly lusts; to say no to disconnecting from God and pursuing other pleasures:

> I cannot continuously say no to this or no to that, unless there is something ten times more attractive to choose. Saying no to my lust, my greed, my needs, and the world's powers takes an enormous amount of energy. The only hope is to find something so obviously real and attractive that I can devote all my energies to saying yes.... One such thing I can say yes to is when I come in touch with the fact that I am loved. Once I have found that in my total brokenness I am still loved, I become free from the compulsion of doing successful things.[7]

Once you and I come to grips with "how wide and long and high and deep" (Ephesians 3:18) God's love for us is, nothing will ever separate us from Him again.

Questions for Reflection and Discussion

1. The love that Oskar Schindler demonstrated to more than twelve hundred Jews was like a seed planted in their hearts. Because they were loved, they passed that love on to others. Where have *you* seen that kind of love demonstrated?

2. Have you ever struggled with not feeling loved by God? Explain. Who or what helped you come to understand and experience the love of God in your life?

3. Selfishness can quickly snuff out the flame of love in our lives. Where have you seen evidence of this? Think of a time recently when selfishness caused a disconnection in your relationship with another person. What did it take to repair the relationship?

4. First Corinthians 13, often called the "Love Chapter" of the Bible, describes God's kind of love and provides the standard by which we are to act toward one another. Come up with a list of things Paul mentions in 1 Corinthians 13:4–8 to describe how love acts. Then share where you most need to grow in loving others.

5. What things have caused you to lean away from God's love? What has God used to draw you back into a warm, intimate relationship with Him?

22. The Game's Already Won!

CTOBER 10, AD 732. On that date, armies in (what is now) Europe, under the leadership of (Christian) Austrasian Mayor of the Palace Charles Martel turned back the army of the Umayyad Caliphate led by (Muslim) Abdul Rahman Al Ghafiqi, governor-general of al-Andalus, between the cities of Poitiers and Tours in what is today France. Charles Martel was victorious and Al Ghafiqi was killed.[1]

As a result, the Muslim armies withdrew from Europe and went back to their traditional Arabic homelands. This battle, now called the Battle of Tours, is marked as the decisive turning point in the struggle between the civilizations of the West and the Middle East. Had the battle gone in favor of the Muslims, all of Europe would be speaking Arabic today instead of their native European languages.[2]

July 1–3, 1863. Union Major General George Meade's Army of the Potomac resisted attacks by Confederate General Robert E. Lee's Army of Northern Virginia at Gettysburg, Pennsylvania. More than twenty-three thousand soldiers were killed, wounded, captured, or reported missing on each side—more than in any other battle in the American War Between the States. The turning point of the battle came on July 3 when the Confederate armies charged Cemetery Ridge under the partial command of Major General George Pickett ("Pickett's Charge") and were repulsed by the Union army defenses. The Confederate armies never recovered from their defeat at Gettysburg. Though the war dragged on for nearly two more years, the Battle of Gettysburg was the decisive battle.

August 8, 1918–November 11, 1918. This period of World War I is known as the Hundred Days Offensive by the Allied Forces (Russia, France, England, Italy, and the United States) against the Central Powers (Germany, Austria-Hungary, the Ottoman Empire, and Bulgaria). This offensive forced the capitulation of the Central Powers and the end of World War I. The war began in 1914, but the Hundred Days Offensive by the Allies broke the back of the Central Powers, signaling that the war was over.

June 6, 1944. This was D-day of World War II—the day Allied Forces invaded the shores of Normandy and began pushing back Hitler's German armies. The nine Allied nations, led by United States general Dwight Eisenhower, accomplished the greatest invasion in military history. The invasion was successful—the outcome of the war was certain, though it took time for hostilities to cease. Indeed, more lives were lost between D-day and V-E Day (Victory in Europe Day, May 7, 1945) than before D-day. But there was no doubt that D-day signaled the end of World War II.

April 23, 1975. United States president Gerald Ford, in a televised speech, declared an end to America's involvement in the war in Vietnam as North Vietnamese forces drew ever closer to Saigon, South Vietnam. By April 30, the fall of Saigon was complete as all U.S. military, diplomatic, and civilian personnel were evacuated. Cameras recorded the frantic efforts of thousands of South Vietnamese who fought for two days, April 29 and 30, to get aboard the U.S. helicopters and escape the encroaching Communist armies. While it took months to "clean up" America's involvement in the Vietnam War, it was over for the United States when Saigon fell.

It was the German-born, Lutheran professor Oscar Cullmann who is famous for noting how most military campaigns have a decisive moment—a turning point—and making the analogy of Jesus Christ's death and resurrection as a spiritual turning point in the cosmic battle between good and evil.[3] And he cites the D-day invasion of the Allied Forces in June 1944 as the prime example.

Leading up to D-day, the citizens of occupied France could only wait patiently for their rescuers to come, as described by Michael Knowles:

> If you had talked to people in the French Underground, and asked them a very simple question, "Do you really think you can beat the

Nazis with their power, their organization, their structures?"—they would have said, "I know we look like a rag-tag force that has no effectiveness whatsoever, but what you don't know is that across the English Channel, even as we talk, a huge invasion force is being assembled. We don't know when it is going to happen, because nobody has told us the day, but a signal will be given, and on that day that huge invasion force will come across the Channel and join up with our feeble efforts and carry us to victory."[4]

God's people in the Old Testament were much like the French Underground prior to D-day. Their prophets had told them that God's Messiah was coming to establish the kingdom of God. They didn't know when or how—they knew only that God had promised victory:

> A shoot will come up from the stump of Jesse;
>> from his roots a Branch will bear fruit.
> The Spirit of the LORD will rest on him—
>> the Spirit of wisdom and of understanding,
>> the Spirit of counsel and of power,
>> the Spirit of knowledge and of the fear of the LORD—
>> and he will delight in the fear of the LORD.
> He will not judge by what he sees with his eyes,
>> or decide by what he hears with his ears;
> but with righteousness he will judge the needy,
>> with justice he will give decisions for the poor of the
>> earth.
> He will strike the earth with the rod of his mouth;
>> with the breath of his lips he will slay the wicked.
> Righteousness will be his belt
>> and faithfulness the sash around his waist.
> The wolf will live with the lamb,
>> the leopard will lie down with the goat,
> the calf and the lion and the yearling together;
>> and a little child will lead them.
> The cow will feed with the bear,
>> their young will lie down together,
>> and the lion will eat straw like the ox.
> The infant will play near the hole of the cobra,

and the young child put his hand into the viper's nest.
They will neither harm nor destroy on all my holy mountain,
for the earth will be full of the knowledge of the LORD
    as the waters cover the sea.
(Isaiah 11:1–9)

And God's D-day arrived! When Jesus Christ died on the cross to cancel out the sin debt of all who believe, Satan's basis of accusation against us was taken away. And when Christ rose from the dead, He received God's mark of approval that His death had been accepted in the court of justice in heaven. The death and resurrection of Jesus were the spiritual D-day in God's big plan—the day the enemy was defeated and the outcome of the war was made certain.

Has the war continued? Yes. Just as Germany continued to fight against the Allied Forces for a year following D-day—even though her fate was sealed—so Satan continues to battle against God's people, even though his final chapter has already been written. He can read Revelation 20:7–10 as well as we can. The outcome of this world's spiritual war is not in doubt.

In this fifth section of *Leaning into God When Life Is Pushing You Away*, we're talking about the God who is love, using 1 Corinthians 13 as our biblical frame of reference for how true love reveals itself. In the previous chapter I said that God is patient (see 1 Corinthians 13:4)—He is patiently seeking to connect with you. And in this chapter I want you to know that God "keeps no record of wrongs" (verse 5). And that's why I have introduced the idea of decisive events—events that shape everything that follows after them; events that are a turning point; events that are watershed moments.

Normally, when we think about not keeping a record of wrongs done to us, we think in terms of forgiving those who have hurt us. But that's not an easy thing to do. The forgiving part is hard enough, but the forgetting part is impossible. The harder we try to forget... well, you know how that goes.

God's love for us is such that He does not keep a record of the wrongs we have done. But we have to understand what changed at the cross of Christ to make that possible.

In the Old Testament, sins had to be forgiven annually on the Day of Atonement (*Yom Kippur*). On that day, in the fall of each year, Israel's high priest would enter the Holy of Holies in the temple to pour out the blood of a sacrificial animal over the lid of the ark of the covenant. The ark contained the stone tablets on which were written the Ten Commandments given by God to Moses on Mount Sinai. They represented all the laws the Israelites were expected to keep—more than six hundred of them. The blood of the sacrificial animal "covered" all the sins committed by the nation during the previous year.

From one Day of Atonement to the next, the Israelites needed to keep a mental record of all the things they had done wrong so as to participate fully in the act of forgiveness on the Day of Atonement. Besides that annual remembrance of their sins, they were required to bring sacrifices for various reasons during the year to cover "incidental" sins committed. The Israelites' sins were never far from them. It was impossible for them to keep "no record of wrongs" since they were continually making sacrifices to receive God's forgiveness.

But with the cross of Christ, everything changed. Like the decisive battles in the various wars I mentioned above, a watershed event took place when Christ died on the cross and rose again from the dead. Nothing was ever the same. If it was impossible in the Old Testament to keep "no record of wrongs," it became totally possible to do so in the New Testament.

The book of Hebrews in the New Testament tells plainly how Christ's journey to the Cross was the decisive battle in human spiritual history—fought once and for all:

> [Christ] also bypassed the sacrifices consisting of goat and calf blood, instead using his own blood as the price to set us free *once and for all*. If that animal blood and the other rituals of purification were effective in cleaning up certain matters of our religion and behavior, think how much more the blood of Christ cleans up our whole lives, inside and out. Through the Spirit, Christ offered himself as an unblemished sacrifice, freeing us from all those dead-end efforts to make ourselves respectable, *so that we can live all out for God.*
>
> (9:12–15 *The Message*, italics added)

> Christ didn't enter the earthly version of the Holy Place; he entered the Place Itself, and *offered himself to God as the sacrifice for our*

sins. He doesn't do this every year as the high priests did under the old plan with blood that was not their own; if that had been the case, he would have to sacrifice himself repeatedly throughout the course of history. But instead *he sacrificed himself once and for all, summing up all the other sacrifices in this sacrifice of himself,* the final solution of sin.

(9:24–26 *The Message*, italics added)

Q. How often did the Jewish high priest have to go into the Holy Place to make atonement for the Israelites' sins?

A. Once each year—year after year.

Q. How often did Jesus Christ go to the cross to make atonement for the sins of the world?

A. Once—and for all!

The words I italicized in the passages are key: Christ sacrificed Himself once, for all time, and put an end to keeping track of our sins. The reason God's love is the kind that "keeps no record of wrongs" is because all the wrongs—past, present, and future—were paid for on the cross. They are no longer an issue with God for those who have accepted the gift of eternal forgiveness for their sins.

In other words, God is not keeping score! The game has already been won—won by Jesus Christ for you and for me when He went to Calvary's cross and willingly shed His own blood once and for all. That is precisely the reason that Jesus' last words before He died were "It is finished" (John 19:30). He accomplished the work God had given Him to do—to put an end to the offering of the blood of bulls and goats that could never permanently wipe away our sins.

The cross was the place where the Old Covenant (Old Testament) of God was fulfilled and the New Covenant (New Testament) of God began. Under the Old Covenant, "God found fault with the people" (Hebrews 8:8 [He kept a record of their wrongs]). But God promised Israel that a "new covenant" was coming (see Jeremiah 31:31), and Jesus announced that it was beginning when He ate the Last Supper with His disciples: "In the same way, after the supper he took the cup, saying, 'This cup is the new covenant in my blood, which is poured out for you'" (Luke 22:20). He became the "mediator of a new covenant" (Hebrews 9:15; 12:24), meaning that all the sins of the whole world were covered by His shed blood (see 1 John 2:2).

And because they are covered, they are out of sight and no longer able to be counted. That's why God's love is a love that "keeps no record of wrongs."

That's a lot of Bible verses to absorb in one sitting. But they are important for all who want to be close to God. I have written in this book about the reasons people lose their relationship with God, and most of them could ultimately be summarized under the heading "Shame and Guilt over Sin, Mistakes, Inadequacy, or Failure." We reach a point in our spiritual experience when we think God has had enough: "Okay, that's it. I've been keeping a record of your wrongs, and you just crossed the line with that last one. I'm finished being patient and forgiving. You're going to have to do something pretty special for Me to forgive that last act of rebellion/immaturity/disobedience."

Have you ever felt that way? I have. And when I do I always come back to the truths in the verses in this chapter. Christ's forgiveness of my sins was once and for all. God will never say to me, or to you, "Enough! That's it! I've had it with you!" God is not keeping score; He is not keeping a record of our wrongs.

That does not mean He takes our sins lightly. In fact, just the opposite. He takes them so seriously that He "gave His only begotten Son" (John 3:16 NKJV) to die for them. What it does mean is this: part of the promise of the New Covenant was that God would change our hearts and minds so that we would want to live for Him: "I will put my law in their minds and write it on their hearts. I will be their God, and they will be my people" (Jeremiah 31:33). He does that by the gift of the Holy Spirit when we become followers of His Son, Jesus Christ.

When the Allied soldiers hit the beaches of Normandy and established themselves in Europe, only one word was necessary to describe the future: *victory!* Yes, they had to march in and accept the victory that was theirs, but the victory was assured because of the decisive D-day invasion.

Are you living today in the victory that the C-Day, the "Cross Day," has provided for you—the day that has caused God to look no longer at your sins but only at the victory Christ won at the cross? Because of what He has done, there is no reason (no mistake, no sin, no inadequacy, no failure) for you ever to be disconnected from Him again.

The victory is yours in Christ!

Questions for Reflection and Discussion

1. Have you ever been falsely accused of something? How did you respond to the false accusation?

2. Scripture tells us that Satan stands before God the Father and falsely accuses us of wrongdoing as Christians. Often we internalize his accusations as feelings of false guilt. Based on what you read in this chapter, how will you respond next time you are struggling with Satan's accusations?

3. God's love is the kind that keeps no record of wrongs because of what Christ accomplished on our behalf on the cross. There is no longer an issue with God for those who have accepted the gift of eternal forgiveness for their sins. Have you accepted this gift? When? What, if any, watershed event in your life caused you to make this decision?

4. What difference does knowing God keeps no record of your wrongs make in your life day to day? Is there anything in your past or present that you are unable to forgive and forget in your own life? What truths in Scripture will help you learn to let go of your own wrongdoing when you find it difficult to do so?

5. What is one important thought or concept you read in this chapter that you want to make a part of your life? How will you do that?

23. Let the Truth of God's Love Jump-Start Your Heart!

DON RICHARDSON WAS LABORIOUSLY crafting sentences in a complex foreign language as he told the Sawi people of New Guinea wonderful truths about how God created the world, and how it was marred by sin. He got to the part about God's Deliverer who had been sent into the world to remedy the problem of evil and sin—and began to lose his audience. A man named Maum yawned out loud and began working on a vine he was fashioning into a bowstring. Other small groups of twos and threes started murmuring conversations among themselves. The tribe called "the Jews" seemed too far away from New Guinea to deserve their interest.

But one day, during part of the Jesus-story Don was telling the Sawi men, they suddenly began listening with rapt attention:

> I was describing Judas Iscariot's betrayal of the Son of God. About halfway through the description, I noted they were all listening intently. They noted the details: for three years Judas had kept close company with Jesus, sharing the same food, traveling the same road.
>
> That any associate of Jesus would have conceived the idea of betraying such an impressive figure was highly unlikely. And if anyone *had* conceived the idea, one of Jesus' inner circle of trusted

disciples would have been the least likely to choose such a course. And yet Judas, one of Jesus' disciples, had chosen to betray Him and carried out the dreadful act alone, without any of the other disciples suspecting his plot.

At the climax of the story, Maum whistled a birdcall of admiration. Kani and several others touched their fingertips to their chests in awe. Still others chuckled.

At first I sat there confused. Then the realization broke through. *They were acclaiming Judas as the hero of the story!* Yes, Judas, the one whom I had portrayed as the satanically motivated enemy of truth and goodness!

A feeling of coldness gripped my spine. I tried to protest that Jesus was good. He was the Son of God, the Savior. It was evil to betray Him. But nothing I said would erase that gleam of savage enjoyment from their eyes.

Kani leaned forward and exclaimed, "That was real *tuwi asonai man*!"

Whatever *tuwi asonai man* meant.

Later, Don Richardson asked his native language interpreter to explain the Sawi phrase Kani had used to describe Judas. He said it was like when the Sawi would capture a baby pig in the jungle, bring it home, and win its affection by providing it with food every day. The pig would become domesticated and not want to return to the jungle. Then, when the pig was a trusting, fattened adult, the Sawi would butcher it for meat.

When Don asked whether this treachery was ever used among people, the interpreter said yes, it was. He told of a stranger who tentatively had visited a friend among the Sawi and found acceptance—so he began visiting often. As soon as he was relaxed among the Sawi, the visitor was killed and eaten. And there were other examples of the Sawis' use of treachery—befriending an animal or a human in order to kill them once their guard was down.

No wonder the Sawi were impressed with Judas. *Tuwi asonai man* meant "to fatten with friendship for an unsuspected slaughter." Treachery was one of the Sawis' highest values.[1]

We are shocked when we read of such treachery—of a place where an otherwise friendly and gentle people could place such a high value on deceit and duplicity. But the Sawi did. To use the apostle Paul's words, they had "exchanged the truth of God for a lie" (Romans 1:25). Somehow, within their isolated culture, they had learned that lying, deceit, and betrayal (not to mention murder and cannibalism) were normal; the rule rather than the exception.

It's not hard to imagine how this could happen. Consider this fictional idea: an infant is kidnapped from its parents by an evil person who raises the child in isolation from the real world. The child is taught that light is dark, black is white, bad is good, and good is bad. Satan is good and God is evil. Selfishness, deceit, lying, and hate are desired values. Everything that is actually true and good in this world is made out to be a lie and bad, and vice versa. Because the child knows no different (except perhaps for the spark of conscience that is quickly extinguished or retrained), he accepts what his authority figure tells him about life in the world—180 degrees opposite to the truth.

Then the child is rescued by his rightful parents and brought out of the Land of Lies in which he was raised and introduced to truth, to reality. Black is black and white is white. Good is good and evil is evil. Down is down and up is up. The task of reorienting and reeducation would be huge. The young child would not only have to learn to distinguish between truth and lies, he would have to learn to trust all over again.

He would, figuratively speaking, need to be "born again"—to start over learning what truth really is. He would have to forget everything that he thought was true and replace it with what was actually true—about himself, about other people, about God, and about how to tell the difference between truth and lies.

The very real experience of Don Richardson, and the fictional story I told, speak to something you and I experience in our own lives: we live our lives with a mix of truth and lies. We may not live in a culture that elevates treachery and deceit to the status of a fine art, but there are other lies in our culture that are just as devastating. We are told that youth is better than aging, that physical beauty is to be desired over spiritual beauty, that possessing wealth is more important than how one attains it, that status and power are more valuable than integrity and good deeds, and on and on.

But besides the values—some true, some not—we absorb from our culture, we also tell ourselves things that are not true. Sometimes the lies we speak to ourselves are based on the lies of the culture: *I know I'm not attractive. No one will ever be interested in a lifetime relationship with me. I'm going to give up thoughts of marriage and family and try to make do as a single person.* And sometimes they are lies we invent ourselves: *I'm better/worse, more deserving/undeserving, less/more likely to succeed than others.* The source of these lies is more subtle, more difficult to identify. But somehow, they become what we believe and result in either pride or poor self-image.

Regardless of who we are and what we believe, our lifetime challenge is to separate truth from error in all dimensions of life—but especially when it comes to what we believe about ourselves. It is possible for people to become so confused about themselves and their places in life, or to arrive at such negative conclusions about themselves, that they shut down spiritually and emotionally.

It is possible to believe the biggest lie of all—*Life is pointless and I am worthless*—and flip the emotional switch that puts one in a "Why bother?" mode. Like a fire that requires fuel and oxygen to continue burning, life requires truth to make it worth living. Lies in life may work in the short term, but they will eventually be exposed and lead to despair for those who believe them.

On February 9, 1996, a railroad train running from Waldwick, New Jersey, to Hoboken, New Jersey, ran through a red signal and crashed into the side of another train at a crossing. The engineers of both trains were killed along with one passenger, and 158 other passengers were injured. A year later the National Transportation Safety Board revealed the cause of the crash: the engineer of the train that ran through the red signal was going blind. For nine years the engineer had been losing his eyesight due to diabetes, but he had kept his condition secret. Even the man's doctor, who knew he was a railroad engineer, did not report his true condition. On the man's annual physical, he lied each year about having diabetes or any other debilitating condition, paying for two eye surgeries out-of-pocket rather than filing an insurance claim. The truth finally came out, as it usually does, in a disastrous way.[2] Whether we believe a lie or are perpetrating a lie, the results are never good.

Continuing in this chapter with the theme that God is love, we find this truth in 1 Corinthians 13:6: "Love does not delight in evil but rejoices with the truth." And because God is love, we can say that He personally delights in the truth. And there is something else God delights in: those He created and loves. It is a true, biblical statement to say that God rejoices when His children are prospering and doing well in life. That is, when His children are living on the basis of truth, not lies:

> The LORD be exalted,
>> who delights in the well-being of his servant.
> (Psalm 35:27)

> The LORD delights in those who fear him,
>> who put their hope in his unfailing love.
> (Psalm 147:11)

> The LORD detests men of perverse heart
>> but he delights in those whose ways are blameless.
> (Proverbs 11:20)

God so desires that His creation lives life on the basis of truth that He sent His own Son to earth to demonstrate truth to the human race. When Pontius Pilate was interviewing Jesus on the night before His crucifixion, he asked Jesus if He was a king. Part of Jesus' answer was, "And for this I came into the world, to testify to the truth. Everyone on the side of truth listens to me" (John 18:37). And Pilate responded, no doubt with a mocking tone, "What is truth?" (verse 38).

It's a reasonable question for one like Pilate, a man who had no benchmark for determining truth. Fortunately, Jesus didn't come into the world to simply point to the truth. Instead, He came into the world *as* the truth: "I am the way and the truth and the life" (John 14:6). We can think of Jesus as truth the way we think of God as love. Everything Jesus said and did was truth. By contrast, everything Satan does is a lie. Jesus once said to a group of people who believed He was lying about His identity, "You belong to your father, the devil, and you want to carry out your father's desire. He was a murderer from the beginning, not holding to the truth, for there is no truth in him. When he lies, he speaks his native language, for he is a liar and the father of lies" (John 8:44).

The phrase, "I tell you the truth" occurs seventy-nine times in the English Bible (New International Version), and seventy-eight of those times occur in the four Gospels, coming from the mouth of Jesus. When Jesus said, "Then you will know the truth, and the truth will set you free" (John 8:32), He could just as well have said, "Then you will know Me, and I will set you free." Jesus was, and is, synonymous with the truth.

Author Mack Stiles related how he led a young man from Sweden named Andreas to faith in Christ. Andreas said to Mack, "I've been told if I decide to follow Jesus, He will meet my needs and my life will get very good." Wanting Andreas to understand the gospel clearly, Mack said, "No, Andreas, no!"—surprising his friend. "Actually, Andreas, you may accept Jesus and find that life goes very badly for you."

"What do you mean?" Andreas asked.

"Well, you may find that your friends reject you, you could lose your job, your family might oppose your decision—there are a lot of bad things that may happen to you if you decide to follow Jesus. Andreas, when Jesus calls you, He calls you to go the way of the cross."

Andreas stared at Mack for a few moments and then said, "Then why would I want to follow Jesus?"

Mack gave him the only ultimate answer: "Andreas, because Jesus is true."[3]

It defies rationality to think that the one true God of the universe could be anything but true and truth. That's why Jesus said, "I am . . . the truth," and it's why He said to God the Father, "Your word is truth" (John 17:17). And Jesus also referred to the Holy Spirit as the "Spirit of truth" (John 14:17; 15:26; 16:13). So God the Father, His Son, His Spirit, and His Word are all "true truth"—what theologian Francis Schaeffer called truth that is always true; truth that never changes.[4]

Sadly, far too many people in our world do not live on the basis of "true truth." It is evident in their inability to discern truth from lies in the world. For instance, the following interview took place as part of a large survey of hundreds of American teenagers concerning their religious beliefs. This exchange was between an interviewer (I) and a fourteen-year-old white conservative Protestant girl from Idaho (T):

I: When you think of God, what image do you have of God?

T: [yawning]

I: What is God like?

T: Um, good. Powerful.

I: Okay, anything else?

T: Tall.

I: Tall?

T: Big.

I: Do you think God is active in people's lives or not?

T: Ah, I don't know.

I: You're not sure?

T: Different people have different views of him.

I: What about your view?

T: What do you mean?

I: Do you think God is active in your life?

T: In my life? Yeah.

I: Yeah, hmm. Would you say you feel close to God or not really?

T: Yeah, I feel close. [yawns]

I: Where do you get your ideas about God?

T: The Bible, my mom, church. Experience.

I: What kind of experience?

T: He's just done a lot of good in my life, so.

I: Like, what are examples of that?

T: I don't know.

I: Well, I'd love to hear. What good has God done in your life?

T: I, well, I have a house, parents, I have the Internet, I have a phone, I have cable.[5]

One of the summary conclusions of this large study of teenagers was that most teens can hardly articulate their own beliefs, that religion seems to operate mostly as an unfocused, invisible dynamic operating in the background of teenagers' lives, and that *many social and cultural forces exert effects that tend to undermine serious religious faith and practice.*[6]

When people who say they believe in God are not grounded in the truth, "social and cultural forces exert effects that tend to undermine serious religious faith and practice." The study shows that's happening to many American youth who say they believe in God, and I don't think it's a stretch to imagine it's happening to many adults as well.

When disappointments and experiences in life take the wind out of our sails, we begin to believe a lie—that life (that is, God) is conspiring against us to ensure our defeat. When that lie is embraced—when one does not know or believe that God is good and that He is love, and that He delights in the success of His children—people shut down totally or to a debilitating degree. They stop expecting blessings, joy, fulfillment, and success. After all, you can't fight (God's) City Hall, so why try?

If you have experienced that kind of shutdown, that kind of disconnect from God, ask yourself whether you have embraced a lie of some sort—a lie from the culture we live in or a lie from the devil himself. Or perhaps a lie that you have convinced yourself is part of your personal reality.

Like a car with a dying battery, you may need the spark of God's truth to jump-start you back to spiritual life—truth like Jeremiah 29:11: "'I know the plans I have for you,' declares the LORD, 'plans to prosper you and not to harm you, plans to give you hope and a future.'" Remember: Jesus said that He and God's Word are both truth. Start by reconnecting with both in order to renew your mind and get back in step with the God who loves you.

Questions for Reflection and Discussion

1. We live our lives with a mix of truth and lies. Some of these lies come from our culture and some come from distorted realities in us. Come up with a list of lies culture perpetuates today. Then create a contrasting truth, based on God's Word, to combat each lie. How many lies of culture have you bought into personally? Which of God's truths do you need to embrace to counteract the lies of culture you've believed?

2. Our lifetime challenge is to separate truth from error in all dimensions of life, but especially as it concerns what we believe about ourselves. What are some lies about *you* that you've believed in the past or perhaps even now believe? Imagine God talking to you. What would He tell you about each of these lies that you believe?

3. Denial, rationalizing, and self-deception keep us believing a lie or perpetuating a lie in our lives. Where have you seen this to be true in the lives of others? In your own life? What were the results of buying into the lie?

4. God delights in our knowing the truth about ourselves. Where in your life have you experienced God's "divine intervention" in such a way that you came to a new reality about yourself? How has the truth set you free?

5. One way to jump-start your heart when you've disconnected from God, because you've bought into the world's lies or your own, is to reconnect with the truth. What are some things you can do this week to reconnect with the truth?

24. Hide Your Mind in the Safety of God's Love

AS LONG AS HE COULD remember, Henry had wanted to marry Glenda. He knew she had a shadowy past and a stained reputation, but he was convinced that by showering her with unconditional love, she would change. After all, prior to meeting him, Glenda had lived around people like herself who treated her poorly. She'd never had the motivation to change; never seen that life could be different. And Henry was committed to showing her the kind of love to which she would remain attracted forever.

Henry prayed and got counsel about his choice of a wife. Humanly speaking, he didn't get much encouragement from his parents and peers. But when he prayed he never felt God saying "No." He knew God was a God of second chances, a God of unconditional love and forgiveness, so he took Glenda for his wife.

It was not long before Glenda became pregnant with their first child. But as the months passed, it was obvious that Glenda had been pregnant when they were married. They had not had sexual relations prior to the marriage, so Henry knew the baby couldn't be his. It appeared that Glenda had brought her past to the doorstep of their lives together and had now brought the child of another man into their family.

But Henry was true to his word. He loved Glenda unconditionally and embraced their new son as if he were his own. And Glenda seemed touched. But her softening was short-lived, and she soon became pregnant again. But when this child was born—a girl—and began to grow, she didn't look like Henry at all. In fact, she seemed like a stranger in their midst. Other matters related to Glenda came to light that made Henry wonder if she had been unfaithful—and she had. She confessed to Henry what she had done, promising to be true. Again, Henry loved her as he had said he would—unconditionally. He made sure that nothing about her adultery was known outside their marriage—and life went on.

In spite of Henry's forgiving love, Glenda lost her moral and spiritual compass altogether. She began to wander from their marriage and home, publicly this time. She returned to her promiscuous lifestyle, working for a high-end escort service. She became almost a captive of the men for whom she worked, with no freedom to leave. Henry was embarrassed and ashamed and did his best to protect his children from their mother's involvements.

Months went by with no word from Glenda. Henry had no way to contact her or see her. It was as if she had disappeared—until one day Henry received a call from the people Glenda worked for: she had become pregnant and given birth to a son. Glenda wanted Henry to come and get the baby.

Henry fell before the Lord, seeking guidance, and was convinced that he received this direction from Him: "Go, show your love to your wife again, though she is loved by another and is an adulteress." And that is what Henry did. When he went to pick up the baby, he asked how much it would take to purchase Glenda out of their sex-trade business, no questions asked. Though it cost Henry everything he had, he paid what it took to protect his wife from further abuse at their hands.

Henry's unconditional love, yet again, protected and provided for the love of his life.

If you know your Bible, you recognized this story. It isn't one we learned in Sunday school. Henry and Glenda are none other than Hosea and Gomer, the characters in the most incredible story of unconditional love in the Bible. Scholars are not in full agreement about the story in the first three chapters of the book of Hosea. Had Gomer been promiscuous and birthed three children before Hosea married her? Or did she become promiscuous after they were married, bearing three children by men other than Hosea?

Regardless of how Hosea came to be married to Gomer, there is little disagreement about God's instructions to the prophet in chapter 3, verse 1: "Go, show your love to your wife again, though she is loved by another and is an adulteress. Love her as the LORD loves the Israelites, though they turn to other gods."

And there is no mistaking Hosea's response: "So I bought her for fifteen shekels of silver and about a homer and a lethek of barley" (verse 2; a "homer and a lethek" is about 430 pounds or 195 kilograms of barley). Gomer's adultery and promiscuity had apparently led her into slavery, out of which Hosea purchased her. Or perhaps she was not enslaved at all, and the money and goods represented a kind of gift to Gomer. Regardless of the reason for the payment, Hosea was doing what he had to do to protect his wife—to get her off the streets and back into a relationship with the husband who loved her.

If you find yourself in a situation similar to Hosea's, I am not encouraging you to use his behavior as a pattern for yourself. The reason God asked His prophet Hosea to undertake such a difficult mission was to use Hosea and Gomer as a parable—a parallel illustration—of His love for the nation of Israel. God's chosen people had been unfaithful to Him time after time. They had wandered away into spiritual adultery, worshiping idols and pagan gods. Yet God sent His prophets to call them back to Himself time after time. God did everything He could to protect the people whom He looked upon as His wife (see Jeremiah 3:8). He "birthed" and "raised" Israel and was committed to her protection:

> When Israel was a child, I loved him,
>   and out of Egypt I called my son.
> But the more I called Israel,
>   the further they went from me.
> They sacrificed to the Baals
>   and they burned incense to images.
> It was I who taught Ephraim to walk,
>   taking them by the arms;
> but they did not realize
>   it was I who healed them.
> I led them with cords of human kindness,
>   with ties of love;
> I lifted the yoke from their neck
>   and bent down to feed them.
>
> (Hosea 11:1–4)

It should come as no surprise that God protects those He loves. The apostle Paul wrote that "[love] always protects" (1 Corinthians 13:7). At the human level, it's not hard to think of the ways perfect love protects—parents and their children being an obvious example. Parents will use anything from tough love to gentle love to protect their children. But spouses demonstrate their love for one another by being protective as well.

In his book *The Ten Laws of Lasting Love*, Paul Pearsall relates the way his wife stepped up to protect him in a time when he was too weak to protect himself. When he was in the hospital battling cancer, his wife was always there to give him an encouraging embrace when the results of a particular test were not what they were hoping for. But one day a doctor entered his hospital room and told Pearsall, "It doesn't look like you're going to make it." I'll let him describe what his wife did:

> Before I could ask a question of this doomsayer, my wife stood up, handed me my robe, adjusted the tubes attached to my body and said, "Let's get out of here. This man is a risk to your health." As she helped me struggle to the door, the doctor approached us. "Stay back," demanded my wife. "Stay away from us."
>
> As we walked together down the hall, the doctor attempted to catch up with us. "Keep going," said my wife, pushing the intravenous stand. "We're going to talk to someone who really knows what is going on." Then she held up her hand to the doctor. "Don't come any closer to us."
>
> The two of us moved as one. We fled to the safety and hope of a doctor who did not confuse diagnosis with verdict. I could never have made that walk toward wellness alone.[1]

What spouse wouldn't want to enjoy that kind of proactive protection from a partner? A wife who did is Sarah Kistan, a Salvation Army worker in Sydney, Australia. On April 28, 1996, she and her husband, Tony, were in a crowded café in Port Arthur, Australia, when a deranged man walked in and began shooting at the patrons. Instinctively, Tony stepped in front of Sarah to shield her from the bullets and was one of the first to fall—one of thirty-four who died that day. His last words, as he lay dying in his wife's arms, were, "I'm going to be with the Lord."[2]

But God protects as well. We know He is protecting, even today, His chosen people Israel, "for God's gifts and his call are irrevocable" (Romans

11:29). And I think He probably protects us more times than we are aware. One of my favorite stories from the Old Testament illustrates that fact. The Hebrew slaves were being led out of Egypt by Moses and needed only to make the short journey around the southeast corner of the Mediterranean Sea and they would be in their Promised Land—a journey of a couple of weeks at the most.

Instead, Moses led them due south into the scorching Sinai desert where he put up with no end of grumbling and complaining from the people. What they didn't know was that God was protecting them from something much worse than burning sands and biting snakes in the desert:

> When Pharaoh let the people go, God did not lead them on the road through the Philistine country, though that was shorter. For God said, "If they face war, they might change their minds and return to Egypt." So God led the people around by the desert road toward the Red Sea. The Israelites went up out of Egypt armed for battle.
> (Exodus 13:17–18)

God knew that the Hebrew slaves would have been no match for the war-happy Philistines who lived on the road to the Promised Land. So He directed them on a detour route—and there is no evidence that Moses ever explained the detour to the people.

Often when I am sitting in a parking lot (disguised as a California freeway) stuck in traffic, knowing I'm going to be late for an appointment, I think of that story from Exodus. Instead of fuming about the stalled traffic and the inconvenience it is causing me, I wonder what the Lord might be protecting me from. Who knows what danger a slight delay in traffic—or any other sudden change in plans—might prevent me from encountering? I choose to believe that God loves me so much that He would change my path or my schedule to protect me from a danger I can't see coming.

As grateful as I am for God's physical protection, there is another kind of protection He provides that is ultimately far more important: the protection of my mind and emotions (my heart). There are lots of physical dangers in this world, but I believe the spiritual dangers make the physical kind pale by comparison. If my mind and emotions are captured by the prevailing thought-systems of this world, I could lose everything. Perhaps not all at once, but over time my values and core beliefs could deteriorate and be replaced by the values of this world.

First John 5:19 says something that doesn't make me afraid, but it does make me live soberly and alertly: "We know that we are children of God, and that the whole world is under the control of the evil one." The evil one is, of course, Satan himself. It is his plan to sow seeds of ungodliness anywhere in the world he can, to discredit God in the most subtle of ways. And it's those subtle messages that I want to guard my mind against. And our loving God has provided the perfect means of protection: the ability to continually renew our minds.

This is a follow-up to the fictional story I told in the previous chapter—about a child who has to relearn truth after being taught lies all his life. *Renewing our minds* is the biblical way of describing that process. It's how we come to enjoy the mental and spiritual protection of God: "Do not conform any longer to the pattern of this world, but be transformed by the renewing of your mind. Then you will be able to test and approve what God's will is—his good, pleasing and perfect will" (Romans 12:2).

If we live our lives in the center of God's will, we will be protected mentally, spiritually, and emotionally. Not necessarily physically—Jesus Himself lived squarely in God's will but was crucified. And all of His disciples and apostles were persecuted for their faithfulness to Him. So physically, we may be called to follow the way of the cross just as Jesus did. But spiritually, emotionally, and mentally, we can be protected.

Remember the difference that protection made in the apostle Peter's life? Before he was filled with the Holy Spirit and became a mature follower of Jesus, Peter was the one who panicked and denied three times that he even knew Jesus (see Matthew 26:69–75). But just a few weeks later, Peter was standing up before a crowd of thousands in Jerusalem and preaching the gospel message of that same Jesus. And from there he only got bolder, defying the Jewish leaders who sought to limit the growth and ministry of the early church in Jerusalem.

What made the difference for Peter? First, the presence of the Holy Spirit, given as a gift to believers in Jesus at Pentecost. And second, the renewing of his mind. He was being protected from thoughts and fears of persecution or even death. He was a different man.

The J. B. Phillips paraphrase of the New Testament renders Romans 12:2 this way: "Don't let the world around you squeeze you into its own mould, but let God re-make you so that your whole attitude of mind is changed." We all are in danger of letting ourselves be squeezed into the shape of this world. But the mind protected by the truth of God can and will resist such pressure.

How is that protection provided? Paul told the Corinthian church it happens this way:

> Though we live in the world, we do not wage war as the world does. The weapons we fight with are not the weapons of the world. On the contrary, they have divine power to demolish strongholds. We demolish arguments and every pretension that sets itself up against the knowledge of God, and we take captive every thought to make it obedient to Christ.
>
> (2 Corinthians 10:3–5)

As the love of God, and especially the Word of God, sinks deep into our hearts and minds, we are able to demolish "any arguments and every pretension" that would seek to destroy our happiness. We don't battle against negative and destructive thoughts and patterns with the "weapons of the world." Rather, we use the weapon God has provided for our protection: "the sword of the Spirit, which is the word of God" (Ephesians 6:17).

Our minds are renewed as we follow the pattern of the psalmist:

> How can a young man keep his way pure?
> > By living according to your word.
> I seek you with all my heart;
> > do not let me stray from your commands.
> I have hidden your word in my heart
> > that I might not sin against you.
> Praise be to you, O LORD;
> > teach me your decrees.
> With my lips I recount
> > all the laws that come from your mouth.
> I rejoice in following your statutes
> > as one rejoices in great riches.
> I meditate on your precepts
> > and consider your ways.
> I delight in your decrees;
> > I will not neglect your word.
>
> (Psalms 119:9–16)

"Every part of Scripture is God-breathed and useful one way or another—showing us truth, exposing our rebellion, correcting our mistakes, training us to live God's way" (2 Timothy 3:16 *The Message*). One of the most loving gifts God has given us is His Word—we neglect it at our peril. If we want to "live God's way," we will avail ourselves of the mental, spiritual, and emotional protection that the truth of His Word provides.

If you are feeling assaulted, overwhelmed, in distress, or in danger, your mind has been unprotected too long. Begin to renew it again by connecting with God where you can always find Him—in His gift to you, the Bible.

Questions for Reflection and Discussion

1. The Old Testament story of Hosea and Gomer demonstrates how perfect love always protects. When have you seen someone step up to protect another person when he or she was too weak to protect him- or herself? When have you done this? When has someone done this for you?

2. Sometimes God intervenes in our lives to protect us from dangers we don't see coming. When have you experienced this? Briefly share that experience and what you ultimately discovered about how God had protected you.

3. When do you tend to feel unprotected or especially vulnerable mentally, spiritually, emotionally? What do you do to protect yourself in these areas of your life? What more might you need to do?

4. What do you think of when you hear the term "spiritual stronghold"? What emotional or mental strongholds have you seen in the lives of others? In your own life? What does it take to break strongholds in our lives?

5. The truth of God's Word provides us with mental, spiritual, and emotional protection. Come up with a list of Scriptures you can use to protect yourself in these three vital areas. Be ready to share your list with your group.

25. God's Love Will Never Fail

I N 1955, JAMES BRACY WAS a young soldier stationed at a San Francisco, California, military base, thousands of miles away from his young bride. In that day, letters were the primary link that kept their love alive. Sallie, James's wife, lived for the mailman's daily arrival in hopes of getting a fresh love letter from James.

On January 28, 1955, James wrote Sallie a letter as he often did and mailed it through the Fort Ord military mail system. But that letter never made it out of the base's postal system, accidentally falling behind a wall in the mailroom. All of James's words of love and expressions of sentiment never made it to his beloved wife. The letter that had been sealed with a kiss lay gathering dust, lost to the world, for nearly half a century.

James's and Sallie's love endured without that letter, thankfully, and they arrived at their fiftieth wedding anniversary. Relaxing and reminiscing on that day, Sallie reminded James of how much his letters had meant to her during the years of his military duty—and how much better it was to know his love face-to-face than just in a letter.

In the weeks prior to their fiftieth anniversary celebration, a construction crew at Fort Ord, California, had been dismantling the old post office facility on the base—and a worker had discovered a letter behind a wall. The construction manager turned the letter over to the postmaster at the U.S. Post Office in Monterey, California, Bob Spadoni. He took on as a personal mission delivering the long-lost letter addressed to Sallie Bracy. Miraculously, through post office records and phone books, he was able to obtain an address for Sallie and sent the letter to her. It arrived just days after James and Sallie's fiftieth-anniversary celebration.

As she read her husband's loving words written nearly a half-century before, Sallie became a twenty-two-year-old young wife all over again. "[His love] meant a lot to me then," she said. "It means even more now."[1]

Fortunately, the lost letter delivered to Sallie Bracy wasn't the only one her husband wrote her during their time of military separation. The absence of one letter, though important, was not enough to make her think that her husband didn't love her. But what if it had been his only letter—and had been lost? She would have lived for all the years of their separation thinking her husband had stopped loving her. She would have thought his silence—his failure to communicate his love—meant he had lost his affection for her. Then, when the lost letter arrived, she would have realized she had been loved all that time! Her disappointment and worry about whether she was loved would have been wasted energy. She was loved the whole time, whether she realized it and benefited from it or not.

I sometimes think that's how we are as God's faith-children. Something will happen that seems to disrupt the flow of communication from God—an experience, a disappointment, even a prolonged feeling—and we begin to question His love. Or even though the Bible is not lost to us, we may stop reading it and reinforcing the truth that God loves us, and it becomes like a lost love letter—or at least one we have stopped reading.

We are so used to human dimensions of love—love "because of" instead of "in spite of"—that almost anything can convince us God's love has stopped. Everything in our human realm is based on performance, beginning from the time we first hear and understand the words "Good boy!" or "Good girl!" We grow up with the understanding that we are loved more when we are good (or perhaps *only* when we are good) than when we are "not good." And "not good" is a nebulous definition that leaves us wondering, *Exactly how good do I have to be in order to be loved?*

As soon as we begin to get report cards in grammar school, the game is fixed in our minds. We get praise from teachers and parents when we do well (and praise obviously equals love in a child's mind), and criticism when we don't. We even are given money (love) for our good grades and other achievements. Parents, of course, mean well with motivations like praise and rewards. Even God has praise and rewards that He plans to distribute when we stand before the throne of Christ one day (see Matthew 25:14–30; 1 Corinthians 3:11–15).

And the system continues throughout our adult lives. We are rewarded and promoted in our vocations on the basis of our performance, so we begin to tie our self-worth and self-esteem to the flow of those external responses from others.

But the truth is that our good performances and bad performances in life, as children and as adults, will vary. We don't always "do good" in life. And because we are so conditioned to equate being loved with doing well, it's easy for us to feel that God's love is as variable as man's. After all, I know when I am not loved by others—I can feel it in my soul. So when I fail to feel God's love, why shouldn't that mean God's love has been cut off from me as well?

The main reason is because the Bible says just the opposite: "Love never fails" (1 Corinthians 13:8). And because God is love (see 1 John 4:8, 16) we could easily say that "God and His love never fail."

When the apostle Paul wrote that "love never fails," he was telling the Christians in Corinth that the God-kind of love is constant. Note his use of the word *always* in 1 Corinthians 13:7: "[Love] always protects, always trusts, always hopes, always perseveres." We can't say the same about human love, because sometimes our love doesn't protect, trust, hope, or persevere. God's love in us can, but our natural human love isn't an "always" kind of love.

So why, if God's love is constantly flowing from His heart to us, do we sometimes feel unloved? Paul anticipated that question and answers it in verse 12: "Now we see but a poor reflection as in a mirror; then we shall see face to face. Now I know in part; then I shall know fully, even as I am fully known." Notice the difference between "now" and "then." Now, we have poor, blurry vision when it comes to seeing God. But then, we will know Him "fully"—"then" being when we enter God's presence for all eternity.

These words of Paul's in verse 12 have become part of the modern English vernacular because of how they were rendered in the original King James (Authorized) Version of the Bible: "For now we see through a glass, darkly. . . ." People use that beautiful phrase to describe things they don't quite understand. And it perhaps has its roots in the seventeenth-century (when the King James Bible was translated) reality that glass, and especially the glass used in mirrors, was not nearly so transparent or reflective as it is now. Looking through a glass window in those days must have been a frustrating experience—the glass might have been cloudy or wavy, either obscuring or transforming what was on the other side. In the apostle Paul's day, of course, there were no glass windows, and mirrors were made of highly polished metal like bronze, making reflections poor at best.

Imagine what it might have been like to look through a seventeenth-century window at something you needed to see—"I can't quite make it out. It looks like—no, wait. Oh, I don't know! I just can't see clearly enough to tell what's happening." Isn't that often how we feel when trying to peer into heaven to see what God is doing during a time in our lives? We desperately want to know why He has allowed such-and-such to happen, or why He seems to have withdrawn His presence and is not answering our prayers. But we can't see—it's cloudy and unclear, like looking "through a glass, darkly."

This is such an important concept for us to understand that I have pulled together four additional translations of 1 Corinthians 13:12. (I hope you're in the habit of reading important verses in more than one Bible version to expand your understanding of the verse's meaning.) Each adds a bit more insight, all the while maintaining the use of the key concepts of "now" and "then":

> We don't yet see things clearly. We're squinting in a fog, peering through a mist. But it won't be long before the weather clears and the sun shines bright! We'll see it all then, see it all as clearly as God sees us, knowing him directly just as he knows us!
> (*The Message*)

> Now we are looking in a mirror that gives only a dim (blurred) reflection [of reality as in a riddle or enigma], but then [when perfection comes] we shall see in reality and face to face! Now I know in part (imperfectly), but then I shall know and understand fully and clearly, even in the same manner as I have been fully and clearly known and understood [by God].
> (*Amplified Bible*)

Now we see a blurred image in a mirror. Then we will see very clearly. Now my knowledge is incomplete. Then I will have complete knowledge as God has complete knowledge of me.
(*God's Word Bible*)

What we see now is like a dim image in a mirror; then we shall see face-to-face. What I know now is only partial; then it will be complete—as complete as God's knowledge of me.
(*Today's English Version*)

Now we see things imperfectly as in a cloudy mirror, but then we will see everything with perfect clarity. All that I know now is partial and incomplete, but then I will know everything completely, just as God now knows me completely.
(*New Living Translation*)

I hope you noticed that Paul never says we're going to see "more clearly" this side of heaven. It's not a matter of becoming more mature, more spiritual, or wiser, and then all of a sudden the blurry becomes sharp. He even included himself when he said "we." Even for the chief of the apostles, God's actions were sometimes not crystal clear.

But there's a difference between trust and understanding. The apostle who said we look through a blurry window now is the same apostle who wrote that love never fails. Even when Paul didn't understand or perceive clearly everything God was doing, he knew that God's love was the motivation for it all. He knew there is no circumstance or situation in life in which God's love is not constantly flowing to us. God is always working in our behalf because He loves us, regardless of how clearly we see His hand through the fuzzy window of our earth-constrained faith. Paul believed in saying plainly, "God's love never fails."

Cal Ripken was known as major-league baseball's "Iron Man" because of his durability. He played in 2,632 consecutive games over a sixteen-season career. He grew up in a baseball family that depended more on demonstrating love than talking about it:

Growing up, "I love you" wasn't spread around too much in our household. Not that it wasn't meant. I could tell every time my dad told me he loved me without saying it. It's just the way things were then.

That part is different in my family. I want my kids to hear it. I tell them, "I love you no matter what," which means, "Whether you're good or bad, happy or sad. It doesn't matter whatever you are. I love you. Unconditionally. Always." It all goes back to security and telling them you'll always be there for them. Maybe you run the risk of telling them you love them so often that it loses meaning. I'll risk it.[2]

God takes the same approach as Cal Ripken—saying "I love you no matter what" again and again in His Word. Yes, God has demonstrated His love for us in many ways, primarily by sending Christ into the world for us: "God demonstrates his own love for us in this: While we were still sinners, Christ died for us" (Romans 5:8). But through those He moved to write the pages of our Bible, He has told us in plain language that there is nothing—*nothing!*—that can or will ever cause God to stop loving us: "I am convinced that neither death nor life, neither angels nor demons, neither the present nor the future, nor any powers, neither height nor depth, nor anything else in all creation, will be able to separate us from the love of God that is in Christ Jesus our Lord" (Romans 8:38–39).

If issues or circumstances are causing you to question God's love for you, you need only ask whether they fall into the category of "anything else in all creation." Paul named some serious spiritual issues that might attempt to block God's love—like angels or demons—but then to bring it down to where you and I live, he included the "anything else" category.

"Anything else" includes your sins, your weaknesses, your failures, your doubts, your expectations about God—anything at all. None of those things are enough to cause God to say, "I don't love you." "I love you" is God's constant refrain, His constant theme that underlies all His actions toward you and in your behalf.

But there is a tension between the performance mentality (*I'm loved because I'm good*) and God's reality (*I'm loved—period*). And the way we live in that place of tension is by choosing to believe that we are loved. The Bible's way of saying it is that we must "reckon" or "count" it to be true. Just as we reckon, or count, ourselves dead to sin in Christ (see Romans 6:11), so we reckon, or count, ourselves to be loved by God (see Genesis 15:6).

The word *reckon* was actually a mathematical, or accounting, term in the ancient Greek language. It literally meant to add up the numbers, or calculate them, to arrive at the bottom line. And the bottom line is that God's love never fails. That is what we must believe when we are looking through a glass darkly and trying to decide whether or not God loves us.

The day is coming when you and I will look back, as Sallie Bracy did when she received her husband's lost love letter, and realize we were loved all along. When we stand before Christ "face to face" we will "know fully" the love of God (1 Corinthians 13:12). Until that day, we are no less loved. But when the difficult times in our lives make the glass fuzzy and cloudy, and it's hard to "feel" God's love, we count it to be true because of what God has done and what He has said.

Don't let a feeling of being unloved keep you from connecting with God. Where your faith takes you, your feelings will follow. Take God at His word: you are loved today and forever.

Questions for Reflection and Discussion

1. Have you ever doubted the love of someone who was very important to you? What was at the heart of your doubt? How did you overcome it?

2. Because we live in a performance-driven society, it is easy for us to tie our self-worth to the flow of external responses we get from others. In what ways do you do this? Give a personal example. What does love that is based on performance look like?

3. Can you think of any ways in which you have been "performing" to gain God's love and acceptance? Where has your performance gotten you?

4. Discuss this quote in your group: "There is no circumstance or situation in life in which God's love is not constantly flowing to us." How do you know this is true? How has God proven to you that His love never fails?

5. Are there any issues or circumstances in your life currently that are causing you to question God's love for you? What do you need to do to let the love of God embrace and hold you at this time in your life?

Part 6

Living for God,
Living with
God—Forever!

26. Grafted for Abundant Life

SOLLY WAS A SUCCESSFUL MAN—depending on how one defines successful. Because he didn't live in the modern era, we know little of him besides the three books he authored and left behind. But their pages reveal three periods of "success" he enjoyed.

In the dawn of his adult years, he wrote a testosterone-filled book on love, sex, and courtship. Considered bold, even bawdy, for the time in which he lived, his book declared the spiritual and sensual joys of a man and a woman finding love and making plans to spend their lives together. His book on love became a classic and is still read today, in its modern translation, by couples young and old.

In the noon period of his adult life, Solly settled down and turned his pen toward the search for wisdom and success. His second book consisted of observations on the human experience—why some people succeed and some people don't. While he was careful to say that a healthy respect for God is the starting point of wisdom, anyone could read his book and benefit from it. Whether one is motivated by a desire to please God or purely to be successful in life, *Solly's Sayings* was a best seller.

But something happened in the late afternoon of Solly's life. Gone was the unbridled innocence and energy of his youth and the reflective maturity of his middle years. It seemed that the older Solly grew, the more bored he became—or maybe *cynical* is a better word. He seemed to have lost touch with the guiding principle of his middle years, that God is the source of stability and meaning in life. We don't know at what age this mid- to late-life crisis began, but when it was over, in his sunset years, he wrote his third book telling what he had tried and what he had learned.

Reading his third book, it's hard to fault his motivation—he was trying to find the true meaning and purpose of life. Indeed, the path he traveled is the path that many before and after him have taken, with mixed results. In fact, one of his own observations in the third book explains the reason why every human being strives for meaning beyond himself or herself: because there is a sense of eternity in the heart of every person. People think, explore, create, debate, and decide because they have a sense that there is more to life than being born, breathing, and dying.

Solly's third book describes everything he did to search for and find meaning. The vehicle for his pursuits was his vast wealth. Seeing there was no particular purpose in just having money, he used it to pursue a life of meaning and happiness. He acquired women, he developed real estate, he hosted banquets and parties galore, he explored the teachings of all the world's wisest people, he lost sight of eternity and used his wealth to live a "You Only Go Around Once" lifestyle—and found it all lacking.

His third book can be summarized this way:

Premise: Life is meaningless, as far as I can tell.
Practice: I'm going to try everything, just to make sure.
Postscript: The only true meaning I can find is in God.

Solly, of course, is our old friend King Solomon from the Old Testament, the author of (in probable chronological order) the biblical books of Song of Solomon (also known as Song of Songs), Proverbs, and Ecclesiastes. While the conclusion to which he came at the end of his third book is a sound one, it's a shame it took him tens of years and zillions of dollars to reach it.

At the beginning of Ecclesiastes, Solomon said what a lot of people in the modern world say in so many words: "'Meaningless! Meaningless!' says the Teacher. 'Utterly meaningless! Everything is meaningless'" (1:2). But at the end of the book, after describing his fruitless search for meaning down all of life's side streets, he presented a more sober assessment of life:

Now all has been heard;
    here is the conclusion of the matter:
Fear God and keep his commandments,

> for this is the whole duty of man.
> For God will bring every deed into judgment,
>   including every hidden thing,
>   whether it is good or evil.
>
> (12:13–14)

After all of Solomon's excursions into the best the world has to offer, he concludes that "the whole duty of man" is to "fear God and keep his commandments." I want to quickly make two points lest Solomon's conclusion be misunderstood. (Some critics might say that God just wore Solomon out—stifled his every attempt to find a little joy in life until Solomon finally relented: "Okay, God. You win! I'll do whatever You say.")

First, the word *fear* in the Old Testament meant several things: honor, respect, defer to, reverence, venerate, worship—and yes, fear. God is big and powerful and should be feared in the literal sense of the word. But that is only part of what Solomon meant. Overall, "fear God" means to recognize Him as the Creator who desires for His human creations to live lives of satisfaction and meaning. We experience meaning and purpose in life when we acknowledge Him to be the Creator who has infused purpose into His creation.

Second, "keep His commandments" doesn't mean in a pharisaical sense where we live our lives by some arbitrary list of rules while God waits to zap us whenever we fail to measure up. Rather, it's like a high-performance car engine that is designed to run at peak efficiency when the right grade of fuel is put in the tank. Will it run on a lesser grade? Yes, but it will cough and sputter and eventually the engine will be ruined. God simply says, "If you will follow these guidelines for your life, you will find yourself happier and more fulfilled than if you don't."

Do we get punished if we don't follow His commandments? Yes, in the same way that the owner of the high-performance car gets punished when his car breaks down because of using cheap fuel. That is, we bring our punishment on ourselves when we choose to live outside the way God designed us to live.

So, Solomon's "conclusion of the matter"—the conclusion of his decades-long search for meaning and purpose in life—was to conform to the way God designed us to live.

The great British writer and apologist C. S. Lewis wrote,

A car is made to run on [gasoline], and it would not run properly on anything else. Now God designed the human machine to run on himself. He himself is the fuel our spirits were designed to burn, or the food our spirits were designed to feed on. There is no other. That is why it is just no good asking God to make us happy in our own way without bothering about religion. God cannot give us a happiness and peace apart from himself, because it is not there. There is no such thing.[1]

Compare that with an article about actor George Clooney that contained some telling insights:

"Most of the time," [Clooney] says, "I wake up and feel like I've somehow missed something. Sleep is something I actually have to make myself do—I don't look forward to it." The restless brown eyes usually snap open at 4:30 a.m. He wakes up feeling wired, ready to get to work. . . . He's 39, but, he says, "people think I'm 42. It cracks me up." There are bags under his eyes. "You can see the years on my face," he says. "I better slow it down. . . ."

Clooney's feeling seems to be this: We only have so much time on this earth, and I'm going to spend mine working. His legacy, he hopes, will be good movies, though his father isn't sure. "My dad keeps getting on me about not having a family," says George. "He says, 'Name one actor from the 1920's.' Well, you can't—not really. Nobody remembers those guys."[2]

With all due respect to a very talented actor, George Clooney's words might have been a paraphrase of Solomon's in Ecclesiastes. Clooney has decided to devote his life to one of the side streets down which Solomon went looking for meaning in life: work. Solomon's work was real-estate development as he built up Jerusalem to be a city that stood out in the ancient world, while George Clooney has chosen the work of acting and making movies. There's certainly nothing wrong with work, or with making movies. But is that all there is?

C. S. Lewis went further on this point:

The Christian says, "Creatures are not born with desires unless satisfaction for those desires exists. A baby feels hunger: well, there is such a thing as food. A duckling wants to swim: well, there is such a thing as water. Men feel sexual desire: well, there is such a thing as sex. If I find in myself a desire which no experience in this world can satisfy, the most probable explanation is that I was made for another world. If none of my earthly pleasures satisfy it, that does not prove that the universe is a fraud. Probably earthly pleasures were never meant to satisfy it, but only to arouse it, to suggest the real thing. If that is so, I must take care, on the one hand, never to despise, or be unthankful for, these earthly blessings, and on the other, never to mistake them for the something else of which they are only a kind of copy, or echo, or mirage. I must keep alive in myself the desire for my true country, which I shall not find till after death; I must never let it get snowed under or turned aside; I must make it the main object of life to press on to that other country and to help others to do the same."[3]

Every human being, if he or she is honest (at least the ones I have met), feels that desire for something beyond this world—a spiritual connection and sense of completeness that nothing in this world can provide. That desire springs from what Solomon felt in his own heart: "[God] has also set eternity in the hearts of men; yet they cannot fathom what God has done from beginning to end" (3:11).

We know there is something there, something beyond the horizon of this world, but we can't figure it out on our own. That is, we can't find God by our own efforts. It is for this reason that God took the initiative and revealed Himself to us. He has done that through creation and the universe (see Psalm 19:1–6; Romans 1:18–20) and through His Word, the Bible (see 2 Timothy 3:16; 2 Peter 1:20–21).

But the primary revelation of God to man is Himself—God incarnate, who came to earth in the person of Jesus of Nazareth: "The Word became flesh and made his dwelling among us. We have seen his glory, the glory of the One and Only, who came from the Father, full of grace and truth" (John 1:14). And Jesus said plainly what He came to do: to find people who were not connected with God (see Luke 19:10) and introduce them to the abundant life God intended every person to experience (John 10:10).

I use the word *abundant* because that's the word Jesus used in John 10:10: "I have come that they may have life, and have it to the full." And what does *abundant* mean? The Greek word used means "more, excessive, to the full." Here are more synonyms: "over and above, more than is necessary, superadded; superior, extraordinary, surpassing, uncommon."[4] It's the same Greek word the apostle Paul used in Ephesians 3:20: "Now to Him who is able to do immeasurably more than all we ask or imagine, according to his power that is at work within us..."

Would you like to have a life that is "immeasurably more" than all you might ask for or imagine? Well, you can. That's the life God sent Jesus to earth to reveal to you. It's a life full of purpose and meaning, discovered once we reconnect with the God who created us. God had a purpose in creating the earth and all that is in it, and we get to participate in that eternal purpose when we come to know Him through His Son, Jesus Christ.

When the time for Jesus to leave the earth drew near, He began to reveal things to His disciples that they would need to know in His absence (see John 14–16). For instance, how to continue living the life He had modeled for them for three years. That would involve the gift of the Holy Spirit, who would be sent to them shortly (see Acts 2), and the concept of abiding, or remaining, in Him (see John 15:9). Knowing they would have the same question that you just had—"What does it mean to remain in Him?"—Jesus used a beautiful metaphor to illustrate: the vine and the branches (see John 15).

Grapevines and vineyards were such a common part of the landscape of the Bible lands that the disciples would have understood this metaphor immediately. Jesus told the disciples that He was the "true vine" from God (John 15:1). (Heretofore, the nation of Israel had been God's "vine"—Psalm 80:8–10; Isaiah 5:1–7; Ezekiel 19:10–14; Jeremiah 2:21.) God was the owner of the vineyard and the disciples were the branches, and this was the point of the illustration: "Remain in me, and I will remain in you. No branch can bear fruit by itself; it must remain in the vine. Neither can you bear fruit unless you remain in me" (verse 4). We must be grafted into Jesus, the true Vine, to receive His life and be able to bear the kind of fruit that leads to the abundant life we desire.

It was the disciples' purpose (then and now) to bear fruit for God's glory (see verse 8), which would happen only if the disciples remained in Jesus—that is, were faithful to continue in the things that He had taught them (see verse 7; Matthew 28:19–20). Jesus said He had remained in

His Father's love by obeying the Father, and we would remain in Jesus' love by carrying out His teachings (see verse 10).

And then Jesus said an amazing thing. He summarized the purpose of the vine metaphor by saying, "I have told you this so that my joy may be in you and that your joy may be complete" (verse 11). This goes all the way back to Solomon's search for joy and meaning in life hundreds of years before. Solomon said that the real purpose and meaning of life was to "fear God and keep His commandments" (Ecclesiastes 12:13). And then Jesus said the same thing: "I have told you [to obey my commands]...that your joy may be complete."

The purpose is not to obey God's guidelines as an end in and of themselves, but as a means to an end. And the end is joy, purpose, and meaning in life—the abundant life that Jesus came to reveal to humankind.

I'm not sure where the idea got started that life with God is a dour, joyless existence, but it definitely happened. Far too many people today are resistant to a relationship with God because they think it means giving up all joy and happiness in life; that they'll have to start wearing black suits with skinny black ties and carry ten-pound black Bibles around with them wherever they go. Or the ladies will have to wear floor-length dresses, put their hair in buns, and give up their makeup. (If that is your style of dress, I mean no offense. It may be your choice, but it's not required to be a follower of Jesus.)

God wants to connect with you and show you the life He created you to experience—a life of joy, purpose, and ultimate meaning, far beyond any life you've ever dreamed of living. But you'll need to remain (or become a believer) in Jesus.

But that's not an obstacle. I've never known anyone who didn't have more joy after knowing Him than they had before. And so will you.

Questions for Reflection and Discussion

1. Even Christians at times get caught up in the "you only go around once" lifestyle. Do an honest inventory of your life. In what ways would you say you've done this? What has your pursuit of the "full life" produced?

2. Every human being feels the desire for a spiritual connection and sense of completeness that nothing in this world can provide.

How do you see this truth played out in the world? How have you experienced this in your own life?

3. Jesus came to find people who were (and are) separated from God (Luke 19:10) and introduce them to the abundant life He intends for them to experience (John 10:10). Describe what you think Jesus meant by an "abundant" life. In what ways have you experienced this kind of life?

4. What would you say your purpose in life is? How would you summarize it in one sentence? How have you pursued your purpose? What has been the result of that pursuit?

5. What is your understanding of the role of the Holy Spirit in helping believers experience more of the abundant life? How would you describe your relationship with the Holy Spirit today?

27. Resisting Distractions— Refocusing on What Truly Matters

"Coach's" records are legendary:

- Ten NCAA men's basketball championships

- Seven NCAA championships in seven consecutive years (1967–1973)

- Most appearances in the NCAA championship Final Four (16)

- Most consecutive Final Four appearances (9)

- Most Final Four victories (21)

- Most consecutive NCAA men's basketball victories (88 during the 1971–73 seasons)

- Thirty-eight straight victories in NCAA tournament play between 1964 and 1974

- Eight undefeated PAC 8 Conference (now PAC 10) seasons

- All-time winning percentage of .813 over forty years of coaching basketball (high school through college)[1]

- First person to be inducted into the National Basketball Hall of Fame as both a player and a coach[2]

Most coaches, regardless of the sport, would be proud to own any one of those records in their lifetimes. But to hold them all? That's why John Wooden, who retired as the coach of the UCLA Bruins men's basketball team in 1975, is considered one of the greatest coaches of all time.

With that kind of legendary history, one would assume that John Wooden's life was and is all about basketball. But that assumption would be wrong. John Wooden's life is all about people first, basketball second.

For instance, in 1946 Wooden was the men's basketball coach at Indiana State University, and his team won the conference title. They were invited to play in the NAIA (National Association of Intercollegiate Athletics) tournament, but Coach Wooden refused the invitation. Why? Because one of his reserve players, Clarence Walker, was an African American, and there was a ban on black athletes playing in the NAIA tournament. The next year, the NAIA changed the policy and again invited Wooden's team to play, and he accepted—and Clarence Walker became the first black athlete to play in the NAIA tournament.[3] For John Wooden, the focus was on people and justice, not on winning basketball games.

Bill Walton was one of Coach Wooden's best players during the glory days at UCLA and remains his close friend to this day:

> [Coach Wooden's] interest and goal were to make you the best basketball player but first to make you the best person. He would never talk wins and losses but what we needed to succeed in life. Once you were a good human being, you had a chance to be a good player. *He never deviated from that....* He never tried to be your friend. He was your teacher, your coach.... He is a man who truly has principles and ideas.... He didn't teach basketball. He taught life. When you're touched by someone that special, it changes your life.... He stopped coaching UCLA 25 years ago. Now he just coaches the world."[4]

Coach Wooden, still mentoring younger people and former players today at age ninety-eight, is a focused individual. But because it's possible to focus on the wrong things in life, he was also a man with priorities: people first and foremost, personal success a distant second, if at all. And *"he never deviated from that."* He knew that if he produced great players without first producing great young people, all the athletic success in the world wouldn't matter. He established his priorities and stayed focused throughout his life, refusing to let lesser things distract him from his mission.

All of us are called to do what John Wooden has done: decide what is most important and stay focused, refusing to be distracted. Because you're reading this book, you have some level of belief that a relationship with God should be an important part of your life. I join you in that belief. And you and I both know that it is just as easy to get distracted from pursuing intimacy with God as it is to get distracted from anything else. We are distractible beings who live in an age filled with interruptions, temptations, and distractions.

But it is not our age that is to blame. Being distracted from our attention to God and spiritual things is the common lot of humanity. John Donne, the seventeenth-century English poet and preacher, wrote, "I neglect God and his angels for the noise of a fly, for the rattling of a coach, for the whining of a door."[5] John Donne, I fear, has been reading my mail! Who among us has not sat down to read our Bibles or to pray about the day's concerns, or just to spend time in meditative contemplation upon God, only to have our minds pulled away by the slightest sound, sight, or suggestive thought?

Even the silence can be a distraction! We are so used to the "noise pollution" of our age that we have learned to work above it. So, when we do find ourselves in a completely quiet place, we are hardly able to stay focused on the Object of our desires, God Himself. C. S. Lewis must have known the feeling, for it was he who wrote,

> The moment you wake up each morning, all your wishes and hopes for the day rush at you like wild animals. And the first job each morning consists in shoving it all back; in listening to that other voice, taking that other point of view, letting that other, larger, stronger, quieter life come flowing in.[6]

Quieting our minds and hearts before God on a regular basis is absolutely critical to developing intimacy with Him. But I want to suggest that there is something larger that will make the disciplines of spiritual intimacy more consistent for you and for me. And that is deciding, and confirming daily, that following Jesus Christ as Savior and Lord is the top priority in our lives.

Recall the distinction I drew in the life of John Wooden between focus and priorities. If our priorities in life are wrong, then all the focus in the world will be wasted. As Christians, our priority in life should be Jesus Christ...the kingdom of God...loving God with all our hearts, souls, minds, and strength. We can phrase the priority a number of different ways, as does the Bible. But they mean the same thing: as a servant of Christ, my life is completely His.

I don't know of anyone in our modern world who has made Christ the priority of his life any clearer than the late William R. "Bill" Bright, the founder and leader of Campus Crusade for Christ International. Bill Bright married Vonette Zachary in 1946, and together they began to grow in their relationship with Christ. He was a young businessman at the time, but they were becoming increasingly involved in Christian work. And they were growing convicted about what they read in the New Testament—how the apostles referred to themselves and others as "slaves [or servants] of Christ." So they decided to follow what to them seemed to be the precedent set in the New Testament: they decided to formally declare themselves (to God) as slaves of Jesus Christ. Many years later, in a conversation with Pastor Rick Warren, Dr. Bright commented on why he and his wife, as a young Christian couple, wrote out a contract with God:

> One Sunday afternoon (I'll not go into details why), God led us to sign a contract—literally to write out a contract of total surrender of our lives to the Lord Jesus Christ—to become His slave.
>
> And, of course, He is our example, our model—Philippians 2:7 speaks of Him becoming a slave. The creator of a couple hundred billion galaxies became a man, the God-man. Paul refers to himself in Romans 1:1 "a slave of Jesus Christ." We felt the most important thing we could do was to become as slaves of Jesus—signing a contract to that effect laid everything we owned or ever would own on the altar, and we've been slaves now for 50 some years, and I must tell you it's the most liberating thing that's ever happened to me.[7]

It is my understanding that, within twenty-four hours of Bill and Vonette Bright signing away their lives to Christ, Dr. Bright felt compelled by the Lord to begin an organization that would take the gospel onto the college campuses of America—the international organization we now know as Campus Crusade for Christ.

Dr. Bright never held up what he and his wife did as a standard for all Christian believers—to prepare and sign contracts making themselves slaves of Christ (though many Christians have followed their example voluntarily). That was simply the practical expression of their own commitment. And they lived by it the rest of their lives. They did not own a house, property, or cars, and had few personal belongings. They raised their own financial support and lived at the same economic level as all other Campus Crusade married staff. When Dr. Bright won the $1.1 million Templeton Prize for Progress in Religion, he donated the money to fund a new Campus Crusade project focused on prayer and fasting. He even cashed in his modest retirement account to establish a spiritual training center in Russia after the fall of the Soviet Union.

Dr. and Mrs. Bright were living examples of the veracity of Matthew 6:33: "Seek first his kingdom and his righteousness, and all these things will be given to you as well." Christ and His kingdom were the Brights' priority, and that made it easier to focus on the daily disciplines and avoid the daily distractions.

I shared Dr. and Mrs. Bright's story to illustrate the primacy of the first choice that followers of Jesus must make. Having a daily quiet time, free from distractions, is not the first choice. It is one of many choices that become expressions of a single priority in life: to be a faithful servant of Christ by putting Him first in all things.

I love the story of the two sisters Mary and Martha in the gospel of Luke. The sisters lived in Bethany, outside Jerusalem, and Martha extended an invitation to Jesus to share a meal in their home. When they arrived, Mary "sat at the Lord's feet listening to what he said. But Martha was distracted by all the preparations that had to be made" (Luke 10:39–40). When Martha complained to Jesus about Mary's lack of help, Jesus said to her, "Martha, Martha...you are worried and upset about many things, but only one thing is needed. Mary has chosen what is better, and it will not be taken away from her" (verses 41–42).

We can get so busy doing things *for* the Lord that we take our eyes *off* the Lord. Mary had the right priority—availing herself of the opportunity to sit at the feet of Jesus and learn from Him. Perhaps Martha's personality type drove her to focus on preparations rather than on people. We don't fault her for that because we see ourselves in her—at least I do. It's so easy to get distracted!

For most of us, something as pronounced as writing out a contract with

God to become a slave of Christ is not how we think or work. And that's okay. But we do need to arrive at the same place: an inner conviction, evidenced by outward manifestations, that we seek God's kingdom first in our life. There are a number of Scripture passages that speak to different aspects of such a priority: Psalms 1:2; 26:8; 27:4; 84:10; Philippians 3:8, 12–14, and many others.

Each biblical writer expressed in his own words what putting God first meant to him. The writers weren't thinking specifically about it at the time; they were just pouring out what they believed through their pens. By virtue of the preservation of their writings in the pages of Scripture, we are privileged to eavesdrop on their hearts and see what kind of people they were—people who longed for nothing in this life more than they longed to live in the presence of God.

Did they ever get distracted? Of course—they were human beings. But somehow, in the aggregate of their lives, they kept God first in what they did.

We may not be leaving a paper trail of writings as they did by which future generations can judge our hearts. But we are leaving traces of evidence behind every day: our daily calendars, our checkbooks, our journals, our photographs, the impressions and impacts we make on others, our actions for those less fortunate, our records of church attendance and participation in worship and service, the deeds we do when no one is looking, the memories of those who know us well....

The sum total of John Wooden's basketball career is easy to judge: people first, personal achievements second. And there will be a sum total of our lives one day that will tell the story of our priorities and our focuses. The value you and I place on being intimately connected with God will be written in our words and deeds.

Take this opportunity to consider your priorities and where God stands among them. The more you choose to make Him the ultimate focus of your life, the deeper and more intimate your relationship with Him will be.

Questions for Reflection and Discussion

1. If someone were to take a look at your daily calendar, checkbook, or the photos in your wallet, what would he or she say is most important in your life?

2. What would *you* say are the top five priorities in your life? What "distractions" keep you from focusing as much time and attention on your priorities as you would like? Would the person closest to you agree that the five things you listed as your top priorities *truly are* your most important priorities? Explain.

3. What distractions tend to steal your focus when it comes to the disciplines of spiritual intimacy (i.e., Bible reading, meditation, prayer)? What have you learned to do to counteract those distractions?

4. What would you say "putting God first" looks like in life? How easy or difficult is it for you to put God first in your life? Be as honest as you can in your answer. Remember that putting God first is about more than just our actions, it's about how we think as well.

5. Consider your priorities and where God stands among them. Is there any priority that repeatedly pulls you away from your relationship with God? Share it with your group and ask them to pray with you that God will show you what you need to change to put God first in your life.

28. Discover the Power of God's Plan for Your Life

OB'S FATHER STARTED A COMPANY from scratch, moving his young family across the country to set up shop in a facility he rented for a few hundred dollars. He was venturing into unknown territory in terms of his marketing ideas, and many established leaders in his industry were critical of his plan. But he would not be deterred. In the beginning, he even went door-to-door to talk to people, to get their feedback, and to invite them to try the product he was developing. He used what he learned to fine-tune his ideas and package his product in a way that would be attractive to consumers.

Young Bob absorbed this activity and energy as a boy growing up, and as a teenager, when his dad's company had established itself and was growing steadily, he spent time helping out in the office. Although it was unspoken during those years, he knew there was an assumption building that he might someday succeed his father as head of the company. And he wasn't opposed to the idea. It seemed like a natural thing to consider.

But by the time Bob was ready to go off to college, his father had become so successful that he (Bob) was now becoming known as "the son of" his father. When he would introduce himself in certain circles, he would be asked, "Are you related to…?" He understood people's interest and didn't mind the connection. He was proud of what his father had accomplished and was happy for his success. The company's product and unique marketing efforts had resulted in worldwide exposure in circles related to the company's focus, so more and more Bob and his sisters found themselves in that shadow.

After college and graduate school, Bob's path led home. He was offered an official position with the company that he gladly accepted. It was a comfortable transition—the succession plan he had imagined as a teenager seemed to be moving forward, though still in an unofficial capacity.

Yet, after a couple of years spent serving in various capacities, Bob began to feel restless. It took him a while to put his finger on why, but he finally concluded that he had never tested his own abilities the way he had seen his father test and develop his. Things had been so easy for Bob—growing up in the business, being the only son among five children, being expected to follow in his father's footsteps and take over the company. He was the only one who wasn't completely comfortable with that scenario. There were things he needed to learn about himself and his own abilities that he didn't feel he could learn in such a protected environment.

Bob knew he needed to go out on his own but dreaded having that conversation with his father. Thankfully, his father listened and, in short order, understood and gave his blessing and support to his son. Bob left the company and did what his father had done: started a small company that grew steadily from the start. In the years he ran his own company he learned what he needed to know—not about business but about himself. How was he unique? How was he different from his father? What path should he pursue in the future? What was God's plan for his life?

If you are familiar with me at all, you know that I am "Bob"—and happy to be! If you don't know me, a word of explanation will help you understand what you have just read. My father, Dr. Robert H. Schuller, was the founding pastor of the Crystal Cathedral church in Garden Grove, California, and the *Hour of Power* television broadcast now seen around the world. He began the church with a vision of taking the gospel of Christ to the unchurched—those who couldn't find a good reason to give even an hour of their Sunday to hearing about God. And those were the people he talked to as he went door-to-door in Garden Grove when we first moved there.

My father rented a local drive-in movie theater for the first few years, and yes, people came in their cars! He stood on top of the concession stand to preach, and people listened to the message through the movie speakers hanging on the window of their car. And Mom played the organ that they brought from Illinois in a trailer behind our car. (You can see why his vision generated no small number of raised eyebrows in our conservative Reformed denomination!)

But God blessed Dad's vision, and his labor and the church grew. Through the church, television, and his books, my father's name became widely known. And it was for that reason I realized it was time for me to stretch my wings and discover who God had called me to be. I left the staff of the Crystal Cathedral and started a church farther down the California coast—one of the hardest, but most fulfilling, times of my life. I learned to trust God through failure and success and came to understand my own gifts.

The book I wrote prior to this book—*Walking in Your Own Shoes: Discover God's Direction for Your Life*—was motivated by the experience I am describing here. As I say in that book, I realized I could never fill my father's shoes, nor should I have. He founded and led the Crystal Cathedral, not me. It would have been wrong to assume automatically that I would step into his shoes and continue his vision. And I am thankful that he understood and agreed with the need I had to find my own path and discover the shoes God had for me to wear.

And I did. The years I spent growing and pastoring a church of my own taught me things about God, myself, other people, and faith that I could never have learned as deeply in any other place. It was definitely part of God's schooling for me (His plan for me) to discover Him and myself. And I am humbled to say that He blessed my desire to find and fill my own shoes. While I am no longer the pastor of the church I started, it is still growing and going strong, touching many lives for Jesus Christ.

As my father's years increased, it became obvious that it was time for him to transition out of full-time preaching on Sundays and into an "emeritus" role at the Crystal Cathedral. So I was invited by the leaders of the church to become the senior pastor, an invitation I felt was God's will for me to accept. Even though it did not end the way I expected or hoped, I still served in that position for nearly three years, baptizing thousands and preaching to millions. Would the same invitation have been issued had I never gone out on my own to pastor my own church? Perhaps—even probably. But when it was issued, I knew that it was coming not because I was the pastor's son and not because I needed a job, but because God had been faithful to use me in the harvest fields on my own.

And as I complete the work on this book, I see new horizons arising in my life—opportunities to stretch my faith and develop new skills beyond the ministry of the Crystal Cathedral. These new opportunities weren't anticipated a year ago, but their presence now is a testament to the ever-increasing and always-unfolding plan of God in our lives. To grow too satisfied and too content is to run the risk of stagnation and self-indulgence. Thus, my dream is to always be ready to embrace God's plan for my life whenever and however it is revealed.

Finding our own paths in life is a lifelong exercise in faith. I can't repeat in this chapter everything I wrote on the subject in *Walking in Your Own Shoes,* but I do want to acknowledge it within the context of the message of this book—connecting, or reconnecting, with God. I know there are many people who feel "lost." Perhaps they were on what they considered to be their lives' paths but hit an obstacle along the way that caused them to crash. It might have been a divorce, a failed business, an experience of abuse, or a crisis of faith.

Whatever the reason, too many people leave their faith because of the pain involved in losing their way. And that leads to the message of this chapter: there is not always a correlation between the smoothness of the path, or your ability to see the path, and the divine source of the path.

Too often, Christians make the mistake of thinking that the smoother and clearer the path, the greater confidence they can have that the path is from God. Conversely, they feel that if the path gets rocky, or if it disappears in front of them and they can no longer find their way, that God has ceased leading them; that He has not been faithful to give them the desires of their hearts. As a result, they become disappointed in God and grow apathetic in their faith—or disconnect from Him altogether as they wander about looking for the path they think they've lost.

But nothing could be further from the truth! From biblical times to the present, there are countless examples of people whose paths have taken them through the rockiest of terrain without destroying their journeys with God. What they had that perhaps some others do not is this: an understanding that God often takes us purposely through difficult places to deepen our faith.

That's not hard to understand, is it? As parents, we do the same thing with our children—divert their paths in spite of their displeasure at our decision in order to build something into their lives (obedience, responsibility, trust, wisdom) that they couldn't learn otherwise. We know things about their futures that they don't know, because we've lived through the growing-up years ourselves. Thus, we tweak their paths (and let them stew in their discontent if they must) in order that they might learn deeper things than convenience and comfort could ever teach.

The great London preacher C. H. Spurgeon knew this truth: "The anvil, the fire and the hammer are the making of us; we do not get fashioned much by anything else. That heavy hammer falling on us helps to shape us; therefore, let affliction and trouble and trial come."

Because metallurgy was just coming into its own in the Old Testament period, we don't find too many references to the anvil, fire, and hammer. But we do find plenty of references to their cultural equivalent: the potter and his wheel. Through the prophet Isaiah, God said,

> Woe to him who quarrels with his Maker,
> to him who is but a potsherd
>   among the potsherds on the ground.
> Does the clay say to the potter,
>   "What are you making?"
> Does your work say,
>   "He has no hands"?
> (Isaiah 45:9)

And through the prophet Jeremiah:

> This is the word that came to Jeremiah from the LORD: "Go down
> to the potter's house, and there I will give you my message." So
> I went down to the potter's house, and I saw him working at the
> wheel. But the pot he was shaping from the clay was marred in his
> hands; so the potter formed it into another pot, shaping it as seemed
> best to him. Then the word of the LORD came to me: "O house

of Israel, can I not do with you as this potter does?" declares the
LORD. "Like clay in the hand of the potter, so are you in my hand, O
house of Israel."
(Jeremiah 18:1–6)

Someone could take these verses and construct a scenario of a malevo-
lent, evil superpower who played with humans like toys, creating them for
some sadistic purpose, and find reason to reject the whole idea. I won't
take time to tear down such a straw man since the Bible makes it clear
that God is good and loving and has only the best intent for those He has
created. Whatever shaping and fashioning He does in our lives (whatever
adjustments He makes to our lives' paths) is only for our good.

There are three ways to think about the path to which God has called
each of His children, moving from general to specific:

First, there is the ultimate path. Every person who has entered into a
faith relationship with God through Jesus Christ has been called on a
path that leads to the same ultimate destination: being conformed to the
image of Jesus Christ. Here is how Paul said it in Romans 8:29: "Those
God foreknew he also predestined to be conformed to the likeness of his
Son, that he might be the firstborn among many brothers."

Every follower of Jesus Christ will ultimately be like Jesus Christ,
conformed to His likeness. It was God's purpose to call a heaven full of
redeemed, perfected human beings to dwell in His presence for eternity
in the likeness of His own Son. And the marvelous thing about God's call
is that the invitation goes out to everyone: "Jesus stood and said in a loud
voice, 'If anyone is thirsty, let him come to me and drink'" (John 7:37).
"Whoever is thirsty, let him come; and whoever wishes, let him take the
free gift of the water of life" (Revelation 22:17).

Anyone in the world who hears that invitation is welcome to come, to
take the path in life that will lead to being restored to the full image of
Adam and Eve, made new in and made possible through "the last Adam"
(1 Corinthians 15:45), Jesus Christ.

Second, there is the personal path. Romans 8:30 says, "Those [God] predestined, he also called; those he called, he also justified; those he justified, he also glorified." Think of the millions God has called to Himself
throughout history, and how different each of their paths has been. God

isn't going to call you in the twentieth or twenty-first century and ask you to revert to living like those He called in the first century. You don't have to be scared of the path God has for you.

Your personal path is best understood in terms of Psalm 139:13–17:

> You created my inmost being;
>> you knit me together in my mother's womb.
> I praise you because I am fearfully and wonderfully made;
>> your works are wonderful,
>> I know that full well.
> My frame was not hidden from you
>> when I was made in the secret place.
> When I was woven together in the depths of the earth,
>> your eyes saw my unformed body.
> All the days ordained for me
>> were written in your book
>> before one of them came to be.
> How precious to me are your thoughts, O God!
>> How vast is the sum of them!

I choose to believe that is true of me, and true of you. But I choose that belief without laboring under the obligation to explain it or understand it in order to have total confidence in it. If I understood how God is able to "ordain" all my days before they come to pass—then I would be God's equal and have no need of Him. But I don't understand the greatness of God, just as I don't understand the intricate details of how the human body works. But I am grateful for them both and am able to have faith in what I know without stumbling in my path over what I don't.

Third, there is the unpredictable path. Further in Romans 8, Paul mentions "trouble or hardship or persecution or famine or nakedness or danger or sword" (verse 35). We don't need to assume that Paul enjoyed these unforeseen parts of God's path for his life any more than we enjoy the hardships that we experience. But Paul did understand this about the obstacles he found in his path: "We know that in all things God works for the good of those who love him, who have been called according to his purpose" (verse 28).

There's the word *called* again. Part of God's calling includes the unforeseen obstacles in our path. And while we are not told ahead of time what they are, we are told that God causes them to be "for the good" of those who have been called into the path of conformity to the life of Christ.

Where are you in relation to God's path for you today? Perhaps you've never started on that path, or perhaps you started but stumbled along the way and are looking for a reason, a way, to get started again. Please don't measure your path by anyone else's, or by what you thought your path should be. Just trust that the path to which God has called you is the one that leads you where He wants you to go—personally and ultimately.

You will find your path in Christ. If you will tell Him that you want to walk with Him again, or perhaps for the first time, you'll find Him ready to walk your path with you.

Questions for Reflection and Discussion

1. Finding our own path in life is a lifelong exercise in faith. Sometimes life's path gets rough and we lose our faith and disconnect from God. Have you ever had this experience? How long did you stay disconnected from God? What, if anything, caused you to reconnect with Him again?

2. Think about how a potter shapes a lump of clay into a beautiful piece of pottery. Remember the importance of heat used to temper the pottery before it's finished. With those two images in mind, describe yourself as a piece of pottery. How "finished" are you? What has God used to shape and temper you through the years?

3. Read Psalm 139:13–17. What do you learn here about God's plan has for your life? What ideas in this passage do you need to embrace in your life right now? What difference will doing so make as you walk through this part of your life?

4. Even as I reflect on the content of this chapter, which was written months ago, and as I write these questions, I am amazed at the way God works in life. In 2008, God unexpectedly and radically changed the direction of my life. Even now I am walking the "unpredictable path" of God's plan for my life. So if that is where *you* are today, believe me—I understand.

    What "unpredictable path" is God taking you on right now?

What is He teaching you about yourself and His plan for your life through this life experience? Who or what is God using to help you get through this experience?

5. God promises to use the unforeseen obstacles in our paths "for good" by using them to conform us to the image of Jesus Christ. Where are you in relation to God's path for you today? Where in your life do you see more of Christ's image in you because of what you are experiencing?

29. Living a Fruitful Life

THE LAST GREAT BONANZA IN the history of North America occurred in the late nineteenth century when gold was discovered along the Klondike River near Dawson City, Yukon, Canada. Thousands of men and women from all over the continent poured into the Yukon territory and labored in freezing winters to extract the precious metal from the ground. Yes, gold was found—more than twelve million ounces.[1] But at an incredible price. The work was brutal, the conditions miserable, the weather unrelenting, and only a few actually struck it rich.

But there's another bonanza brewing in North America, and this time those getting rich are doing nothing harder than walking to their mailboxes to pick up huge checks. (There is the labor involved in meeting with lawyers and financial planners to figure out what to do with all the newfound money, but so far no one is complaining about that.)

The new bonanza is happening in an area of Montana, North Dakota, and Saskatchewan, Canada, about the size of West Virginia—something called the Bakken Formation, home to an estimated 4.3 billion barrels of recoverable oil. Farmers in the region who have been scratching a living out of the hard-packed soil for decades have suddenly become millionaires by selling the drilling rights to oil companies. They've been living on top of untapped wealth for years without realizing it.

Actually, geologists discovered oil in the area as far back as 1951, but the price of oil was so low they couldn't afford to drill for it. But when oil surged past $100 per barrel, recovering the oil in the Bakken Formation suddenly became profitable. As long as the market price of oil per barrel stays above $75, the drilling will continue. And the farmers will continue making the trip to the mailbox to pick up their checks.

Bruce Gjovig of the University of North Dakota's Center for Innovation calculates that two new millionaires were being created daily in September 2008. In August 2008, eighty rigs were drilling in western North Dakota alone, a record for that state. But some property owners aren't happy. They sold off the mineral rights to their property (the rights to what lies beneath the surface) in hard times for pennies per acre, rights that are now worth up to $1,500 per acre. Besides losing the mineral rights income, they lose the oil royalties—income that will amount to millions of dollars.[2]

For those who have struck it rich, only one thing is necessary to enjoy the newfound wealth: cooperation with the companies that can provide it.

It's not often that we experience windfall profits in life. We are used to working hard for everything we have, and rightfully so. God told Adam, after he lost access to the beautiful Garden of Eden, that life would be difficult:

> Because you listened to your wife and ate from the tree about
> which I commanded you, "You must not eat of it,"
>> Cursed is the ground because of you;
>>> through painful toil you will eat of it
>>> all the days of your life.
>> It will produce thorns and thistles for you,
>>> and you will eat the plants of the field.
>> By the sweat of your brow
>>> you will eat your food
>> until you return to the ground,
>>> since from it you were taken;
>> for dust you are
>>> and to dust you will return.
>
> (Genesis 3:17–19)

Whether we are farmers like the people in North Dakota and Montana, who know the reality of battling the "thorns and thistles... by the sweat of [their] brow" or not, all of us know the implications of God's words to Adam. While there are some exceptions, the rule for 99 percent of the human race is that we have to work for what we get. Every day we rise and face the same challenge: we labor for what we have. It's hard to imagine what it must be like for those who are sitting back and becoming millionaires without doing anything except saying yes to a gift of unimagined wealth.

Maybe that's why it's hard for some followers of Jesus to grasp the idea of the ministry of the Holy Spirit in their lives. We're helped somewhat by working through the concept of grace when we come to believe in Christ. Receiving forgiveness of our sins and the promise of eternal life *freely by grace* is hard to comprehend, we're so used to working for what we get. Grace is often explained with the acronym "God's Riches At Christ's Expense," and that's a fair definition. Grace is free to us because Christ paid the price by His death on the cross. As those guilty of sin, we could not pay our own debt; we needed a sinless person to die in our place, and that's what Christ did. He paid the price so God could freely grant us the gifts of forgiveness and eternal life (see Ephesians 2:8–9).

It takes most of our spiritual pilgrimage with Christ to separate the work we do in the world to earn our living from the free gift of salvation for which we are asked to do nothing except believe and receive. It's the ultimate way in which the kingdom of God is different from the kingdom of this world.

After getting the free gift of salvation (mostly) settled in our minds, we discover that the Christian life is a wholly different kind of life than we were used to living. Before meeting Jesus, we knew we were supposed to be nice, patient, kind, helpful, and loving in our relationships with others. But now we are given a new model for life—the sinless person of Jesus. And as hard as we try, we find ourselves unable to be as spiritually consistent as He was. In fact, we get frustrated trying and failing.

And then we learn that God has provided a second gift. Not only were we unable to save ourselves, we are unable to live for Christ by ourselves. As is often said, "The Christian life is not hard—it's impossible!" The gift of the Holy Spirit is the second gift God has provided in order that we might live a kingdom life, a life that pleases God, a life that mirrors the life of Jesus himself.

Salvation is a gift: "The wages of sin is death, but the gift of God is eternal life in Christ Jesus our Lord" (Romans 6:23).

And the Holy Spirit is a gift: "Repent and be baptized, every one of you, in the name of Jesus Christ for the forgiveness of your sins. And you will receive the gift of the Holy Spirit" (Acts 2:38).

Jesus had promised the disciples that the Father would send the Holy Spirit after He (Jesus) left them to return to the Father (see John 14:16ff.; 16:5–16). The purpose of the Spirit would be to manifest the life of Christ and the mind of Christ through each person who received the gift of the Spirit through faith in Christ; to be a comforter, counselor, and guide for the disciples in the absence of Jesus.

In fact, Jesus said it was better for the disciples that He go away and that the Spirit should come (see John 16:7). That is the whole basis for Jesus' telling the disciples that they would do greater works in the world than He did (see John 14:12). When Jesus was on the earth physically He could be in only one place at one time; His ministry was limited to one person or group at a time. But with Him living inside each disciple through the presence of the Holy Spirit, He could minister to the whole world through His followers. As the church grew, Jesus' presence on earth grew as well. Through His followers, Jesus was able to cover the earth with His teaching and ministry—that is, do "greater things" through them than He did alone.

When it came to explaining this idea to the early church—the reality of the Holy Spirit living in the life of every Christian—the apostle Paul talked about it in terms of spiritual gifts (the works of Jesus Christ) and spiritual fruit (the character of Jesus Christ). Every Christian was to be empowered by the Holy Spirit to do certain works that Jesus did when He was on earth, and to display a kind of godliness that would set His followers apart from the rest of the world: "By this all men will know that you are my disciples, if you love one another" (John 13:35).

Both our "doing" for Christ (spiritual gifts) and our "being" like Christ (spiritual fruit) are totally beyond our human capacity. There is nothing we can do to acquire spiritual gifts or spiritual fruit on our own. If we are to manifest them, it will be only because we have said yes to the Spirit in our lives.

The apostles Paul and Peter mention spiritual gifts in four different places in the New Testament: Romans 12; 1 Corinthians 12; Ephesians 4; and 1 Peter 4. And in each of those four places, the lists of the gifts mentioned are different. The fact that there is not one set list of spiritual gifts that is duplicated whenever gifts are mentioned leads me to believe that there is no set list—that the gifts of the Holy Spirit are the manifestations of the work Jesus chooses to do through His followers in a given circumstance.

It's easy to see why Paul and Peter gave names to the gifts: teaching, mercy, administration, healing, prophecy, and so on—it helps to name them when discussing various tasks within the church. But just as it would be impossible to develop a definitive list of the works Jesus did ("Here are the seventeen works Jesus did while on earth. . . ."), neither should we attempt to limit the works of Jesus through His followers to a certain list. Those works would certainly include the gifts Paul and Peter mentioned, but they could also include others that were not mentioned.

For example, the apostle Barnabas was so known for his ability to encourage other believers that he was nicknamed "Son of Encouragement" (Acts 4:36). Encouragement is not mentioned as a spiritual gift in the New Testament, yet we would be safe in attributing Barnabas's ministry in Christ to Him.

The fruit of the Holy Spirit is mentioned in only one passage in the New Testament: Galatians 5:22–23. The nine manifestations (character qualities) of the Spirit listed are love, joy, peace, patience, kindness, goodness, faithfulness, gentleness, and self-control. But as with the gifts of the Spirit, these nine are not the only character qualities of Jesus Christ that we ought to see in the lives of His followers.

Paul listed these nine qualities in order to contrast them with "acts of the sinful nature" manifested in the lives of those who are not indwelt by the Spirit: sexual immorality, impurity, hatred, selfish ambition, and others (see Galatians 5:19–21). That list is certainly not exhaustive, nor should we think the list of the fruit of the Spirit is exhaustive.

The point of both the gifts of the Spirit and the fruit of the Spirit is to manifest the living Lord, Jesus Christ, in and through the life of every Christian. And because the gifts and the fruit are Spirit-born, they cannot be generated by human effort. To manifest Christ's life through ours, we simply have to say yes to the Spirit's desire to glorify Christ in our lives. Paul calls this being "filled with the Holy Spirit," contrasting it with being filled with wine (Ephesians 5:18).

In other words, we will display the character of whatever we are filled with: wine manifests itself in drunkenness and lack of self-control, and the Holy Spirit manifests Himself through the works and character of Jesus Christ.

I have known people who wanted to give up on the Christian life because they couldn't be loving like Jesus, joyful like Jesus, peaceful like

Jesus, or *anything* like Jesus. And they were right! We can't be like Jesus in our own strength or by our own efforts. The life of Christ in us is a gift that we receive, a life that we yield to, not something we produce on our own. The apostle Paul put it this way: "I have been crucified with Christ and I no longer live, but Christ lives in me. The life I live in the body, I live by faith in the Son of God, who loved me and gave himself for me" (Galatians 2:20).

I read about a family who paid a visit to the Grand Coulee Dam in Washington State, the largest electric producer in the United States and fourth largest in the world.[3] But when they entered the visitors' center to look around, they discovered it was dark—all the lights in the center were off and none of the displays were illuminated. They suddenly realized that there was no power in the visitors' center. Just as we might experience a power outage in our home on occasion, the visitors' center at the nation's biggest source of electric power was in a power-out situation.[4]

It might seem odd for there to be no power available just a few hundred feet from where massive amounts of power are being generated, but that was the case. Just so, some Christians who have been given the gift of the Holy Spirit are living in a powerless fashion because they have not learned to yield to the Spirit and allow Him to reproduce the life of Christ through them. We can short-circuit the power of the Spirit by grieving (see Ephesians 4:30) or quenching (see 1 Thessalonians 5:19) the Spirit. He doesn't leave us, but He doesn't fight for control either. He waits until we reach a point of despair with our own abilities and ask Him to fill us again.

If you have despaired of ever being able to live the Christian life, gaining victory over sin and experiencing the love, joy, peace, patience, kindness, goodness, faithfulness, gentleness, and self-control that you desire, I have good news! You can't achieve these realities on your own, but the Holy Spirit can produce them in and through you.

If you would like the Holy Spirit to fill your heart and mind with the presence of Jesus, just ask Him to do so. If there is anything in your life that you know is contrary to God's will for you, confess it to Him and receive His forgiveness (see 1 John 1:9). Then ask the Holy Spirit to take control of your life and manifest His gifts and fruit through you. Should you stumble, continue to ask God's forgiveness and ask the Spirit to fill you again. Because it is God's will, those are prayers that will always be answered.

The power of the Spirit is the greatest untapped spiritual bonanza in Christendom. And all it takes to live a life of spiritual wealth is to say yes!

Questions for Reflection and Discussion

1. Tell about a time you received something of value that either you didn't work for or you didn't deserve.

2. Ephesians 2:8–9 reminds us that forgiveness and eternal life can't be earned; they are God's gift to us. Did you find God's grace easy or difficult to understand and accept? Explain. How do people who find it difficult to accept grace often live?

3. God also gives all Christians the gift of the Spirit to be their Comforter, Counselor, and Guide. When has the Holy Spirit provided comfort, counsel, or guidance in your life? Give one or two examples.

4. What is the difference between a spiritual gift and spiritual fruit? What spiritual gift(s) have you seen manifested in your life? What evidence of spiritual fruit is there in your life? Remember, human effort cannot produce either of these in our lives.

5. How do we as Christians short-circuit the power of the Holy Spirit in our lives? Give some specific examples of ways in which we do this. What does it take to get the Spirit flowing freely in our life again?

30. Power to Live Forever

UGANDAN ANGLICAN BISHOP FESTO KIVEN-GERE was known as the "Billy Graham of Africa" before leukemia took his life in 1988. When he spoke out against the brutal dictator Idi Amin, he had to flee to neighboring Rwanda in 1973—but not before witnessing an event that same year that helped spark a spiritual revival in his country. In his own words:

February 10 began as a sad day for us in Kabale. People were commanded to come to the stadium and witness the execution. Death permeated the atmosphere. A silent crowd of about three thousand was there to watch.

I had permission from the authorities to speak to the men before they died, and two of my fellow ministers were with me.

They brought the men in a truck and unloaded them. They were handcuffed, and their feet were chained. The firing squad stood at attention. As we walked into the center of the stadium, I was wondering what to say. How do you give the gospel to doomed men who are probably seething with rage?

We approached them from behind, and as they turned to look at us, what a sight! Their faces were all alight with an unmistakable glow and radiance. Before we could say anything, one of them burst out:

"Bishop, thank you for coming! I wanted to tell you. The day I was arrested, in my prison cell, I asked the Lord Jesus to come into my heart. He came in and forgave me all my sins! Heaven is now open, and there is nothing between me and my God! Please tell my wife and children that I am going to be with Jesus. Ask them to accept him into their lives as I did."

The other two men told similar stories, excitedly raising their hands which rattled their handcuffs.

I felt that what I needed to do was to talk to the soldiers, not to the condemned. So I translated what the men had said into a language the soldiers understood. The military men were standing there with guns cocked and bewilderment on their faces. They were so dumbfounded that they forgot to put the hoods over the men's faces!

The three faced the firing squad standing close together. They looked toward the people and began to wave, handcuffs and all. The people waved back. Then shots were fired, and the three were with Jesus.

We stood in front of them, our own hearts throbbing with joy, mingled with tears. It was a day never to be forgotten. Though dead, the men spoke loudly to all of Kigezi District and beyond, so that there was an upsurge of life in Christ, which challenges death and defeats it.

The next Sunday, I was preaching to a huge crowd in the home town of one of the executed men. Again, the feel of death was over the congregation. But when I gave them the testimony of their man, and how he died, there erupted a great song of praise to Jesus! Many turned to the Lord there.[1]

We come to the final chapter in this book about leaning into God, and there is no more important and appropriate subject to talk about than death. As someone has said, "The last time I looked, the statistics on death were exactly 100 percent. Everybody dies." This is not a subject for the poor, the downtrodden, the unfortunate, or the mistreated. No, death is the Great Leveler in all of life, something that makes equals of us all. Human beings are equal in the sight of God and in the sight of death.

So many jokes have been made about death that we lose sight of death itself: "When you die you can either make an ash of yourself (cremation) or a fuel of yourself (burial)." "When was the last time you saw a U-Haul trailer behind a hearse?" Woody Allen has apparently thought a lot about death: "I don't want to achieve immortality through my work; I want to achieve immortality through not dying." "It's not that I'm afraid to die. I just don't want to be there when it happens." "Death is one of the few things that can be done as easily as lying down."

You can almost judge how serious a particular issue is in modern cultures by how many jokes are told about it: death, marriage, government, sex, and others. When we know something is important but aren't quite sure what to say or believe about it, we try to ease the tension with a joke. I guess the thought is that if we distract ourselves with laughter, the serious issue will go away, at least temporarily.

But death isn't going away. In fact, you and I are closer to it today than we were yesterday; closer this afternoon or evening than we were this morning. I say that not to be morbid, but to be honest. And to be biblical. The Bible does not avoid the subject of death. Indeed, it addresses it head-on: "Man is destined to die once, and after that to face judgment" (Hebrews 9:27).

That verse contains both of the realities about death that concern people. First, the fact of death itself: *Will it be sudden or drawn out? Untimely or when I am old? Painful or easy? Will I be missed or forgotten?* And second, the after-death questions: *Is there life after death? Is there a heaven and a hell? Can I know what my destiny will be? Will I face judgment?*

These are real questions to which the average person has given no small amount of thought—even people with religious beliefs find themselves not sure about the after-death facts of life. When singer-songwriter Roseanne Cash lost both her parents, Johnny and June Carter Cash, in 2003, she "was just feeling bitter." But her uncertainty led her to a ministerial friend at a mainline church in New York City:

> I went in and said, "I just want to know where they are." And
> he touched my hand and said, "I don't know." It was a beautiful
> moment, and it changed everything. If he had said, "Oh, honey,
> they're in heaven with the angels," I would have hated that. But
> he respected me enough to give me permission to explore my own
> doubts.[2]

With all due respect to Ms. Cash, the minister she consulted, and the memory of her believing-in-Christ parents, I'm not sure that "I don't know" is the most hopeful answer one might give to questions about life after death. It certainly is not the biblical answer. The apostle Paul stated succinctly that, for those whose faith is in Christ, "to be away from the body [is to be] at home with the Lord" (2 Corinthians 5:8).

Compare "I don't know" with the approach Prime Minister Winston Churchill took to his own funeral. Not surprisingly, he planned it well ahead of time and to a "T." As an Anglican, he had his funeral conducted in the massive St. Paul's Cathedral in London, using the eloquent Anglican funeral liturgy. When the funeral service came to a close with the benediction, Churchill had specified that a bugler, positioned high in the dome of St. Paul's, should play "Taps," the universally recognized signal that the day is over. But then Churchill surprised everyone by having a second bugler, on the opposite side of the dome, burst into "Reveille," played in British military camps as the signal to rise for a new day: "It's time to get up. It's time to get up. It's time to get up in the morning."

Churchill's funeral service was his way of saying that "Taps" was not to be the last word for him or for those whose faith is in Christ. A new day of resurrection from the dead—a glorious "reveille"—is yet to come.[3]

That's a realistic approach to death—the ability to acknowledge its approach, to plan one's own funeral with great expectation, and to go to the grave with utter confidence that death is a transitional, not a terminal, experience.

The beloved German pastor Dietrich Bonhoeffer, who was hanged by the Nazis for his subversive opposition to Adolf Hitler, approached his own death with a similar confidence:

> Through the half-open door in one room of the huts I saw Pastor Bonhoeffer, before taking off his prison garb, kneeling on the floor praying fervently to his God. I was most deeply moved by the way this lovable man prayed, so devout and so certain that God heard his prayer. At the place of execution, he again said a short prayer and then climbed the steps to the gallows, brave and composed. His death ensued after a few seconds. In almost fifty years that I worked as a doctor, I have hardly ever seen a man die so entirely submissive to the will of God.[4]

From whence comes that kind of confidence? It comes from

conviction—conviction that the resurrection of Jesus Christ from the dead in Jerusalem, around AD 30–33, was a time-and-space event that gives the average person reason to believe that death is *not final*! That death is a *defeated foe*! That death is a portal from temporal life to *eternal life*!

A study by the Christian researcher George Barna in October 2007 revealed that 83 percent of mainline Protestants in America, 95 percent of non-mainline Protestants, and 82 percent of Catholics embrace what the Bible says about Christ's resurrection as being literally true.[5] That leaves a good number of people in each of those Christian communities who don't believe that Christ was literally raised from the dead. And yet the apostle Paul said that the resurrection of Christ is the linchpin of the faith! Remove the resurrection of Christ, and the entire edifice comes tumbling down.

Here's what Paul said in 1 Corinthians 15:14–19, in the contemporary translation called *The Message*, which puts Paul's words into remarkable focus:

> Face it—if there's no resurrection for Christ, everything we've told you is smoke and mirrors, and everything you've staked your life on is smoke and mirrors. Not only that, but we would be guilty of telling a string of barefaced lies about God, all these affidavits we passed on to you verifying that God raised up Christ—sheer fabrications, if there's no resurrection.
>
> If corpses can't be raised, then Christ wasn't, because he was indeed dead. And if Christ wasn't raised, then all you're doing is wandering about in the dark, as lost as ever. It's even worse for those who died hoping in Christ and resurrection, because they're already in their graves. If all we get out of Christ is a little inspiration for a few short years, we're a pretty sorry lot.

You may want to read those words again—they explain why the resurrection of Christ is the central validating act of Christianity and the key to life after death. Notice what Paul says:

1. If Christ was not literally raised from the dead, Christianity is "smoke and mirrors."

2. If Christ was not literally raised from the dead, Paul and the apostles were all liars.

3. If Christ was not literally raised from the dead, those who called themselves Christians were still lost, guilty of unforgiven sins.

4. If Christ was not literally raised from the dead, those who died hoping to be raised from the dead would never come out of their graves.

5. If Christ was not literally raised from the dead, then there was nothing to Christ's life except an inspiring three years of religious preaching.

6. If Christ was not literally raised from the dead, Christians are a "sorry lot"—duped, deceived, and hopeless.

Given what Paul says about the importance of the Resurrection, I wonder about the motivation of those who attend Christian churches without belief in the Resurrection. Perhaps they are there for uplifting music and messages from the pulpit. But they can't be there for the central theme of Christianity, that Jesus Christ has conquered the grave and proved that resurrection and reunion with God unto eternal life is a possibility for all who put their faith in Him.

Without the resurrection of Christ, there is no resurrection for Christ's followers. And without the hope of the resurrection unto eternal life, there is no hope in this life. Having that message restated and reconfirmed week after week is the message of hope that all who face death need. It is the reality of Christ's resurrection that makes the reality of our own resurrection a valid focus and confident hope.

But consider what is true if Christ was resurrected (evidence for which Paul presents in 1 Corinthians 15:1–8): Christianity is true, the apostles are trustworthy spiritual guides, our sins are forgiven, the dead in Christ will come out of their graves, and the last two thousand years of expansion of the Christian church has been a movement of truth and integrity.

It was Jesus' own words about overcoming death that His resurrection validated, and which give hope to all who will face death. He spoke those words when His friend Lazarus died in the village of Bethany on the outskirts of Jerusalem (see John 11:1–44). Jesus was some distance from Bethany when He received word that Lazarus was sick, but He deliberately stayed where He was for two more days (see verse 6). When He did finally arrive, Lazarus had been dead for four days, and the deceased's sister Martha was not happy that Jesus had delayed His arrival: "'Lord,' Martha said to Jesus, 'if you had been here, my brother would not have died'" (verse 21).

Martha, like many today, was focused on death—doing everything possible to keep a person alive. But Jesus was focused on life! And He delayed His arrival in order to show Lazarus's friends and family that eternal life trumps death every time. Jesus called forth Lazarus out of the tomb and ordered that his grave clothes be stripped away. He raised Lazarus from the dead in order to prove that death is not the end of life—the same message He later reinforced by His own resurrection.

And He said to Martha the words that every person who fears death, or wonders about death and life thereafter, needs to hear: "I am the resurrection and the life. He who believes in me will live, even though he dies; and whoever lives and believes in me will never die. *Do you believe this?*" (verses 25–26, italics added). And Martha answered, "Yes, Lord . . . I believe that you are the Christ, the Son of God, who was to come into the world" (verse 27).

That's what Martha believed, but the question is, Do *you* believe this? If you do, then you have no reason to fear, or wonder about, death. For death is not really the end of you. Jesus said in John 17:3 that eternal life is knowing God the Father and Jesus the Son. If you know God personally, you already have eternal life—now, while you are living on earth. So when you die physically, your eternal life continues into eternity. Your reborn spirit simply slips out of your body and goes to heaven to await the consummation of God's work here on earth and the resurrection of your body when Christ returns.

Death is simply a transition from eternal life on earth to eternal life in heaven. And it is offered to all who place their faith in the One who conquered death in order to "free those who all their lives were held in slavery by their fear of death" (Hebrews 2:15). This beautiful imagery by Henry Van Dyke is a perfect picture of what it means to leave one realm and enter another at the same time:

> I am standing at the seashore. A ship at my side spreads her
> white sails to the morning breeze and starts for the blue ocean.
> I stand and watch her until, at length, she hangs like a speck of
> white cloud, just where the sea and sky come to mingle with each

other....And just at the moment when someone at my side says: "There, she is gone!" there are other eyes watching her coming, and other voices ready to take up the glad shout: "Here she comes!" And that is dying.[6]

If death—that of a loved one or the contemplation of your own—has caused you to question God's love, I beg you to take the words of Jesus to heart. If you will connect with Him on earth, you will remain connected with Him for eternity. In Jesus you have the power to live forever with Him!

I pray that this book has strengthened your connection with God, both now and as you anticipate eternity. Nothing can separate you from God's love in Christ. May that truth be your daily experience as you live for Him and long to see Him face-to-face.

Questions for Reflection and Discussion

1. Death is not an easy subject for us to talk about. But as Christians we don't have to fear the subject of death. What questions about death have you wrestled with from time to time?

2. When have you come face-to-face with the reality of death? How did you deal with it?

3. Has the death of a loved one or the contemplation of your own ever caused you to question God's love? How did you deal with it?

4. What difference does knowing that Jesus Christ conquered death through His own resurrection and reunion with God in heaven make in your life? Try to explain it in practical terms.

5. How has this book encouraged you to lean into God rather than away from Him? Mention one or two life-changing ideas you will take away from reading and discussing this book.

NOTES

Introduction

1. http://www.barna.org/FlexPage.aspx?Page=Topic&TopicID=2 and http://www.barna.org/FlexPage.aspx?Page=Topic&TopicID=10

2. Cathy Lynn Grossman, "Survey: More Have Dropped Dogma for Spirituality in U.S.," USAToday.com, June 23, 2008, http://www.usatoday.com/news/religion/2008-06-23-pew-religions_n.htm.

3. See my books *Possibility Living* (coauthored with Douglas Di Siena) (San Francisco: HarperSanFrancisco, 2000), 114–18; *Getting Through What You're Going Through* (Nashville: Nelson Books, 1986), ix–xviii, 89–92; and *Power to Grow Beyond Yourself* (Grand Rapids, MI: Revell, 1987), 141–59.

1: Reconnecting When Disconnected by Guilt

1. Details of Martin Luther's life were summarized from the article by James S. Kittelson titled "The Accidental Revolutionary," in *Christian History*, April 1992.

2. Edward K. Rowell and *Leadership*, eds., *1001 Quotes, Illustrations and Humorous Stories for Preachers, Teachers and Writers* (Grand Rapids, MI: Baker, 1996, 1997), 72.

3. Anonymous. See Mark Water, *The New Encyclopedia of Christian Quotations* (Grand Rapids, MI: Baker, 2000), 219.

4. Roy B. Zuck, *The Speaker's Quote Book* (Grand Rapids, MI: Kregel, 1997), 182.

5. Rowell, *1001 Quotes*, 215.

6. Julia H. Johnson, "Grace Greater Than Our Sin," © 1938 Hope Publishing Co., owner.

7. Leonard Jones, "Not Guilty," ©1998 EagleStar Productions, a division of MorningStar Fellowship Church (www.MorningStarMinistries.org). Used by permission.

3: Finding Forgiveness After Fits of Rebellion

1. Ronald P. Jensen and Gina Page, *Spiritual Growth: A Workbook for Group Study* (Costa Mesa, CA: R & G Publishing, 1997).

4: Accepting Mercy When Weighed Down by Regrets

1. Summarized from wikipedia.com, s.v. "Mickey Mantle"; and Mickey Mantle with Jill Lieber, "Time in a Bottle," *Sports Illustrated*, April 18, 1994.

2. John Ayto, *Dictionary of Word Origins—The Histories of More Than 8,000 English-Language Words* (New York: Arcade Publishing, 1990), 437.

5: Finding Freedom When Isolated Through Humiliation

1. Audrey Hector, "Sexual Abuse of Children," Christian Answers Network Web site (Gilbert, AZ: Eden Communications, 1996), URL: http://www.christiananswers.net/q-eden/childsexual abuse.html; italics added.

2. As repeated weekly on his radio program *A Prairie Home Companion* in the commercial for "Beebopareebop Rhubarb Pie."

3. From Evelin Linder's article "Humiliation and Dignity: Regional Conflicts in the Global Village" in Intervention International's *Journal of Mental Health, Psychosocial Work and Counseling in Areas of Armed Conflict*, January 2003. (See http://www.interventionjournal.com/index4.html; cited at http://www.beyondintractability.org/essay/Humiliation/.)

4. "Boy, 12, Commits Suicide Before Beginning School," *Chicago Tribune*, August 27, 1996, sec. 1.

6: Tapping into Faith When Debilitated by Fear

1. See http://phobialist.com/index.html.

2. Both from *New Scientist*, March 6, 1999. Cited in *Perfect Illustrations*, compiled by the editors of *Preaching Today* (Wheaton, IL: Tyndale House, 2002), 94.

3. Paul Martin, *The Sickening Mind* (New York: HarperCollins, 1997), 3–4. Cited in *More Perfect Illustrations*, compiled by the editors of *Preaching Today* (Wheaton, IL: Tyndale House, 2003), 102–3.

7: Plugging into Renewed Confidence When Crushed by Disappointment

1. Juliette Cunliffe, *The Encyclopedia of Dog Breeds* (Bath, UK: Paragon Publishing, 2002), 78–79.

2. Craig Brian Larson and *Leadership Journal, 750 Engaging Illustrations for Preachers, Teachers, & Writers* (Grand Rapids: Baker Books, 2002), 426.

3. See *The NIV Study Bible* (Grand Rapids, MI: Zondervan, 1985), note on Isaiah 40:31.

8: Claiming Courage When Derailed by Anxiety

1. Lucinda Bassett, *From Panic to Power: Proven Techniques to Calm Your Anxieties, Conquer Your Fears, and Put You in Control of Your Life* (New York: HarperCollins, 1995).

2. Lucinda Bassett's story is summarized from my interview with her on the *Hour of Power* television program, January 11, 2004, and from her Web site: http://www.stresscenter.com.

3. Haddon Robinson, "The Disciple's Prayer," *Preaching Today*, no. 117.

9: Finding Direction When Lost and Confused

1. See various online resources on Robert Robinson and the hymn discussed, such as STEM Publishing (http://www.stempublishing.com/hymns/biographies/robinson.html), Glimpses of Christian History (http://chi.gospelcom.net/DAILYF/2003/06/daily-06-09-2003.shtml), and Wikipedia, s.v. "Come Thou Fount of Every Blessing" (http://en.wikipedia.org/wiki/Come_Thou_Fount_of_Every_ Blessing).

2. See http://www.usatoday.com/news/nation/2007-09-03-hikers_N.htm.

3. W. E. Vine, Merrill F. Unger, and William White, Jr., *Vine's Complete Expository Dictionary of Old and New Testament Words* (Nashville: Thomas Nelson Publishers, 1996), p. 525.

10: Exercising Blind Belief When Weakened by Trials

1. Rusty Dornin, "Blind Iraq War Vets Learn to Ski" (and accompanying video), at CNN.com (http://www.cnn.com/2008/US/02/18/blind.veterans/index.html#cnnSTCText), February 18, 2008; all italics added.

2. Wikipedia, http://en.wikipedia.org/wiki/Leap_of_faith.

3. Copyrighted 1965, 1968 by Campus Crusade for Christ, New Life Publications. New Life Publications, P.O. Box 593684, Orlando, FL 32859.

11: Finding Wholeness Through Prayer When Debilitated by Brokenness

1. http://www.tcpalm.com/news/2008/jun/23/good-you-tracey-bailey/; http://www.aaeteachers .org/bailey.shtml; Tracey Bailey, "Lesson of a Lifetime," *Guideposts*, April 1997.

2. Bill Hybels, *Too Busy Not to Pray* (Downers Grove, IL: InterVarsity Press, 1988), 74.

3. Oswald Chambers, *My Utmost for His Highest: An Updated Version in Today's Language*, ed. James Reimann (Grand Rapids, MI: Discovery House, 1992), reading for August 6.

4. Lorraine Kisly, *Christian Teachings on the Practice of Prayer: From the Early Church to the Present* (Boston: New Seeds, 2006), 62–63.

5. Harry Verploegh, ed., *3000 Quotations from the Writings of George MacDonald* (Grand Rapids, MI: Revell, 1996), 260.

6. C. S. Lewis, ed., *George MacDonald: 365 Readings* (New York: Collier Books, 1947), 33.

7. Thomas Watson, "The English Puritan," cited in Kisly, *Christian Teachings*, 112.

12: Receiving Spiritual Health Through Praise When Disabled by Dis-ease

1. Taken from http://www.outreachofhope.org, http://www.davedravecky.com; and http:// en.wikipedia.org/wiki/Dave_Dravecky. Final quote from Rowell, *1001 Quotes*, 50.

2. John Ayto, *Dictionary of Word Origins: The Histories of More Than 8,000 English-Language Words* (New York: Arcade Publishing, 1990), 577.

3. C. S. Lewis, *Reflections on the Psalms* (New York: Walker & Co., 1985), 95.

4. Roy B. Zuck, *The Speaker's Quote Book* (Grand Rapids, MI: Kregel, 1997), 293.

5. Ibid., 425–26.

6. Craig Brain Larson and *Leadership*, eds., *750 Engaging Illustrations for Preachers, Teachers, and Writers* (Grand Rapids, MI: Baker, 2002), 163.

13: Rediscovering Joy When Overcome by Grief

1. The names of the five stages are Kübler-Ross's; the examples of responses are mine. See *On Death and Dying* (New York: Simon & Schuster, 1969).

2. R. Kent Hughes, *1001 Great Stories & "Quotes"* (Wheaton, IL: Tyndale House, 1998), 193–94.

14: Learning to Forgive When Gripped by Bitterness

1. From an article by Adam Myrick in *Southwestern News* (Fall 2000), cited in David P. Barrett, ed., *Perfect Illustrations for Every Topic and Occasion* (Wheaton, IL: Tyndale House, 2002), 115–16.

2. Glenn E. Schaeffer, "Kids of the Kingdom." *Christian Reader*, September–October 1997, cited in Barrett, *Perfect Illustrations for Every Topic and Occasion*, 173.

3. Diana Garland, *Family Ministry: A Comprehensive Guide* (Downers Grove, IL: InterVarsity Press, 1999), 358. See also http://en.wikipedia.org/wiki/Butler_-_Fitzgerald_dispute.

15: Seeking Restoration When Shattered by Rejection

1. As told by Ray Stedman in *The Birth of the Body*, cited by Charles R. Swindoll, *The Tale of the Tardy Oxcart* (Nashville: Thomas Nelson, 1998), 8.
2. "Weaver's Inner Growth," in *The Week*, August 15, 2008.
3. R. Kent Hughes, *1001 Great Stories & "Quotes"* (Wheaton, IL: Tyndale House, 1998), 347.
4. Craig Brian Larson and *Leadership*, eds., *750 Engaging Illustrations for Preachers, Teachers, and Writers* (Grand Rapids, MI: Baker, 2002), 589. See also http://www.theopedia .com/G._Campbell_Morgan.
5. C. S. Lewis, *The Problem of Pain* (New York: HarperOne, 2001), 16.
6. Bart D. Ehrman, *God's Problem: How the Bible Fails to Answer Our Most Important Question—Why We Suffer* (New York: HarperOne, 2008).
7. Harold S. Kushner, *When Bad Things Happen to Good People* (New York: Avon, 1983).
8. Madeleine L'Engle, *Walking on Water: Reflections on Faith and Art* (New York: North Point Press, 1995), cited in Barrett, *Perfect Illustrations*, 229.
9. See http://www.worldisround.com/articles/73022/photo1920.html.

16: In Whom Do You Trust? Getting to Know Your Power Source

1. See http://www.blessitt.com/?q=nicaragua.
2. See http://www.law.cornell.edu/supct/html/historics/USSC_CR_0465_0668_ZD.html.
3. See http://en.wikipedia.org/wiki/In_God_We_Trust.

17: Turning Wishes into Reality When Dreams Are Dashed

1. All quotes from Lisa Beamer with Ken Abraham, *Let's Roll: Ordinary People, Extraordinary Courage* (Wheaton, IL: Tyndale House, 2003), 59–64; italics added.
2. Ibid., 99; italics added.
3. Ibid., 119; italics added.
4. Ibid., 124; italics added.
5. Ibid., 139; italics added.

18: Living Vigilantly to Keep from Drifting Off Course

1. John and Jean Silverwood, *Black Wave* (New York: Random House, 2008). Quote taken from an excerpt from *Black Wave* reprinted in *The Week*, September 5, 2008.
2. See http://www.tscpulpitseries.org/english/1990s/ts920706.html.
3. Cited in Craig Brian Larson, *750 Engaging Illustrations for Preachers, Teachers, and Writers* (Grand Rapids, MI: Baker, 2002), 294.

19: Putting Up Sails, Praying for Wind

1. Tom Perkins, *Valley Boy—The Education of Tom Perkins* (New York: Gotham Books, 2007), 251.
2. Annie Dillard, "Total Eclipse," in *The Annie Dillard Reader* (New York: HarperCollins, 1994), 11–12.

20: The Grand Irony: When Holding On Is Letting Go

1. Lewis Smedes, "The Power of Promises," in Thomas G. Long and Cornelius Plantinga, eds., *A Chorus of Witnesses: Model Sermons for Today's Preacher* (Grand Rapids, MI: Eerdmans, 1994), 156–57; italics added.
2. *The Life Promises Bible* (Grand Rapids, MI: Zondervan, 2001), 194.
3. Liz Szabo, "A Katrina Survivor Stands Fast in Her Faith," *USA Today*, July 19, 2007, http://www.usatoday.com/news/religion/2007-07-18-katrina-faith_N.htm; italics added.

21: God's Love Burns Bright Forever

1. See http://en.wikipedia.org/wiki/Schindlerjuden.
2. See http://www.oskarschindler.com/6.htm.
3. See http://www.taize.fr/en_rubrique8.html.
4. For short videos of such a Taizé candlelight service, see http://www.youtube.com/watch ?v=JdW6oGG8hRY&feature=related and http://www.youtube.com/watch?v=73ptUCEEwmI& feature=related.
5. Max Lucado, *A Gentle Thunder: Hearing God Through the Storm* (Nashville: Thomas Nelson, 2001), 122.
6. Brent Curtis and John Eldredge, *The Sacred Romance* (Nashville: Thomas Nelson, 1997), 106.
7. Terry Muck, "Hearing God's Voice and Obeying His Word," *Leadership Journal*, Winter 1982.

22: The Game's Already Won!

1. See http://en.wikipedia.org/wiki/Battle_of_tours.
2. Frank S. Mead, *The Decisive Battles of Christianity* (New York: Grosset & Dunlap, 1936, 1937), 67–77.
3. Oscar Cullmann, *Christ and Time: The Primitive Christian Conception of Time and History,* trans. Floyd V. Filson (Philadelphia: Westminster, 1964), 84.
4. Michael P. Knowles, *The Folly of Preaching* (Grand Rapids, MI: Eerdmans, 2007), 41.

23: Let the Truth of God's Love Jump-Start Your Heart!

1. Don Richardson, *Peace Child* (Seattle, WA: YWAM Publishing, 2004), 141–43.
2. Matthew L. Wald, "Engineer in '96 Rail Crash Hid His Failing Sight from Railroad," *New York Times*, March 26, 1997, sec. A.
3. J. Mack Stiles, "Ready to Answer," *Discipleship Journal*, March–April 1997.
4. See http://www.labri.org/england/resources/Learning-from-Francis-Schaeffer.pdf.
5. Christian Smith with Melinda Lundquist Denton, *Soul Searching: The Religious and Spiritual Lives of American Teenagers* (New York: Oxford University Press, 2005), 135.
6. Ibid., 263; italics added.

24: Hide Your Mind in the Safety of God's Love

1. Paul Pearsall, *The Ten Laws of Lasting Love* (New York: Simon & Schuster, 1993). Cited in *Reader's Digest*, March 1995.
2. Ramon Williams, "News Clips: Powerful Last Words," *Christian Reader*, July–August 1996.

25: God's Love Will Never Fail

1. *Jefferson City News Tribune* (Jefferson, Missouri), April 25, 2001. Cited in Craig Brian Larson, *More Perfect Illustrations* (Wheaton, IL: Tyndale House, 2003), 18–19.
2. From *Dad's Magazine*, June–July 2000, cited in Larson, *More Perfect Illustrations*, 97.

26: Grafted for Abundant Life

1. C. S. Lewis, *Mere Christianity* (New York: HarperCollins, 1952), 50.
2. Doug Stanton, "Why George Clooney Never Sleeps," *Men's Journal*, July 2000.
3. Lewis, *Mere Christianity*, 136–37.
4. Joseph Henry Thayer, *Thayer's Greek-English Lexicon of the New Testament*, electronic version, s.v. "perisso/ß."

27: Resisting Distractions—Refocusing on What Truly Matters

1. See http://www.coachwooden.com; tab "The Journey."
2. See http://uclabruins.cstv.com/sports/m-baskbl/spec-rel/ucla-wooden-page.html.
3. See http://www.coachwooden.com; tab "Timeline"; italics added.
4. Hal Bock, Associated Press, "A Coach for All Seasons," *Spokane-Review*, December 4, 2000.
5. Mark Water, comp., *The New Encyclopedia of Christian Quotations* (Grand Rapids, MI: Baker, 2000), 284.
6. C. S. Lewis, *Mere Christianity: A Revised and Amplified Edition, with a New Introduction, of the Three Books, Broadcast Talks, Christian Behaviour, and Beyond Personality* (New York: Harper-Collins, 2001), 198.
7. See http://legacy.pastors.com/RWMT/article.asp?ID=59&ArtID=2072.

29: Living a Fruitful Life

1. See http://en.wikipedia.org/wiki/Yukon_gold_rush.
2. Summarized from http://www.usatoday.com/money/industries/energy/2008-09-09-dakota-drilling_N.htm.
3. See http://en.wikipedia.org/wiki/Grand_Coulee_Dam.
4. Craig Brian Larson, ed., *More Perfect Illustrations for Every Topic and Occasion* (Wheaton, IL: Tyndale House, 2003), 212.

30: Power to Live Forever

1. As found in Colin Chapman, *The Case for Christianity* (Lion Hudson plc, 1981), cited in Craig Brian Larson and *Leadership*, eds., *750 Engaging Illustrations for Preachers, Teachers, and Writers* (Grand Rapids, MI: Baker, 2002), 143–44.
2. Elysa Gardner, "For Roseanne Cash, Death Brings a Test of Faith," *USA Today*, January 26, 2006.
3. Larson, *750 Engaging Illustrations*, 140.
4. The words of the German prison doctor who observed Bonhoeffer's hanging, as cited in Mark Water, comp., *The New Encyclopedia of Christian Quotations* (Grand Rapids, MI: Baker, 2000), 252.
5. See http://www.barna.org/FlexPage.aspx?Page=BarnaUpdate&BarnaUpdateID=282.
6. *Our Daily Bread*, April 24, 2008, http://www.rbc.org/devotionals/our-daily-bread/2008/04/24/devotion.aspx.